Imaginary Cities of Gold

RENEWALS 458-4574
DATE DUE

Imaginary Cities of Gold

The Spanish Quest for Treasure in North America

PETER O. KOCH

McFarland & Company, Inc., Publishers

Jefferson, North Carolina, and London

LIBRARY OF CONGRESS CATALOGUING-IN-PUBLICATION DATA

Koch, Peter O., 1953–
    Imaginary cities of gold : the Spanish quest for treasure in
North America / Peter O. Koch.
       p.   cm.
    Includes bibliographical references and index.

    ISBN 978-0-7864-4381-9
    softcover : 50# alkaline paper ∞

    1. America — Discovery and exploration — Spanish.
2. Núñez Cabeza de Vaca, Alvar, 16th cent.   3. Coronado,
Francisco Vásquez de, 1510–1554.   4. Soto, Hernando de, ca.
1500–1542.   5. Explorers— America — Biography.   6. Explorers—
Spain — Biography.   7. Geographical myths.   I. Title.
E123.K65   2009
970.01'6 — dc22   2009006678

British Library cataloguing data are available

Cover image ©2009 Shutterstock

Manufactured in the United States of America

McFarland & Company, Inc., Publishers
  Box 611, Jefferson, North Carolina 28640
    www.mcfarlandpub.com

For Abelene, Sara, Alex, and Eric; and for my extended
family, Betty, Augusto, Mabelle, Joel, Meng, and
Alpha: your love and support mean everything.

Let the curious reader consider whether there is not much to ponder in this that I am writing. What men have there been in the world who have shown such daring?

— Bernal Diaz del Castillo

They were all groping in the darkness, because they did not understand what the Indians were saying.

— Fray Bartolomé de Las Casas

TABLE OF CONTENTS

PREFACE

Nearly a century before a small company of hopeful English colonists sought to plant a permanent settlement at Jamestown, Spanish colonists, who had already established a foothold in North America, were busy planning expeditions to explore, conquer, and settle the mysterious lands that lay just to the north of Cuba and Mexico. Their curiosity piqued by native tales of lands teeming with a natural supply of precious metals and gems, and uncharted regions that were home to many strange and wondrous sights, some of which seemed to correspond with ancient European lore, a great many Spaniards were willing to risk everything, including their lives, for the chance to find treasures said to surpass even their wildest dreams.

A mere twenty years after Christopher Columbus established the first truly permanent European settlement in the Americas, a conquistador by the name of Juan Ponce de León sailed from Puerto Rico in search of the island of Bimini, a land that the natives had told him was rich with gold and home to a magical spring of water that could revive both body and soul. While he failed to find either of these attractive items, this legendary explorer did happen to discover an unfamiliar territory that he christened Pascua Florida, a region that soon became the focus of intense Spanish speculation, most of which was fueled by native stories of extraordinarily wealthy kingdoms just waiting to be claimed for the greater glory of Spain.

Rumors of Hernán Cortés's discovery of Tenochtitlan, a New World city that surpassed the size and magnificence of any contemporary Old World city, spread quickly throughout the Spanish colonies in the West Indies. It stood to reason that if there was one such opulent kingdom then surely there must be others just waiting to be discovered. Such reasoning rekindled Juan Ponce de León's desire to return to Pascua Florida. This renewed quest for gold and glory came to an abrupt end when the Spanish commander suffered an arrow wound that proved fatal.

The dream of finding Florida's legendary wealth did not, however, die with the passing of Juan Ponce de León. There would soon follow a successive number of expeditions to this region, all of which were led by Spanish commanders who were thoroughly convinced that they possessed the where-withal to succeed where their predecessors had failed. Pánfilo de Narváez, a Spanish conquistador blinded by greed, arrogance, and the loss of one eye, was next in line to take up the search for the ever-elusive rich empires of Florida, especially a wealthy realm the natives called Apalachee. This ill-fated expedition suffered one loss after another until there were but four survivors, one of whom was an officer by the name of Álvar Núñez Cabeza de Vaca.

After more than seven years living among various tribes that wandered across much of Texas, New Mexico, and northern Mexico, Cabeza de Vaca and his three comrades finally found their way back to civilization. These four survivors were escorted to Mexico City, the Spanish capital of New Spain that was built over the ruins of Tenochtitlan, the city that was once the very heart of the Aztec empire. Besides returning with a profound respect for the indigenous peoples of the Americas, Cabeza de Vaca and his comrades returned with splendid stories of lands that held out the promise of yielding a great many earthly rewards.

The most promising of the tales told by the survivors of the Narváez expedition centered around a region to the distant north that the four men never set eyes on but had been told was a major source of the kind of met-als and gems that were so dear to the hearts of every European. The natives would call this golden realm Cibola, which they claimed was home to seven cities, each of which either equaled or eclipsed the magnificent wealth once stored at the principal cities of the Aztecs of Mexico or the Incas of Peru. To Christian ears, the Seven Cities of Cibola sounded very similar to the oft told Iberian tale of the Seven Cities of Antillia, the glorious and unmapped cities founded during the eighth century A.D. by seven pious Portuguese priests and their faithful followers after having barely escaped the wrath of an invad-ing horde of Arabs and Moors by sailing westward across the Atlantic Ocean.

Gossip and speculation over the many treasures that awaited at Cibola ignited numerous calls for the launching of a major expedition to find and claim this splendid region for Spain. A cautious Antonio de Mendoza, the viceroy of New Spain, responded by sending a small scouting party — led by Fray Marcos de Niza, a devout priest who had once beheld the incredible wealth that was housed at Cuzco, and guided by Esteban, a Moor and Span-ish slave who was one of the four survivors of the Narváez expedition — which was expected to discover a direct route to the legendary Seven Cities of Cibola. Esteban would forfeit his life for the opportunity to be the first to catch a glimpse of Cibola, while Fray Marcos would return with wondrous stories of having seen a large and towering city that appeared to be made entirely of gold. Needless to say, many Spanish settlers were now convinced that Cibola truly was a realm worthy of being claimed for Spain.

Francisco Vásquez de Coronado was appointed to lead a large expeditionary force charged with laying claim to the Seven Cities of Cibola. The success of this mission seemed assured with the addition of Fray Marcos as its guide. However, instead of finding a golden city larger than Mexico City, Coronado and his soldiers were disappointed to discover that Hawikuh, one of the Seven Cities of Cibola, was simply a small pueblo consisting of a few buildings made of clay and rock. Unable to find any items of value at Cibola, Coronado then turned his attention to finding Quivira, a region that a self-serving native guide claimed had an abundance of gold. Coronado's army would spend nearly two years trekking across the barren lands of northern Mexico, Arizona, New Mexico, Texas, Oklahoma, and Kansas only to discover that the golden cities of Cibola and Quivira were simply an illusion.

While Coronado and his troops were searching for the rich native empires first mentioned by the four survivors of the Narvaez expedition, Hernando de Soto was leading an even larger army of eager conquistadors through the swamps and forests of Florida to find the wealthy native kingdoms that had eluded Panfilo de Narvaez. Don Hernando de Soto had earned for himself the fame and fortune that every conquistador who ever sailed to the New World dreamed of acquiring but few ever realized. Not one to rest on his laurels, de Soto decided to risk all that he had on the chance to find even greater fortune and glory in the province of Florida. The success of this venture appeared certain, thanks to information provided by Álvar Núñez Cabeza de Vaca upon his return to Spain.

Landing along the shores of present day Tampa Bay, Hernando de Soto and his troops set off along narrow native trails that passed through extremely treacherous terrain only to discover that Anhaica, the prominent town of the Apalachee province, had none of the gold, silver, or precious gems that everyone expected to find. The de Soto expedition would continue to cut a path of death and destruction across much of Florida, Georgia, Louisiana, Mississippi, North Carolina, Oklahoma, Tennessee, and Texas with little to show for their efforts except a handful of freshwater pearls. The long list of trials and tribulations that accrued on this venture would factor into the death of roughly half the members of the expedition, including Hernando de Soto, who was buried beneath the waters of the Mississippi — the river he is frequently credited with discovering.

Hostile encounters, harsh terrain, a lack of food, and debilitating illnesses were prominent among the many circumstances that conspired against the quest of the Spanish conquistadors to explore, conquer, and settle the southeastern and southwestern regions that are now part of the United States of America. However, there were other, less conspicuous, factors that clearly escaped the notice of the Spaniards and all too often are ignored or glossed

over by historical accounts of this epic period in America's history. The inhabitants of these New World regions were clever enough to realize that the surest
way to rid themselves of Spanish intruders was to fill their heads with stories
of distant lands rich with gold and other precious items, tales calculated to
send the Spaniards far from their own town or to deliver them into the lands
of their enemy, where they would either kill or be killed by a rival tribe. Time
and time again, the conquistadors, whose sense of direction was almost
entirely guided by far-fetched native yarns, were disappointed to discover
that these elaborate tales of faraway rich kingdoms failed to live up to their
lofty expectations.

While there have been many past and recent books that address the epic
adventures of Álvar Núñez Cabeza de Vaca, Francisco Vázquez de Coronado,
or Hernando de Soto in North America, there are few works that collectively
deal with these individual efforts as part of a larger topic that revolves around
Spain's determined effort to enhance its emerging empire in the New World.
This book, which is the fourth entry in a series of studies that examines the
events surrounding the very first encounters between European explorers and
the indigenous peoples of the Americas, focuses on the various circumstances
that surround and connect these disastrous attempts to conquer, settle, and
exploit an unknown region thought to be the source of untold wealth. Had
these Spanish expeditions been successful then, the Anglo-America that exists
today may have never come to pass. However, a case can be made that the
Spanish seeds planted some five centuries ago have now begun to flower.

During the course of researching and writing this book, I have encountered a number of works, especially those penned by contemporary historians, that were overly concerned with condemning the actions of every single
conquistador who set foot on America's soil; or promoting their own theories regarding the specific routes undertaken by these Spanish expeditions;
or espousing their beliefs as to why certain historical accounts, especially
their own, should take precedence over that of another; or any combination
of the aforementioned. While such opinions and theories clearly have a valid
place in the academic and somewhat arcane field of historiography, they
should not, however, be accorded more weight than the actual events that were
an integral part of America's history.

My research for this work focused on the chance meetings and interac-
tions that took place between the conquistadors and the indigenous population. This book is also devoted to providing a better understanding of the
various circumstances that led to these expeditions and the particular events
that ultimately contributed to each failure.

1

THE LURE OF THE QUEST

The Magical Waters of Bimini

On March 3, 1513, three ships hoisted their anchors at the Port of San German, a harbor that supported a Spanish settlement located at the western end of Puerto Rico, and sailed off in search of the island of Bimini, a land that the natives of Borinquen claimed was rich in immeasurable ways. The Spanish commander of this small expedition was eager to find this neighboring island that, besides having a natural abundance of gold and precious gems, was home to a mystical fountain that could revive the vigor of youth and restore good health to anyone who drank or bathed in its crystal clear waters. Firmly planted in the mind of this wealthy, middle-aged conquistador was the tale of a mighty Arawak chief who many years earlier had set off in a canoe in search of the magical waters of Bimini. The fact that the chief never returned to his island home was interpreted as a sign that he had discovered the mysteries of this land and therefore did not wish to leave such an earthly paradise.

Such a tale of restorative waters was certainly not without precedent: Sir John Mandeville, a legendary knight whose tales of adventure were well known throughout European circles, wrote of having happened upon a Well of Youth that could heal any known malady and rekindle long-lost youthful exuberance to whoever drank three times from its waters. The wandering knight claimed that he drank three times from this well, and then he declared: "Ever since that time I have felt the better and healthier, and I think I shall do so until such time as God in his grace causes me to pass out of this mortal life."[1] The regenerative powers of the Well of Youth seems to have been fleeting, for the adventurer concludes his tale by saying, "I am now come to rest, a man worn out by age and travel and the feebleness of my body, and certain other causes which force me to rest."[2] The fact that John Mandeville was simply the imaginary creation of an extremely clever writer was not yet known to the many readers of this intriguing tale. He was, at the moment, considered by many as reliable a source on the mysterious regions of a world just waiting to be revealed as the renowned Marco Polo.

It had been nearly twenty years since Juan Ponce de León, the proud son of a prominent Spanish family from Tervås de San Campos, a town situated in the northwestern province of Valladolid, had sailed to the New World in search of fame and fortune. A veteran of the wars against the Moors of Spain, a young Juan had the distinction of participating in the conquest of Granada, a celebrated victory that unified Spain under the rule of a zealously devout Christian king and queen. He was just nineteen years old when he signed on for Christopher Columbus' Second Enterprise of the Indies. King Ferdinand and Queen Isabella had seen enough evidence of gold and spices brought back by Columbus on his epic voyage across the uncharted waters of the Atlantic to convince them that this Italian explorer in the employ of Spain had discovered a back door to the fabulous wealth of the Far East. The Spanish sovereigns authorized the Admiral of the Ocean Sea to lead a second expedition, an armada of seventeen ships carrying fifteen hundred eager settlers, to establish a permanent settlement that would serve as a depot for trade with the mighty and wealthy potentates of the Orient.

All who sailed on this expedition expected to be greeted at the island of Hispaniola by the forty men who had been left behind by Christopher Columbus. They were told that these soldiers occupied a fort built from the wreckage of the Santa Maria, where they were expected to pass the time carrying on trade with the extremely friendly natives or mining the rich land for the copious amounts of gold and gems believed to exist there. One can only imagine the disappointment felt by all when, after reaching Hispaniola, they found that the fort had been burned to the ground and all of the Spanish settlers had been slaughtered by the natives. It mattered little, except perhaps to the ever-optimistic Columbus, that such carnage was simply a long overdue response by the natives to the numerous atrocities perpetrated by the Spaniards who had remained at Hispaniola. The frustration of the newly arrived colonists was soon compounded by the realization that this island was not home to anywhere near as many precious minerals and stones as they had been led to believe.

The Tainos, who are also known as the Arawaks, paid dearly for having taken up arms to defend their way of life. Over the next two decades they would find themselves subjugated into submission in order that they might serve at the leisure of their Spanish overlords. Those who did not die by the sword were forced to toil in the mines digging for gold or cultivating the land to produce the crops that would temporarily satisfy the insatiable desires and needs of the Spanish settlers. Few Spaniards struck as much fear in the hearts of the natives as did Juan Ponce de León. His bright red locks and beard were a reflection of the fiery temperament possessed by this young commander who led campaigns that conquered most of the tribes along the eastern region of

Hispaniola. A grateful Nicolás de Ovando, who had replaced Christopher Columbus as governor of the island, rewarded Ponce de León with the governorship of the province of Higuey.

From the natives who were his subjects, Juan Ponce de León heard enticing stories of great wealth just waiting to be uncovered on the neighboring island of Borinquen, an isle he had briefly seen from aboard one of the admiral's ships just prior to the fleet's arrival at Hispaniola. The ambitious Spanish commander requested and was granted the right to explore, conquer, and settle this island that held out the promise of surrendering many earthly rewards. Governor Ovando's one stipulation was that before any wealth was to be shared, Ponce would have to first conquer all the aggressive Carib tribes that made their home on Borinquen. The Caribs were a notorious warlike race who, because of their propensity for feasting on the flesh of others, were greatly feared by the generally peaceful island tribes and viewed with a sense of awe and trepidation by the Spaniards. In their huge dugout canoes, large groups of Carib warriors periodically rowed across the gulf of water that separated them from Hispaniola to launch raids on Taino villages. The prisoners were transported back to the Carib villages where the captured men were butchered and eaten. The majority of the Taino women were kept as sex slaves and the children they gave birth to were served up at a special banquet. Governor Ovando wanted Ponce to put an end to these Carib incursions that posed a threat to his already dwindling labor force.

After agreeing to Nicolás de Ovando's terms, Juan Ponce de León began his conquest of Borinquen in 1508 with a mere one hundred well-armed soldiers. Even though they were greatly outnumbered, the conquistadors, due in part to their superior weapons and military tactics, were able to eliminate the Carib threat and forcefully subjugate most of the Arawak tribes of this island within just a year. The bold Ponce de León had earned his right to an appointment as governor of an island that was to be renamed Puerto Rico.

The conquistadors had an easily recognizable Achilles heel that the natives of the New World were quick to exploit. Blinded by their lust for gold, the Spaniards were willing to entertain any tale, regardless of how outlandish it might sound, that spoke of the precious metal that was so valuable to them. While some of these tales of rich kingdoms waiting to be discovered contained an element of truth, the avaricious Spaniards were slow to pick up on the fact that such places were always very far away from the tribes they were currently tormenting. Taking their cue from the natives of Hispaniola, the natives of Borinquen fed the conquistadors similar tales of distant lands containing wealth that exceeded their wildest expectations. They were clever enough to add a bit of local lore that made their tale even more alluring to Juan Ponce de León. The natives told the governor of a land called Bimini, an island not only rich with gold but where there could also be found a fountain of water blessed with the magical power to restore health and wash away the ravages of time.

Juan Ponce de León's term as governor of the island he had recently conquered and settled was cut short in 1509 by the unexpected arrival of a newly appointed "Admiral of the Ocean and Governor of Hispaniola." This was the year that Diego Colón, the eldest son of Christopher Columbus, who, after having won a protracted legal battle to inherit the titles and property of his famous father, arrived at Santo Domingo to assume his appointment as governor of Hispaniola and viceroy of all the West Indies. One of Diego's first official acts was to purge from office every appointment made by his predecessor, Nicolás de Ovando, the governor who had been extremely unkind to his father during a time when he desperately needed his help. Ponce de León found himself an early casualty of Diego's vendetta, a decree that granted him the freedom to pursue the treasures that awaited on the island of Bimini. The lure of an expedition to discover the whereabouts of this wondrous land prompted Ponce de León to return to Spain to seek royal approval to explore and settle the island of Bimini, a patent that King Ferdinand granted him on February 23, 1512.

Approximately two hundred hopeful men placed their full trust in Juan Ponce de León's belief in the claims of the Borinquin natives. Their commander, in turn, placed his full faith in the ability of Antonio Alaminos, a pilot who had previously sailed with Christopher Columbus, to locate the mysterious island that the Indians had mentioned. The flotilla, which consisted of two caravels, the *Santa Maria de Consolacion* and the *Santiago*, and one bergantina, the *San Cristóbal*, latched on to a gentle breeze that carried them out of Añasco Bay. The ships skirted along the chain of small islands collectively known as the Bahamas, and on the second day of April 1513 the explorers came upon the pristine shores of what appeared to be an exceptionally large island. In tribute to the time of the season and the splendid scent of the flora that permeated the air, Ponce de León christened his discovery Pascua Florida, the Floral Easter. They dropped anchor at an inlet located in the vicinity of present-day Daytona Beach and on the following day the commander went ashore to claim the land for both Spain and himself.

Setting sail again on April 8, the expedition proceeded on a northerly course. The skillful pilot and his resolute commander decided to reverse their course after finding that the strong currents ran contrary to their intended route. As they trekked southward along the eastern shore of Florida's coast, every Spaniard kept an eye peeled for any promising signs of exceptionally rich native kingdoms or seemingly extraordinary fountains of flowing water.

They did discover several springs of water that proved sweet enough to satisfy their thirst but none which were possessed with the medicinal value they all so desperately craved. Ponce made a point to stop at any village they sighted in hopes of learning if the objects of his desire were nearby. At one such stop, the Spaniards unexpectedly came under attack and were forced to make a hasty retreat to the safety of their ships, but not soon enough to prevent the death of one of their comrades.

The expedition resumed its southerly course and soon reached the Cape of Florida, which appeared to confirm that Florida was an island, though it certainly seemed much larger than most. While making their way around this vast promontory, the Spaniards passed by the small group of islands now known as the Florida Keys. It was at one of these islets that a group of natives paddled out toward the Spanish ships as if they were coming to extend a warm welcome to their homeland. These expectations were quickly shattered when the Spaniards noticed that the Indians placed their hands on the ship's cables in an apparent attempt to tow their boat toward the island. Ponce de León ordered his men to chase the natives off and this pursuit continued on land, where the soldiers dismantled several native canoes and took four women of the tribe as their prisoners.

Antonio Alaminos steered the ships northward along the western coast of the Florida Peninsula until they reached a promising bay now known as Charlotte Harbor. Sensing that this might be a good spot to resume their search for the fabulous treasures they sought, Ponce de León ordered the anchors to be dropped and for the men to go ashore and begin establishing a camp. All were unaware of the fact that their movements were being closely watched by the Calusa, a tribe that did not take kindly to strangers who trespassed upon their lands. The Calusa had learned a great deal about the Spaniards from Cuban natives who had been forced to seek refuge in the Calusa homeland. According to some accounts, Ponce's troops were greeted by an Indian who knew enough Spanish to tell them to wait where they were for the arrival of their revered chief.

The Calusa were a confederation of many chiefdoms who owed their fealty to a supreme chief, to whom tribute was paid with a bountiful offering of animal skins, feathers, food, and prisoners of war, the latter of which were often served up as sacrificial offerings to honor the gods during religious ceremonies. The tribes made their homes along the inner waterways adjacent to Florida's southwest coastline, which provided them with a steady diet of fish and shellfish to complement the wild game they hunted for sustenance. The inexhaustible supply of seashells was used in the making of jewelry, utensils, tools, and spearheads for hunting. Like most of the natives encountered in Florida, the Calusa went about naked except for a loincloth, which only modestly covered the parts considered shameful to Spanish eyes. However, unlike most of the natives encountered so far, the Calusa men were just as tall, and many were considerably taller, than the Spaniards.

Juan Ponce de León and his men would soon discover just how fierce and determined these Calusa warriors were when it came to protecting their borders. Chief Calusa, a local ruler who bore the same name as his tribe, led an imposing armada of eighty large canoes filled with a great many armed warriors that caught the Spaniards by surprise. A hailstorm of unleashed arrows forced the frightened soldiers to quickly weigh anchor and seek refuge at a nearby island, where they hoped to have an opportunity to make much needed repairs to the ships. Those plans were altered by the renewed attack of Calusa's warriors. The aggressive nature of these natives was a disconcerting sight to a crew already frustrated by their lack of success in finding anything of value and discouraging enough to convince a disappointed Ponce de León that the time had come to return to Puerto Rico.

The disillusioned adventurers sailed southward until they docked at a small group of islands that Ponce de León christened the Tortugas because they were home to a great many sea turtles. While there, the famished soldiers filled their bellies with the turtles, seals, and pelicans they were able to capture. While feasting on this bountiful catch, a decision was made to chart a course to the closer coast of Cuba instead of home, but somehow they missed their intended destination and unexpectedly found themselves along the unfamiliar shores of the Yucatan Peninsula.

Juan Ponce de León apparently viewed their failure to reach Cuba as a sign that they should resume their search for the elusive Fountain of Youth. While hoping to avoid another encounter with the hostile Calusa, the commander decided to retrace as best he could the route that had brought them to this remote region. Antonio Alaminos managed to safely guide the three ships back to the Bahamas, at which point it was decided that the expedition would be divided into two groups in an earnest effort to thoroughly search as many islands as possible. Alaminos took the helm of the *San Cristobal* while Ponce de León took command of the other two ships. Each party set off in different directions to search among the many isles of the Bahamas for the one that might be the fabled island of Bimini. In September of 1513, after the *Santa Maria de Consolación* was lost to the ravages of the sea, a frustrated Ponce de León returned to Puerto Rico with the *Santiago*—which also carried the rescued crew of the other ship—without anything of value to show for their six month long search. Antonio Alaminos and his crew, unfortunately, had to endure a more perilous experience. After a successive series of difficulties, the weary crew of the *San Cristobal* found themselves hopelessly

SEEKING THE FOUNTAIN OF YOUTH.

Juan Ponce de León and comrades seeking the fountain of youth.

stranded upon one of the numerous islets of the Bahamas. They were rescued by a ship piloted by Diego Miruelo and found their way back to Puerto Rico four months after Ponce and his crew had returned.

Juan Ponce de León returned to Spain in 1514 to seek another grant to search for Bimini as well as an additional patent to explore the large island he had discovered and christened Pascua Florida. He brought with him an offering of five hundred gold pesos, all of which was from his own coffers and none of which had been obtained during his last expedition. He reasoned that since he had already learned where not to look, it therefore would be easier for a second expedition to find the naturally rich land of Bimini. Peter Martyr de Anghiera, an Italian who served as chaplain to the Spanish court and who was also an avid historian, reported that same year the story of Juan Ponce de León's search for an island having "a spring of running water of such marvellous virtue, that the water therof being drunk, perhaps with some diet, makes old men young again."[3] Ponce returned to Puerto Rico with all the grants that he requested, but he had to put his plans for a follow-up expedition on hold after being ordered back into service by King Ferdinand to help track down the neighboring island Caribs who were suddenly launching raids against the native labor force of Puerto Rico.

Into the West

Tales of rich New World kingdoms just waiting to be discovered soon took a turn to the west, an interest that was, to a large extent, kindled by the intriguing stories told by the pilot Antonio Alaminos. Like so many other restless conquistadors who were eager to stake a claim to a hardy share of gold and glory, Alaminos migrated to Cuba in hopes of hitching his star to another daring expedition. This native of Palos had sailed to the West Indies in 1502 as a member of the final voyage of the "Admiral of the Ocean Sea." While searching for the ever elusive Strait of Malaaca, a passage that many believed would lead to the infinite treasures of the Far East, the Columbus expedition encountered a large native canoe along the coast of Central America that was transporting a great quantity of cacao beans, copper hatchets, blankets and elegant garments. These Mayan merchants invited Christopher Columbus to visit their homeland, which they said was just a bit further up the coast. The admiral, however, had his own strict schedule to maintain, and therefore was unwilling to stray from his charted course. The vivid memory of this brief encounter coupled with the recent experience of his voyage to the Yucatan as pilot of the Juan Ponce de León expedition had given Antonio Alaminos reason to believe that perhaps the better chance for achieving enduring fame and fortune could be found directly to the west of Cuba.

Lope Ocha de Caycedo and Cristóbal Morante took a keen interest in the stories of Antonio Alaminos, and soon the three began formulating plans for an expedition of their own. Since a venture of this size and scope was well beyond their combined financial means, the trio spoke of their aim to sail westward "to seek and discover new lands and give ourselves an employment" to Francisco de Córdoba, a wealthy merchant and landowner who was known to finance expeditions that dabbled in the lucrative trade of native slaves. Fascinated by the rich possibilities of such a venture, Córdoba pledged not only his full financial support but also his services as captain of the expedition. Diego Velázquez, the governor of Cuba, was also intrigued with their plan. In addition to granting an official sanction to this westward excursion, Governor Velázquez contributed enough funds to procure an additional ship.

On February 8, 1517, Antonio Alaminos piloted three ships carrying a crew of one hundred ten men, all of whom were under the command of Francisco de Córdoba, out of the port of Ajaruco to seek out new lands endowed with untold possibilities. Two of these ships were the large naos, which had hulls spacious enough to haul the tremendous store of treasures they expected to obtain on this journey. To facilitate their trade with the natives, the Spaniards made sure they brought an abundant supply of the various trinkets that had served them so well in the past, especially the cheap colored glass beads that the island natives seemed to adore.

Francisco de Córdoba and his men found their way to the tip of the Yucatan Peninsula where they experienced promising meetings with the Mayans, an Indian civilization that, by all appearances, seemed far more advanced than any native culture the Spaniards had previously encountered in the New World. Unfortunately, all of these meetings turned into deadly confrontations. The first such bloody skirmish occurred at a place the explorers christened Cape Catoche. When the battle ended in favor of the Spaniards, the victorious soldiers rewarded themselves with the numerous golden items they found inside the sacred Mayan temples. The wary Spaniards then proceeded by boat to Champoton where, shortly after coming ashore, a battle occurred that this time ended in favor of the Mayans. Forty-eight Spaniards fell before a ferocious onslaught and all would have surely perished had they not made a hasty retreat to the safety of their ships. All of the survivors, except for one, suffered wounds from the battle, and five of these injured soldiers died shortly after setting sail.

The life-threatening problems that Córdoba, Alaminos, and the rest of the survivors now faced were compounded by the fact that they had inadvertently left behind the casks brought ashore to fill with fresh water and that one of their boats had sprung so many leaks that they had no choice but to run the ship aground and salvage what they could before putting her to the torch. Considering that they barely had enough able-bodied men to handle even two ships, there was little concern over the loss of this one vessel. In a region sorely lacking in rivers or streams, the far greater worry was finding fresh water before all perished of thirst. Several soldiers expressed a desire to return to Cuba but there was a concern among many that few of them had the strength to survive even this relatively short voyage.

Antonio Alaminos dangled the possibility of another course of action, one that offered his disheartened comrades a continued chance to find the fortune they all craved. After careful consideration of their present bearings and a thorough review of his nautical charts, Alaminos calculated that a voyage to Florida, the land he had sailed to as the pilot for Ponce de León's expedition, would make for a faster landfall than the neighboring island of Cuba. While there was a genuine concern that the indigenous tribes of Florida were every bit as warlike as the Mayans of the Yucatan, Alaminos emphasized that they could take comfort in the knowledge that this was a land that certainly had no shortage of freshwater. More likely than not, Alaminos reminded a wounded and bedridden Francisco de Córdoba about the native tale of a fountain that flowed with invigorating waters that could heal both the body and the soul. An added attraction was that this "celebrated spring" was located in a land that was naturally rich in gold and precious gems, which just might be what the Calusa were determined to keep the Juan Ponce de León expedition from discovering. Córdoba placed his fate and that of his crew in the hands of Alaminos.

Just as promised, Antonio Alaminos steered the two ships to a region abundant with freshwater. The chief pilot had managed to guide the crew to the very same Florida shore where he and Juan Ponce de León had their injurious encounter with the Calusa tribe. With their captain too weak to even get out of his bunk, it was up to Alaminos to lead a company of men ashore to gather water and food. Once on land, the men bathed their wounds and filled their bellies before beginning to load the barrels with freshwater for the rest of the troops. The Spaniards were interrupted in their task by an abrupt call to arms from a soldier who, along with another soldier named Berrio, had been posted as a lookout. The men suddenly had to shield themselves from a torrent of arrows unleashed by Calusa warriors who rapidly descended upon them from both land and water. Ten Spaniards were seriously wounded during a desperate race back to the ships, one of whom was Alaminos. An arrow found its way into the neck of the chief pilot but fortunately for him, and the rest of the crew, it was not a fatal wound.

Alaminos and his men made their escape by capturing a native canoe and paddling back to their ship. All of the men who had gone ashore were accounted for except Berrio, the only soldier who had survived the brutal engagement with the Mayans at Champoton without a scratch. A search was immediately conducted for their missing comrade but it was to no avail. It was at this point that the frustrated and fatigued survivors of this expedition agreed that the time had come to return to Cuba.

After the two boats docked at the port of Havana, a feeble Francisco de Córdoba went to meet with Diego Velázquez to issue a detailed report of the expedition's findings. Though disturbed to hear that more than half of the crew had perished on this mission, most at the hands of natives who had fiercely defended their homeland, the governor was delighted to learn from the captain that these hostile Mayans were obviously a far more advanced civilization than the tribes that inhabited the islands already conquered by the Spaniards. This conclusion was supported by Córdoba's tale of Mayan towns built with carved stone, a building achievement vastly superior to the typical reed huts that housed the island tribes, and the elegant attire worn by the Mayans, a stark contrast to the nearly naked natives the Spaniards were used to encountering. Naturally, the gold that Córdoba and his crew seized from the temples at Cape Catoche was sufficient reason to warrant another expedition to explore the lands to the west of Cuba. Just ten days after his return to Cuba, Francisco de Córdoba succumbed to the terrible wounds he had received at Champoton.

In 1518, Antonio Alaminos signed on as chief pilot for the follow-up expedition to the Yucatan. This flotilla of four ships was placed under the command of Juan Grijalva, a young and inexperienced officer whose defining qualification was the fact that he was the nephew of Governor Diego Velázquez. Two hundred forty soldiers of fortune signed on for this hopeful voyage, a list that included a bold and dashing officer by the name of Pedro de Alvarado and a future historian by the name of Bernal Díaz del Castillo. While this mission experienced better success at forcefully dealing with the belligerent Mayans, and even avenged the terrible loss suffered by Córdoba's troops at Champoton, Grijalva failed to establish a permanent settlement in this hostile region, an oversight that Diego Velázquez was unwilling to forgive his young nephew. However, the governor was delighted to see that this expedition had returned with an even larger quantity of gold and additional reports of a naturally rich land that seemed ripe for the taking.

The ambitious Diego Velázquez decided to send yet another expedition to the Yucatan, this time with explicit instructions to claim, conquer, and settle this promising region in the name of Spain and, more important, for the greater glory of the governor. Diego chose Hernán Cortés as the commander of this third venture to the Yucatan. Cortés had served with distinction in Velázquez's conquest of Cuba, and for his loyal service he was rewarded with an encomienda to call his own and an appointment as the official notary of Asunción de Baracoa, the first Spanish settlement on Cuba. Though the two had become good friends, with each taking the other into their confidence, it was a volatile relationship that at one point landed Cortés in prison on a charge of treason. While the two men temporarily resolved their differences, had Pánfilo de Narváez, the governor's favorite officer, not been in Spain at that time attending to personal affairs, the course of human events might have taken a drastically different turn.

Hernán Cortés set out across the Yucatan Channel on February 19, 1519, at the head of an imposing fleet of eleven ships that carried five hundred eight soldiers and one hundred sailors, as well as a great many Cuban natives and several African slaves who were brought along to help shoulder some of the burden. Pedro de Alvarado served as second-in-command and Antonio Alaminos enlisted as the chief pilot for this epic adventure. Shortly after landing along the shores of the Yucatan Peninsula, Cortés complied with the decree of the governor and laid claim to the region for Spain. However, Hernán reasoned that, since he and his men were taking all the risks in conquering and settling this land, the glory and rewards of this expedition belonged to him and his troops. While pledging his continued allegiance to the Crown, Cortés severed all ties with the governor of Cuba and established an independent governing body that was answerable to him.

When Diego Velázquez learned that he had been betrayed by Hernán Cortés, the governor sent a fleet of nineteen ships carrying a heavily armed force numbering more than eleven hundred soldiers to the Yucatan to crush the rebellion. Pánfilo de Narváez, who had recently returned from Spain, was given command of this mission sent to avenge a terrible injustice committed against the governor. Narváez was instructed to continue with the conquest and settlement of the Yucatan once he had defeated the rebel force and sent the captured Cortés back to Cuba. Unfortunately, the arrogant Narváez underestimated the military cunning of his adversary, and it was he who found himself languishing inside a prison cell after his army was defeated by a much smaller force. Besides having to endure the humiliation of such a defeat, Pánfilo de Narváez suffered the loss of an eye, which had been plucked out by the pointed lance of a soldier loyal to Hernán Cortés.

Reinforced by the captured troops of Narváez and carefully forged alliances with a number of disaffected native tribes, Cortés eventually succeeded in toppling the rich and mighty empire lorded over by the Aztecs. Rumors of Cortés' discovery of a magnificent inland city that exceeded the size and splendor of any contemporary European city spread quickly throughout the Spanish colonies in the New World, and soon everyone was eager to sign on for any upcoming expedition, of which there was suddenly no shortage, to find and conquer other native empires. It stood to reason that if there was one such lavish kingdom, then surely there must be more just waiting to be discovered.

A Renewed Interest in Florida

The ongoing adventures of Hernán Cortés and his troops in Mexico rekindled Juan Ponce de León's desire to return to Pascua Florida, the land he had discovered and for which he held the rights to conquer and settle for Spain. He undoubtedly heard the stories of how the mighty Aztecs had driven the Spaniards out of Tenochtitlan, the capital of the Aztec empire, and how they were putting up a staunch defense against a renewed Spanish offensive that included the enlisted aid of thousands of native warriors eager to bring an end to the harsh reign of the Mexica, a victory that Cortés and his allies did not achieve until August 13, 1521. Such tales probably reminded Ponce de León of just how fiercely the Calusa had defended their homeland and possibly caused him to consider that maybe the they too had something of great value they wished to keep hidden from the prying eyes of outsiders.

Ponce de León's return to Florida began on February 15, 1521, a date, according to most accounts, he set sail with two hundred settlers, several priests, fifty horses, and a large number of domesticated animals, to lay the foundations for a permanent colony along the western shores of Florida. Though still hopeful of finding the elusive treasures of Bimini, Ponce was now more interested in learning about the domain of the Calusa. Those painful memories of his first encounter with this warlike tribe were soothed by the news that Diego Miruelo, who is believed to be the same Diego Miruelo that rescued Antonio Alaminos, had sailed in 1516 to the very same region and supposedly carried on a profitable trade with the Calusa tribes. An unscathed Miruelo returned to Cuba to report that Florida was a rich and bountiful land. The numerous pieces of silver and gold he had obtained on this voyage were offered up as proof to the truthfulness of his bold claims. What Miruelo and his comrades failed to realize was that the precious metals they brought back had once belonged to Spain. The Calusa and other coastal tribes, especially those along the Florida Keys, often collected gold and other precious articles that washed ashore from Spanish shipwrecks and these items frequently circulated between tribes as a form of currency used for barter or tribute.

The prospective Spanish settlers landed in the vicinity of Charlotte Harbor, near where the previous expeditions of Juan Ponce de León and Francisco de Córdoba had encountered hostile resistance from the Calusa. The hopes and dreams of all who joined this expedition were dashed the moment they realized that the Calusa had no intention of sharing their land with anyone else. The Calusa warriors launched an attack shortly after the Spaniards came ashore, an unrelenting assault that claimed the lives of many would-be colonists. An arrow pierced the thigh of Ponce de León and because of the angry way that his deep wound festered many believed it was the result of a poisoned arrow, a deadly concoction that was part of the Calusa arsenal. The survivors abandoned their plans to settle Florida and sailed at once for Havana, the closest Spanish port, in order that their commander could receive proper medical attention. Despite the best efforts of all who were concerned for his welfare, Juan Ponce de León passed away in July of 1521. The dream of uncovering the hidden wealth of Florida, however, did not die with the passing of Ponce de León. There would be several more expeditions to this region, all of which were led by commanders who were convinced that they had the wherewithal to succeed where the Spanish discoverer of Florida had failed.

While Ponce de León was still probing the west coast of Florida, another Spanish expedition was venturing up along the eastern shores of the same peninsula in search of slaves to serve the various needs of the Spanish settlements. Lucás Vázquez de Ayllón, a wealthy and high ranking official, had sent a single ship on a slaving excursion under the command of Francisco Gordillo to the Lucayos (Bahamas) in the year 1521. Ayllón had come to the New World in 1502 aboard the fleet that accompanied Nicolás de Ovando, the newly appointed governor of Hispaniola. Allyon sailed to Mexico in 1520 as a royal judge charged by the Royal Audiencia of St. Domingo with monitoring and mediating the escalating dispute between Hernán Cortés and Diego Velázquez over rights to the lands currently being explored by the future conqueror of the Aztec empire. Pánfilo de Narváez, the officer who had been sent by the governor of Cuba to arrest Cortés, showed his sheer contempt for Ayllón's persistent attempts to intercede by having him arrested and forcibly placed on a ship that was supposed to carry him to Cuba. The judge, however, used his powers of persuasion to compel the captain of the ship to return him to the more politically hospitable climate at Hispaniola.

Content to return to less threatening affairs of business, Ayllón sent Francisco Gordillo off in search of island natives who could be sold for a tidy profit at the local slave market. Upon reaching the Bahamas, Gordillo was disappointed to learn that the indigenous population of this region had already been picked clean by a steady stream of other such Spanish slaving expeditions. The Lucayans were excellent swimmers and because of this recognized skill they were pressed into serving the Spaniards' avaricious need to retrieve pearls and, on occasion, to recover sunken treasure from the ocean floor. Captain Gordillo met up with Pedro de Quejo, another Spanish captain who had sailed to Andros Island for the same purpose. The two dissatisfied captains decided to join forces and they soon sailed northwest in search of other lands where Indians could be found.

Continuing northward, the joint expedition touched along the eastern shores of North America until both ships docked at a harbor near present-day Cape Fear, North Carolina, in June of 1521. There are a number of historians who contend that this expedition never made it past the boundary of South Carolina, but regardless of which latitude was reached, most accounts agree that the captains did go ashore, with each capturing as many as seventy natives to bring back to their respective benefactors. Unfortunately, the majority of the captured Indians died during the return journey, with starvation being the suspected reason for most of these deaths.

One of the few enslaved survivors was baptized with the Christian name of Francisco and assigned as a personal servant to Lucás Vázquez de Aylón. The converted native told his master that he hailed from a fabulous realm that was called Chicora, a wealthy kingdom that possessed a natural abundance of the lustrous pearls that the Spaniards cherished. Francisco also claimed that his homeland was ruled by a blond-haired giant named Datha who, just like the Spaniards, had many horses that he called his own. He claimed that Datha ruled a vast kingdom heavily populated with fair-haired people whose golden locks reached all the way down to their heels. Even though this native servant bore the physical characteristics common to most natives encountered in the New World — raven black hair and a copper complexion — the Spaniards were so enthralled with his tale that many took to calling him El Chicorano.

The tale told by El Chicorano coupled with the freely circulated stories of Diego Miruelo, the master of a ship who claimed to have carried on trade with the Floridians, was enough to convince Lucás Vázquez de Ayllón that the Florida region was home to a kingdom equal to, or even greater than, the magnificent Aztec empire that Hernán Cortés had discovered and conquered. Ayllón returned to Spain in 1523 to seek a charter that would permit him to further explore and settle the region where Francisco Gordillo had sailed, the land that his native servant once called home. To bolster his proposal, Ayllon brought El Chicorano with him so that he could give a first-hand account of the vast store of riches that awaited at the province of Chicora. Charles V, the grandson of Ferdinand and Isabella who inherited the Spanish throne in 1516 and was elected as the Holy Roman Emperor three years later, relished the idea of laying claim to another rich native empire and therefore enthusiastically embraced Ayllón's plan for establishing a colony. The emperor appointed Ayllón as Adelantado of a region that was to be called New Andalusia. He was also granted the right to explore some eight hundred leagues of this new land in order to find the legendary kingdom of Chicora, establish a permanent settlement in the Florida region, and to seek out a passage that would lead to the Spice Islands.

Upon his return to Santo Domingo, Ayllón sent out two reconnaissance ships to plot a course and determine a suitable spot to found his colony, one preferably close to the kingdom of Chicora, while he remained at Hispaniola to make detailed preparations for the upcoming conquest and settlement of New Andalusia. The number of ships that Ayllón procured for his expedition varies with each account: one lists only three ships, another says four, and one claims there were six. Rumors of the fabulous riches waiting to be found at the province of Chicora were compelling enough to convince five hundred men and women at Hispaniola that Ayllón's venture was one well worth joining. The judge made sure that their inventory included plenty of livestock, between eighty and ninety horses, approximately one hundred African slaves, and every conceivable provision that would help ensure the success of this venture.

Everyone's great expectations for success were bolstered by the addition of Diego Miruelo as the expedition's navigator. All, including Ayllón, were convinced that Miruelo would be able to lead them to one of the many native places of trade he so frequently spoke of as possessing sizable amounts of precious metals, a region most must have concluded was part of the kingdom of Chicora, which, in turn, was a province that grew grander in size and wealth with each retelling of the tale. The Ayllon expedition set sail in July of 1526 but got off to an inauspicious start when Miruelo seemed to have great difficulty remembering the precise whereabouts of his previous profitable encounters. The problems of the expedition were compounded by the loss of the flagship after it ran aground during a search up one of the rivers that emptied into the Atlantic. Frustrated by his own inability to locate what he had promised to find and plagued by a growing sense that those around him had begun to doubt the veracity of his many splendid stories, Miruelo slid into a melancholy that continued to worsen until he no longer possessed the will to live, a state of suffering that led to his premature death.

Though the death of the navigator was viewed as an ominous sign by many, the expedition continued northward along the coast of North America in search of an ideal spot to establish a colony. Where exactly the remaining ships finally dropped anchor is still a source of debate amongst historians. Some believe it was along the Sapelo Sound in Georgia, others say it was at the mouth of the Pee Dee River in South Carolina, and many contend they settled at the Cape Fear River near Wilmington, North Carolina. The one thing that all seem to agree on regarding the founding of this Spanish settlement, which preceded the English colony of Jamestown by eighty years, is that it was christened San Miguel de Guadalupe.

The site where Lucás Vázquez de Ayllón chose to establish his colony proved inhospitable in more ways than the Spanish settlers were prepared to handle. They arrived too late to plant crops and since their food supply was nearly depleted, the colonists had to expend a great deal of time and energy foraging for sustenance in unfamiliar terrain. The natives that Ayllón had counted on as an interim source of food steered clear of any contact with those they knew were of the same race of men who had previously come ashore to kidnap their people. Adding to their mounting list of woes was the sudden desertion of Francisco Chicorano and several other natives, which gave many Spaniards good reason to believe that the Datha tale was merely a clever ruse that earned the native servant a trip back home. This unexpected loss left Ayllón without any guides or interpreters.

The Spaniards also discovered that they shared their colony with a host of germ carrying mosquitoes and soon many colonists, most of whom were already weak from a lack of food, began to complain of uncontrollable chills and fever. The settlers were also unprepared for the drastic drop in temperature ushered in by autumnal winds that made an early appearance. After having watched many of his followers perish from a rampant fever epidemic, Ayllón found himself suddenly stricken with similar symptoms and, after much suffering, he passed away on October 18, 1526. The looming threat of a long and bleak winter was incentive enough for the survivors to abandon this ill-fated colony. An effort was made to return Ayllón's body to Santo Domingo but the small boat used to tow his corpse was swept out to sea. Only one hundred of the settlers found their way back to Hispaniola, disease and famine claiming the others, who had died in vain.

2

THE NARVÁEZ EXPEDITION

Narváez's Preparations

Pánfilo de Narváez would spend nearly three years at Vera Cruz as a prisoner of Hernán Cortés, the man he had been sent to bring to justice by Diego Velázquez, the governor of Cuba. He certainly had plenty of time to reflect upon all his past deeds, and, while there were many successes to savor, it was this recent failure that would haunt him for all his days remaining.

Like so many other young men of his era, Pánfilo de Narváez believed that the West Indies offered the promise of greater opportunities for success than his homeland of Spain could ever possibly offer. Narváez reached the New World sometime around 1498 and immediately enlisted in the ongoing military campaigns to subjugate the tribes that inhabited lands now claimed by Spain as part of its emerging empire. His large stature, broad frame, bright red beard, and booming voice cast a commanding presence that contributed considerably to his steady rise in rank. Narváez served with distinction in the wars against the indigenous peoples of Hispaniola and Jamaica, but it was the conquest of Cuba that earned him the wealth and recognition he craved so dearly. His string of victories over tribes ill-equipped to counter the superior weapons and refined warfare tactics of the Spanish soldiers had swelled Narváez's confidence to a point where he believed it was his bold strategies that made the difference in the outcome of these battles. It was an arrogance that frequently led him to underestimate his enemy and ultimately resulted in his humiliating defeat at the hands of Hernán Cortés, a soldier who once served under him. A humbled Narváez lost not only his command and an eye during a brief battle with a smaller army under the command of Cortés, but also the favorable reputation he had worked so hard to establish. Adding insult to injury, Pánfilo was forced to watch as his triumphant foe was accorded titles and accolades for a conquest that, by his reckoning, rightfully belonged to him.

In 1523, nearly two years after the fall of the Aztec Empire, Hernán Cortés felt confident enough with his own stature to permit Pánfilo de

Narváez to return to Cuba. The conqueror of Mexico was, at that moment, a celebrated figure at the Spanish court, and a grateful Emperor Charles V appointed him governor and captain-general of the rich tract of land he had added to the rapidly expanding empire of Spain. With his honor and pride cut to the quick, a despondent Narváez returned to Cuba wearing a silk patch to conceal his barren eye socket. Pánfilo was heartened to learn that, thanks to the skillful direction of his wife, María de Valenzuela, his holdings and wealth had greatly increased during his long absence.

With a renewed sense of confidence, Pánfilo de Narváez returned to Spain in early 1525 with the objective of obtaining a grant to lead his own expedition, one that hopefully would add to the coffers of the Spanish Crown and thereby restore his badly tarnished reputation. He was to spend the next year and a half seeking permission and funding to lead an expedition that, in his own words, was "to serve your Majesty by the exploration, conquest and populating of certain lands in the Ocean Sea, asking that the subjugation of the countries there are from the Río de Palmas to Florida might be given me ... for me, my heirs and successors."[1]

Narváez had brazenly proposed to take over claims to the extensive land grants that were awarded beforehand to two other explorers: Francisco de Garay and Juan Ponce de León, both of whom were now deceased. Garay had been granted territory just to the north of New Spain, lands that were once lorded over by the Aztecs and were now governed by Hernán Cortés, but Garay had died under suspicious circumstances shortly after having dined with the conqueror of Mexico. It had been five years since Ponce de León, who held title to the lands he called Florida, had expired from an arrow wound received while attempting to settle the region granted to him by King Ferdinand, the grandfather of Emperor Charles V.

After many months of intense negotiations, during which time many favors had to be called in and a great many promises had to be made, Pánfilo de Narváez was finally given the opportunity to redeem himself. On December 11, 1526, Emperor Charles granted him a patent to explore, conquer, and settle Florida "from one sea to the other." Ironically, it was the expedition of his nemesis that provided the one-eyed Narváez with a chance to restore his good name and return to the good grace of the emperor.

Delighted by the native wealth that had been accumulated by Hernán Cortés and his troops during the conquest of the Aztec Empire, the Spanish Crown hoped that Pánfilo de Narváez could locate a city equal to the opulence of Tenochtitlan. There was reason to believe that Florida was the most logical location for another vast and rich native empire. The tenacious resistance offered by the Calusa Indians on two separate occasions to keep Ponce de León from claiming their land was viewed by many as a sign that they were determined to protect something of great value, much like the Aztecs, who had valiantly defended their city of Tenochtitlan even when all hope of victory had long since passed. Florida was no longer thought of as an island but recognized as the peninsula of a much larger land mass that extended northward and westward for an unknown distance. With the combined rights to the land grants of both Francisco de Garay and Juan Ponce de León and all the lands that lay in between, Narváez held claim to a region of extraordinary breadth and untold possibilities.

Álvar Núñez Cabeza de Vaca, an ambitious Spanish officer assigned to the house of the duke of Medina Sidonia, learned of the upcoming expedition to the New World under the command of Pánfilo de Narváez and was eager to enlist. Like so many other Spanish citizens of his era, Cabeza de Vaca was captivated by the stories of daring expeditions led by such illustrious adventurers as Christopher Columbus and Hernán Cortés. His sense of adventure was also inspired by the celebrated accomplishments of his paternal grandfather, Pedro de Vera Mendoza, the Spanish conqueror of the Gran Canaria, the third largest of the chain of islands off the northwest coast of Africa collectively known as the Canary Islands.

Cabeza de Vaca was born at Jerez de la Frontera, near the port city of Cádiz, sometime around 1490. The origin of this peculiar family surname can be traced back to the family legend of a peasant ancestor named Alhajá, who, in the year 1212, is said to have helped the cause of King Sancho of Navarre by marking an unguarded pass in the Sierra Morenas with the skull of a cow. This secret passage through the mountains helped the Christian soldiers surprise and defeat an army of Moors at the battle of Las Navas de Tolosa. A grateful king rewarded his loyal subject with the "Cow's Head" surname, a title that the family carried with pride, for it helped elevate them into the lesser ranks of Spanish nobility. It was a family name that certainly served Álvar Núñez well, and even today he is best remembered as simply Cabeza de Vaca.

The eldest of four children, Cabeza de Vaca was the recipient of a well rounded education that helped him to cultivate a refined manner, an essential quality for the making of a gentleman. He grew to be tall and well built, and he took to sporting a red beard to signify his maturity. His noble lineage helped earn him employment in 1503 at the house of the duke of Medina Sidonia, a benefactor whom he served until the time he sailed to the New World. During a two year period that ended in 1513, Cabeza de Vaca saw service in the Italian campaigns, participating in the battles of both Ravenna and Bologna. He was recognized for his valiant service with the honorable appointment of royal standard bearer of Gaeta, a city near Naples. He married shortly after returning from Italy, and in 1521 Cabeza de Vaca served at the battle of Puente de la Reina, in Navarre, where the Spanish army defeated an invading French force.

Cabeza de Vaca's status at the royal court earned him an appointment as treasurer of the upcoming Narváez expedition that was planning to conquer and colonize the Florida region. He was also awarded the post of provost, and because of these appointed titles Cabeza de Vaca was, much to the chagrin of Pánfilo de Narváez, generally recognized as being second-in-command of the expedition. Many of the officers were personally selected by Narváez but the commander had no say over royal appointments such as the treasurer, and this situation would prove to be a constant source of friction between the two highest ranking officers of this campaign. Other royal appointments that Pánfilo de Narváez had no choice but to accept included Alonso de Solís, as royal factor and inspector of mines, and Alonso Enríquez as comptroller.

Among the enlisted officers, Captain Alonso del Castillo, the son of a prominent doctor who practiced medicine at their hometown of Salamanca, and Andrés Dorantes from Béjar, who signed on as Captain of the Infantry, were two of the most notable. Dorantes was accompanied on this journey by his slave, a dark-skinned Moroccan christened with the name of Esteban (aka Estevan or Estevanico). This native of Azamor was born around 1500 and forced into slavery in 1513 after he was captured by Portuguese raiders. Andrés Dorantes purchased the rights to Esteban in 1520, and since all slaves brought to Spain were required to submit to the tenets of Christianity, the Moor had most likely been forced to convert to the faith of the Christians.

Five well provisioned ships, all of which were caravels, set sail from the fortified seaport of Sanlúcar de Barrameda on June 17, 1527, to begin the eagerly anticipated search for the rich native kingdoms that had twice escaped the notice of Juan Ponce de León. The flotilla that Narváez assembled carried approximately six hundred enlisted soldiers of fortune, none of whom were paid a salary from the Crown but all of whom were willing to serve for the promise of a share of the tremendous rewards expected to come from this venture. They also brought with them a great many horses and a full arsenal of weapons to aid in the conquest of Florida. Included in their armory were many swords, crossbows, lances, daggers, halberds, which were poles with sharpened blades shaped like a cleaver, and several arquebuses, the awkward forerunner of the musket. The horses were supplied with armor to protect them from the weapons of the natives.

The Narváez fleet charted a course to the island of Hispaniola, an Atlantic crossing that ended when the ships docked at Santo Domingo after nearly three months at sea. Here the commander spent forty-five days gathering additional supplies and rounding up more horses for the upcoming expedition to Florida. Narváez also purchased another vessel during his stay at the island. But all of these gains could not offset the numerous losses suffered from an unforeseen circumstance. News of Lucás Vázquez de Ayllón's disastrous effort to establish a colony to the north had reached Hispaniola and this resulted in the sudden change of heart of one hundred forty soldiers who promptly decided to desert Narváez's command.

Fearing that the loss of men would continue to swell, Narváez sailed at once for Cuba, the island he had called home ever since he helped Diego Velázquez in 1511 take it away from the Ciboney and Taino tribes who dwelled there. While docked at Santiago, Narváez met with Vasco Porcallo de Figueroa, an old comrade who served in the conquest of Cuba and who was now one of the wealthiest landowners on the island. He was also a notoriously cruel slave master. It is said that during one of his more extreme fits of rage, Porcallo castrated several native slaves who failed to meet his expectations and forced them to eat their own genitalia. It is also said that when he learned many of his slaves were plotting to take their own life by eating dirt, Vasco promised them that he too would take his own life in order that he might continue to torment them in the hereafter for all eternity.

Vasco Porcallo offered to sell Pánfilo de Narváez some horses and supplies from his land holdings at the port town of Trinidad, a place that had been founded by both conquistadors. The entire expedition set sail for Trinidad, a distance of slightly more than one hundred fifty miles. Halfway there, however, Narváez decided to send Cabeza de Vaca and Porcallo on ahead with just two ships to procure the additional provisions while he remained behind at the Gulf of Guacanayabo with the four other ships.

After reaching Trinidad, the captain of the two vessels, an officer by the name of Pantoja, went ashore with Porcallo to conduct business. Cabeza de Vaca was summoned ashore shortly thereafter to assist in the intricate matters of this transaction, while the rest of the men remained aboard the anchored boats. The ominous formation of clouds noticed by the crew was a clear sign that a gathering storm was about to descend upon them. Thirty members of the crew made it to shore before the full fury of the storm materialized. This sudden hurricane slammed the island with such force that it completely destroyed the two ships and claimed the lives of more than fifty soldiers and twenty horses. Cabeza de Vaca, Vasco Porcallo, Captain Pantoja and the rest of the survivors sifted through the scattered wreckage and tended to those who were not as fortunate as they. Fearing that a similar fate had befallen Narváez, the men at Trinidad resigned themselves to the thought that their grand adventure had ended before it even had a chance to begin. Their spirits were revived by the unexpected appearance of Pánfilo de Narváez and his four vessels, all having survived the wrath of the storm intact by taking shelter in a nearby harbor.

Narváez was ready to continue with his quest, just as if nothing had happened, but bad weather lingered around to threaten the island for several more days. Storms of this magnitude greatly frightened the troops and many expressed a desire to delay plans for their departure until the end of winter. Compelled by the elements and the wishes of his men to temporarily postpone his expedition, Narváez made use of this time by making much needed repairs to the ships. They ventured to the town of Jagua where the impatient commander was able to obtain two ships and additional recruits to replace those lost to the storm. Narváez also managed to obtain the services of an experienced pilot carrying the familiar last name of Miruelo. There is still speculation about the true identity of this pilot who had been to Río de las Palmas, which rested along the westernmost region of Narváez's extensive land grant. He was very possibly a relative of the navigator by the same name who several years earlier obtained a small quantity of gold through trade with the natives of Florida and who had recently passed away while serving as the chief pilot of the ill-fated Ayllón expedition. There are some historians who believe that his true name was Diego Fernández de Mirnedo, a pilot who sailed to Mexico in 1523 to help Francisco Garay, the governor of Jamaica, establish a colony at Panuco.

The ships left Jagua and sailed further west along the coast of Cuba in an effort to replenish the provisions that had been used up during the long winter wait. Another disastrous setback occurred when the boats were accidentally run aground on sandbars, where they floundered for more than a fortnight until a storm released the hulls from the firm grip of the ocean floor. Plans for continuing to sail along the coast of Cuba were dashed when a sudden storm pushed them far out into the Gulf of Mexico. Narváez thought there had already been enough delays and decided at that moment to steer a course for Río de las Palmas, which rested to the north of Santisteban de Puerto. It had always had been his plan to begin the conquest from the west, where there was already an established Spanish settlement, and steadily work his way toward the east, a region populated by hostile natives who had previously resisted the explorative efforts of Juan Ponce de León and Francisco de Córdoba. It was a route that Narváez hoped would reveal a back door to the rich kingdoms that the Calusa were obviously trying to keep the Spaniards from finding.

In Search of Apalachee

Unfortunately for all aboard the ships, the wind and the sea conspired against the sailors' determined efforts to reach the western shores of Narváez's vast land grant. The fact that Miruelo had proven to be a less than competent navigator also offers another explanation as to why the expedition failed to arrive at its intended destination. It was generally assumed by the crew that the land sighted on April 7, 1528, after nearly a month at sea, was just to the east of Río de las Palmas. Convinced that he knew of a nearby suitable harbor from a previous venture, Miruelo had the flotilla head south shortly after land was sighted. One of the ships was lost along the coast; where, when and why are still unclear.

Even though he had lost his bearings, Miruelo managed to locate Boca Ciega Bay, a promising passage just to the north of the entrance to Tampa Bay, which, in turn, was to the north of where Juan Ponce de León had twice made landfall. The conquistadors were soon treated to the sight of several well constructed round houses, one of which sat atop a man-made earthen mound. All took this as a sign that they had already happened upon the realm of an advanced civilization similar to those discovered in Mexico. Eager to learn more about this place, Narváez sent Alonso Enríquez, the comptroller, ashore with a small group of soldiers. As a token of their peaceful intentions, these Spanish emissaries brought an assortment of trinkets to offer the natives; some were gifts and some were meant for carrying on trade.

The natives who came out to meet Alonso Enríquez were unlike any the Spaniards were accustomed to meeting. These Florida Indians were of considerable height — taller than most of the soldiers — and their bodies were decorated with a great many tattoos. Many of the men and women who lived among the tribes of this southeastern region had elaborate tattoos etched upon their faces, limbs, and torsos, which were markings of noteworthy deeds or close family ties. The men wore only a breechclout to cover their privates while the topless women wore skirts that provided merely a modest amount of coverage. Following an exchange of pleasantries, Enríquez showed these natives a sample of corn, which was the staple of the civilized tribes of Mexico, and gold, a precious metal that seemed to be a common commodity of such cultured people. Much to the dismay of the Spaniards, the Indians made it quite clear that they possessed neither of these items. The best that Enríquez could do at this point was to trade some of his gewgaws for a more than fair quantity of food, mostly fish and venison. The comptroller then returned to the ships to report these tidings to his commander.

On the following day, Pánfilo de Narváez personally led approximately forty soldiers, including Cabeza de Vaca, toward the nearby village to meet with the natives who had carried on trade with Enríquez. The Spaniards were disappointed to see that the town, which consisted of just "seven or eight houses" and one fairly large mound, upon which there stood a house that seemed to have been built for the ruler, had recently been abandoned. The Spaniards took advantage of this opportunity to rummage through every hut

and their efforts were rewarded with the discovery of a solitary gold ornament. One account says the item was a gold disk, while Cabeza de Vaca
remembered that it was a gold rattle. Most likely, this precious item was salvaged from a Spanish shipwreck, but to many wishful Spaniards, this article
served as evidence that this was indeed a land of great wealth. Those who
were disappointed by the lack of valuables at this village found encouragement in the words of the veteran conquistadors who told them that tribes
along the coast were generally primitive and poor.

Narváez formally staked a claim to this region for Spain by reading aloud
the "El Requerimiento," the legal document that entitled him to take possession of the land for his God, his king, and himself. After the return of their
commander, the rest of the soldiers disembarked as did the horses, which,
because of the long voyage, had dwindled from eighty to around forty-two
gaunt and wobbly legged steeds. The following day, while the Spaniards were
still busy unloading the ships and making camp, a delegation of Indians
stepped out of the woods and with signs and gestures tried as best they could
to get Narváez and his men to leave their land. Much to the dismay of the
natives, the Spaniards chose to ignore their request and continued setting up
camp.

Convinced that these Indians were attempting to prevent him from discovering something of monumental importance, Pánfilo de Narváez headed
inland with another group of forty plus soldiers, a company that once again
included Cabeza de Vaca, to scour the surrounding region. A march northward brought the explorers to the mouth of a large bay they called Bahia de
la Cruz, which was the western stretch of the large inlet now known as Tampa
Bay. Narváez quickly returned to camp to inform Miruelo that he had most
likely sighted the harbor that the pilot had been looking for. He ordered Miruelo to take the brigantine and search for the mouth of the Río de las Palmas
so they could get their bearings and the expedition could get back on track.
In the event that he was unable to find the Spanish settlement situated near
the river, Miruelo was instructed to return to Havana to gather more provisions before rejoining the expedition. Miruelo immediately set sail but since
the port he sought was on the other side of the Gulf of Mexico, the baffled
pilot had a difficult time locating terrain that corresponded with either his
memory or his charts.

After the brigantine left, Narváez took the same company of men who
had joined him on the previous excursion and followed a native trail that went
northward along the shore of the bay. The commander hoped that this path
would either lead to a village where food could be found or reunite him with
Miruelo at the port the pilot was presently seeking. This trail led them to an
encounter with four Indians, who, after being shown some samples of maize,

promised to guide the conquistadors to a place where corn could be found. The Spaniards had surmised from their recent experience in Mexico that native tribes who grew corn were generally more civilized and wealthier than the natives who were forced to spend much of their time hunting and gathering food for their tribe.

True to their word, the Indians led the Spaniards to a village near the bay where they found corn that was not yet ready to be harvested. A further search of the area led to the surprise discovery of some familiar fabrics, European styled shoes, some bits of iron, a few pieces of gold, and several merchant crates, all of which were the washed ashore remnants of a Spanish shipwreck. Narváez's men were shocked to discover that inside the Castilian crates were corpses draped in deer skin. Whether these were the bodies of deceased Spaniards, Indians, or a combination thereof remains unclear. The natives were probably using these boxes as temporary caskets for those who were to be interred during a mass ceremony at their ancestral burial grounds. Disgusted by what he saw, Narváez ordered the burning of all the crates and their gruesome contents.

Many of the natives gathered to confront Narváez and his men the following day, making signs and gestures that appeared as if they were trying to shoo away these disrespectful Spaniards who were steadily sifting through their personal belongings. Violence erupted when Pánfilo de Narváez refused to comply with their request. The brief altercation ended in favor of the Spaniards, who immediately resumed their search for items they deemed worth taking. Narváez, an officer who was known for his cruelty toward the island natives, began torturing the inhabitants of this village in an attempt to learn where he could find more gold. The Indians they happened upon had no gold other than that which they salvaged from Spanish shipwrecks. The only means available to end their suffering was to tell Narváez what he wanted to hear. Several tortured natives pointed north while blurting out "Apalachen! Apalachen!" to indicate this was the place where much gold could be found. Narváez believed he had successfully persuaded the natives to reveal the rich secret of Florida, a vast treasure they had been trying to keep from the Spaniards ever since the first expedition of Juan Ponce de León.

A chief by the name of Hirrihigua made the fatal mistake of complaining to Narváez about the ransacking of his village and the torture of his people. The Spanish commander responded by unleashing dogs on the chief's mother. Greyhounds, bloodhounds, mastiffs, and wolfhounds were among the breeds of large dogs that the Spaniards used to strike fear in the natives they sought to subjugate. Hirrihigua was forced to watch in horror as his beloved mother was savagely torn to pieces and devoured by a pack of ravenous dogs. Narváez then turned his wrath on the chief by having Hirrihigua's nose chopped off so closely that it severed a noticeable portion of his lips. Though permitted to live, Chief Hirrihigua would forever be haunted by the painful memories of that day.

Convinced that the Apalachen realm was much closer than indicated, Narváez compelled the natives who had spoken of this place to serve as his guides. The Spaniards marched for an additional ten or more leagues before they came upon another village, which had been abandoned in anticipation of their arrival. Seeing that this native town consisted of just a dozen or so huts and housed no precious metals or stones, Narváez was now ready to concede that Apalachee was still a long way off. The gold and glory that awaited would have to wait just a little longer while he took some time to organize a much larger regiment of conquistadors.

Narváez and his men rejoined their comrades still camped near the ships, all of whom they regaled with their enticing findings from the natives of a golden realm known as Apalachee, a city that was believed to be every bit as rich and magnificent as Tenochtitlan. Narváez called a meeting of his officers and told them that he intended to conduct a quick probe overland for Apalachee while the ships continued on a northerly course along the coast in search of the settlement of Santisteban del Puerto, which was to the south of the Río de las Palmas. The commander and his cronies were convinced that the Panuco region was a mere ten to fifteen days away, which they based on the calculations of the absent pilot Miruelo. Both parties were to search for the Spanish settlement, and the expedition that reached this destination first was to wait there until the other party arrived, after which they would jointly resume the march to find Apalachee.

Several officers, including Cabeza de Vaca, questioned the soundness of Narváez's proposal. They countered that it would be more advisable to remain with the ships until a suitable harbor had been located and a base established before setting off in search of an unknown kingdom in an unfamiliar land. This contingent of concerned conquistadors felt it would be reckless to head inland without knowing exactly where the ships were docked. It was also pointed out that they had no one to serve as an interpreter, their supply of food had become precariously low, and most of the horses were still too weak to undertake such an arduous journey. Cabeza and the officers who shared his concerns were quick to learn that Pánfilo de Narváez was not one to heed the advice of a subordinate.

Angered that all the officers did not fully agree with his plan, Narváez took out his mounting frustration on Cabeza de Vaca, his most vocal critic, by attempting to shame the treasurer into submission. In the presence of the other officers, Narváez told Cabeza de Vaca that if he was afraid to venture to Apalachee without knowing where the boats were docked then perhaps he should remain with the ships. Though he still disagreed with his commander, Cabeza de Vaca did not wish to be thought a coward by his comrades and therefore declined such a denigrating offer. After the meeting was adjourned, Narváez sent a message to Cabeza de Vaca beseeching him to reconsider his offer. Whether the commander truly believed that the treasurer was the best man to command the ships or just saw this as an opportunity to rid himself of an officer who did not share his views remains unclear. Cabeza de Vaca again made it clear that he had no intention of changing his mind. Narváez even came in person to try to persuade him into taking charge of the ships, but being the proud Spaniard that he was, Cabeza de Vaca replied "that I preferred risking my life to placing my honor in jeopardy."[2] A judge by the name of Caravallo became Narváez's second choice as commander of the ships that were to sail northward.

Having chosen to ignore the voice of reason, the stubborn Narváez proceeded with the plan that called for dividing his forces. He took three hundred soldiers, forty of whom were cavalry, on an overland expedition to the north while the ships with a crew of roughly one hundred, ten of whom were the women that had accompanied the expedition from Cuba, set sail in search of Santisteban del Puerto. Cabeza de Vaca and the rest of the officers were included in the group that followed Pánfilo de Narváez. The commander decided to head back to the region where they had found corn and evidence of a Spanish shipwreck before setting off in search of Apalachee. Since there was a concern that Miruelo and his crew would wonder what had become of them once they found their way back to the Spanish camp, a cross was erected along the beach with a letter attached that told of Narváez's plan to find Apalachee. The note also instructed them to follow a similar path as soon as possible and to make sure to bring all the supplies they had procured on their voyage.

Leaving behind a pristine beach, Narváez and his men followed a native trail that many believed would soon lead them to signs of civilization and all the rewards that such a discovery entailed. Their spirits, however, began to wane as they found themselves having to trudge through numerous swamps and wade across many streams while hacking their way through the dense vegetation of a heavily forested region. The Spaniards quickly discovered that the swamplands of this region were a vast breeding ground for blood sucking mosquitoes and leeches and were also home to a host of man-eating alligators and poisonous snakes. Besides the difficult terrain, the soldiers had to battle the stifling heat and humidity that weighed heavily on their armored bodies and the swarms of giant flies and pesky gnats that never gave them a moment's piece. The difficulties of this treacherous trek would eventually claim the lives of several soldiers.

The weary Spaniards marched inland for fifteen grueling days without sighting either a village or any natives. Their food supply, which was precariously low at the start of this venture, was now nearly exhausted. Narváez and his men came to the Withlacoochee River, which, because of the strong currents, made for a very difficult crossing. Once across, the Spaniards encountered a band of warriors several hundred strong who barred the way. Without an interpreter to allay the concerns of those who inhabited this land, the tension between these two determined forces quickly escalated into an armed confrontation. The desperate soldiers prevailed and in the process they captured several of their adversaries, whom they compelled to lead them to their village. Here the famished conquistadors filled their bellies with maize and helped themselves to whatever else they desired.

After having learned from the natives that the ocean was not very far away, Narváez sent a scouting party that included Cabeza de Vaca and Captain Alonso del Castillo to locate the coast. The patrol soon returned to report that the shore was indeed near and that they had come to the mouth of a river that emptied into a bay. Believing that this was one of the rivers of the Panuco region, Narváez sent another expeditionary force under the command of Captain Valenzuela to locate the port that Miruello and Carvallo were separately searching to find. Valenzuela returned after several days to report that he had explored the bay, which he determined was too shallow for any ships, and was unable to locate either a Spanish port or settlement.

Anxious to renew his search for the golden realm of Apalachee, Pánfilo de Narváez convinced himself that he was within the vicinity of Panuco and therefore the ships would be waiting somewhere nearby when he made his triumphant return. Ignoring his own orders about waiting until the other expedition arrived before setting off on a quest for gold and glory, Narváez led his men away from the coast to resume the hunt for Apalachee. Guided by the natives they had previously captured, the Spaniards were soon met by a native lord called Dulchanchellin, who was accompanied by a large entourage of warriors and servants. The commander met with the chief and managed to communicate through signs that he and his men were in search of Apalachee. Dulchanchellin made it clear that he was familiar with the Apalachen, for they were an enemy of his people. This was music to the ears of Narváez. He knew from personal experience that Hernán Cortés had engineered the conquest of Tenochtitlan by forging alliances with the native tribes that were either vassals or enemies of the Aztecs. Narváez was delighted to learn that Dulchanchellin was not only eager to show them the way to Apalachee but also willing to aid the Spaniards in a campaign of conquest.

The first casualties of the inland march to Apalachee were Juan Velázquez, a relative of the former governor of Cuba, and his faithful horse, both of whom drowned while making a foolhardy attempt to cross the Suwan-nee River. Juan thought he could prove to the others that this river could be crossed without the aid of a boat. Both rider and horse were swept into the deep end of the river by the swift current and, following an exhaustive strug-gle to extricate themselves, their cries for help were soon suffocated by the raging water. The natives later found the lifeless bodies of both man and beast downriver. After giving their fallen comrade a proper burial, the Spaniards butchered the dead horse so that it could serve as sustenance for the fam-ished soldiers.

Narváez and his men were led to Dulchanchellin's village, where they were given enough maize to relieve their hunger. Feeling comfortable among their new-found allies, the Spaniards waited patiently for the natives to return with the water they promised to fetch for them. The tranquility of the moment was shattered by the whiz of an arrow that narrowly missed one of the sol-diers. It was then that the Spaniards noticed the entire village had been aban-doned. Bewildered and bothered by the treachery of those whom he thought were willing to aid in the conquest of Apalachee, Narváez placed his men on full alert while preparations were made for an early morning departure. The Spaniards were relieved that the night passed without incident, and at dawn's first light they made a hasty departure along a beaten path that all hoped would safely lead them to where they wished to go.

The wary conquistadors had not traveled very far before they encoun-tered a band of Dulchanchellin's warriors, all of whom were armed and painted for war. As the Spaniards prepared for battle, the warriors suddenly slipped back into the woods, which the natives thereafter used to conceal their movements while they continued to track the fleeing Spaniards. Most likely, Dulchanchellin's warriors simply wanted to make sure that these intruders understood they were not welcome in their province and that they were prepared to follow them all the way to the border of their homeland to make sure they did not attempt to return. Narváez was understandably concerned by these tactics and laid an ambush that led to the capture of three or possibly four warriors, who were all retained as guides. The surprise attack also brought an end to the perceived threat posed by the natives, as Chief Dulchanchellin and his warriors quickly retired to the safety of their village.

A Disappointing Discovery

The path through the dense forest that led to Apalachee was obstructed by a large number of fallen trees, many of which were felled by bolts of light-ning hurled from the terrible tempests that frequently plague this region.

Their fifty-five day long march since parting ways with the ships concluded on June 25, the day they finally reached the Apalachen province. It was at the site where the city of Tallahassee now stands that Pánfilo de Narváez and his men realized they had been misled. Instead of sighting a great city, one which they had been led to believe would rival the magnificence and wealth of Tenochtitlan, the Spaniards saw that the main town of Apalachee was nothing more than a humble village of forty crude huts situated near a lake that was surrounded by thick woods and numerous lagoons, some of which were too deep to cross by foot or on horse.

Narváez instructed Cabeza de Vaca to assemble a squadron of men and take the town by force. Slightly more than sixty Spaniards, nine of whom were on horseback, descended upon the unsuspecting inhabitants with such speed that they were able to lay claim to the village without a struggle. The celebration of their swift victory ended when the soldiers discovered that they had merely conquered a town inhabited by old men, women, and small children, none of whom were prepared to offer any serious resistance. The Spaniards soon learned that most of the male residents were either away tending to their nearby fields or off on a hunting expedition. Disappointment set in once it was realized that the village had little to offer in the way of material wealth; and as for gold, there was none to be found anywhere. Their only consolation was that they did find, just as their guides had promised, a large quantity of maize and other appetizing food items to fill their bellies.

A number of Apalachen men were near enough to hear the commotion and quickly returned to confront the Spaniards. Taking cover behind the trees, the natives pulled back on their longbows and released flat tipped arrows with enough force to penetrate deep inside the thick trunk of an oak tree and, as later demonstrated, with enough power to easily pierce Spanish armor. The arrows rained down on the Spaniards faster than they could load their weapons and even after they were loaded the soldiers could not see who was shooting at them. The natives killed the horse of Alonso Solís, the only Spanish casualty on that day, during the ensuing counterattack of the conquistadors.

The armed Apalachens were driven off, but only for the moment. Those who fled deep into the woods went to warn their fellow hunters and farmers of what had occurred. Two days after Narváez had laid claim to the village, the majority of the Apalachen men returned to demand that the Spaniards relinquish what was rightfully theirs. Negotiations led to the release of the women and children. But Narváez was unwilling to give up the village or one of their chiefs, whom the commander retained as leverage in bargaining for food and to ensure the safety of his men. It was a decision that all the Spaniards would soon regret.

Once the women and children were out of harm's way, approximately two hundred strategically positioned warriors let loose a barrage of arrows. In a determined effort to drive out those who had trespassed upon their land, the Apalachens set fire to their own village. The Spaniards rushed from the burning huts and, after gathering their weapons, charged toward the direction of the incoming arrows. By this time, however, the warriors had cleverly taken advantage of the surrounding woods and lagoons to conceal themselves from plain sight. They soon revealed their hidden locations with yet another round of arrows before seeking new places to hide. Sensing a trap, Narváez had his men return to safer ground.

Cabeza de Vaca, who saw an arrow whizz past his nose before becoming firmly embedded in a tree, provided a lasting testament to native skill with the bow and arrow: "All the Indians we had seen from Florida to here are archers, and as they are of large build and go about naked, from a distance they appear to be giants. They are a people wonderfully well built, very lean and of great strength and agility. The bows they use are as an arm [and] eleven or twelve spans long so that they can shoot arrows at two hundred paces with such great skill that they never miss their target."[3] The tension was set so taut on the bowstring cords, which were made from thongs of deer skin, that even the strongest Spaniard found it difficult to pull the string back as far as his face. The skill of the Apalachee warriors with wooden longbows nearly as large as a man would be a fatal lesson later learned by many Spaniards.

The following day another group of Apalachen warriors, a tribe from a neighboring village, launched an attack from a different direction. Once again, the Spaniards found their enemy to be an extremely difficult target to locate, but they still found a way to fend off their attackers. Each fierce altercation resulted in the death of one person, both being Apalachen warriors. After these two incidents, the natives resorted to guerilla tactics in an effort to drive off the Spaniards. They harassed Narváez and his men with sporadic rounds of arrows released from their longbows, a tactic that succeeded in stirring up much anguish among the troops.

Still hoping that there was some truth to the native tales of great wealth that could be found at Apalachee, Narváez sent out three separate reconnaissance expeditions. All soon returned to report that there was little to see except for more trees and more lagoons. The frustrated commander then questioned the native chief he had retained about the location of all the fabulously rich cities of Apalachee. He was disappointed to learn that this was the largest and richest village of the entire Apalachen province. When Narváez inquired about where he could find a town larger than this one the chief replied that the nearest would be Aute, a village that rested near the ocean and was roughly a nine day march to the south. The detained chief also told his captor that at Aute he would find many splendid items that would be to his liking and enough food to fully satisfy his large army.

Much to the delight of the disillusioned troops, Pánfilo de Narváez announced that the time had come to leave the Apalachen province. They had spent nearly a month dodging arrows and chasing an unseen enemy in order to defend their claim to a village that had nothing more to offer than basic food and water, and even those items were in short supply. Simple tasks such as collecting freshwater were fraught with peril. Don Pedro, a Mexican prince from Texcoco who Narváez expected to serve as an emissary and translator at the courts of the rich kingdoms he expected to discover on this expedition, was ambushed and killed by Apalachee warriors while he was attempting to quench his thirst. It was hoped by all that a return to the coast would lead to a much welcome reunion with their comrades aboard the ships.

Needless to say, the Apalachens were delighted to see that the Spaniards were finally leaving their village and therefore made no effort to oppose their exodus. However, this did not mean that they were willing to forget and forgive the conquistadors for their many transgressions. With the aid of a native guide who knew the way to Aute, Narváez and his troops were able to navigate the rugged terrain at a fairly brisk pace on their first day. On the following day the expedition came upon a large lagoon that had to be crossed. Once mired in the middle with water up to their chests, the Spaniards discovered they had walked into a trap. A sudden bombardment of arrows rained down on them from several directions and succeeded in wounding several startled soldiers and horses. Narváez gave the order to return fire only to discover that their powder was soaking wet, thereby rendering their arquebuses useless. The Spaniards were limited to shots of the crossbow, but when they took aim they found that the warriors, who had taken cover behind the trees, were not in their sights. Even when the soldiers could get off a shot, the Apalachens, who emerged just long enough to let fly another arrow, were able to get off several shots with their longbows in the time it took the Spaniards to reload their cumbersome crossbows.

The besieged Spaniards were forced to make a frantic dash across the lagoon. Their efforts, however, were slowed by the soft bed of the swamp, which caused their feet to get stuck, their heavy armor, which weighed them down, and the steady stream of arrows whizzing overhead, which forced them to keep low. Even when the end of the lagoon was in sight the Spaniards saw that a large force of Apalachee warriors were waiting for them to emerge. Frustrated by these events, Narváez ordered a desperate charge at the warriors who were harassing them. Their bold effort succeeded in causing the Apalachen archers to scatter to new hiding places, which provided the Spaniards an opportunity to safely escape this watery trap. While elated to reach safer ground, the Spaniards were discouraged to learn that their native captives, including their guide to Aute, had escaped during the fracas.

The Apalachen warriors continued to pursue and harass the conquistadors at every turn. Silently stalking their prey, the natives would emerge from the woods to attack the soldiers, exposing themselves just long enough to unleash their loaded bows at the Spaniards and then skillfully concealing themselves from sight before the enemy had a chance to return fire. Many Spaniards fell during this desperate flight back to the Gulf of Mexico, some from the sting of arrows while others were overcome with swamp fever. The weary soldiers exited one swamp only to become mired in another, one that was often larger than the previous one. Luckily, the Apalachen warriors, who were satisfied that the Spaniards had finally passed the boundary of their province, were no longer pursuing them.

Eight days of steady marching while constantly having to look over their shoulders had brought the Spaniards very close to Aute. Unfortunately, the path they followed led them directly into yet another ambush. The Aute Indians had learned of the Spaniards' approach and, once the soldiers were in range, launched an attack from the rear that killed the servant of an officer named Avellaneda, who, after hearing the screams of the young retainer, rushed to his aid. Avellaneda's valiant effort was cut short by an arrow that penetrated his neck, a mortal wound that caused him to suffer terribly before death provided welcome relief. Several other Spaniards were wounded before the Aute assault was finally repulsed.

The starved and exhausted Spaniards reached the village of Aute the following day only to discover that the natives had chosen to deprive them of the comfort of the native homes and the satisfaction of food from the native fields by setting fire to them prior to seeking shelter in the nearby woods. After sifting through the charred remains, Narváez and his men were relieved to find some maize and squash that had escaped the blaze of the fire. Unfortunately, there was not enough food to sustain an army of this size for very long. The predicament of the soldiers grew even more precarious with the rapid spread of a fever that weakened the minds and bodies of a great many men. Narváez was included in the group stricken with this debilitating ailment.

After two days at Aute, Narváez sent Cabeza de Vaca, Andrés Dorantes, Alonso del Castillo, Fray Juan Suárez and fifty soldiers on a mission to locate the reportedly nearby ocean, where they hoped to find Spanish ships patiently waiting for them. The Aute warriors saw that the Spaniards had divided their forces and used this opportunity to launch a night raid against those who remained at their village. While Narváez and his men still had enough strength to fend off this assault, many of the soldiers began to worry that Aute was

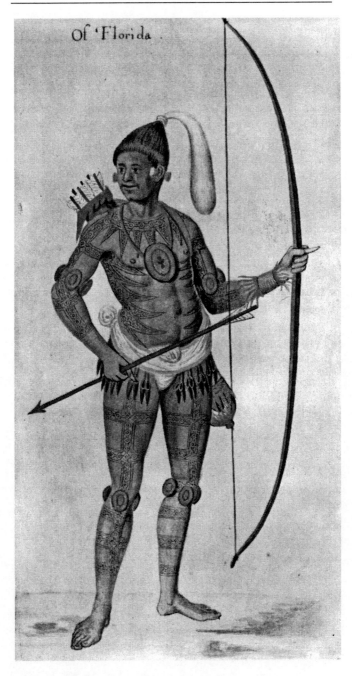

Florida warrior proudly displaying his numerous tattoos and the longbow that struck fear into the hearts of the Spanish explorers.

about to turn into another Apalachee, and, if this was to be the case, there was a growing concern among them that, given their present condition, they could not hold out for very long.

Shortly thereafter, Cabeza de Vaca and his companions returned to report that they had happened upon a bay where there were many oysters to feast upon; but as for the ocean, it was still a long way off. Though disappointed by this report, Narváez decided it would be best to wait along the shore, where there was the remote possibility of sighting the ships, rather then stay at Aute, where there was no hope of relief from the threat of attack. The commander also feared, and rightly so, that if he remained much longer at Aute the men might be driven to mutiny.

The Bay of Horses

The entire company left Aute the following day. While their intended destination was said to be less than a one day march, their pace was slowed by the fact that there were more sickly soldiers than the horses could possibly accommodate. The strange illness that sapped their strength grew worse with each passing day and no one knew how to treat this dreadful malady. Thankfully, they reached the inland bay that same day. Unable to locate the ships that had been sent to search for Panuco and too weak to continue on foot, the despondent troops had little choice but to remain where they were. Though many of the healthier members still wished to continue the quest to locate cities of gold, there were few who relished the thought of marching inland where they would surely be tracked by natives eager to exact further revenge. A sense of panic and desperation began to set in when it finally dawned on all that they were marooned upon this inhospitable land. Such discontent fueled murmurings of an uprising, especially among the upper class cavaliers, a conspiracy that Narváez was able to quell by involving the conspirators in the decision over the best course of action to follow, one which the commander had already decided upon.

Narváez had found a way to restore the blighted hope of his troops by putting them to work constructing boats that, it was to be hoped, would carry them all to safety. Such a daunting task was complicated by the fact that among the troops there was but one carpenter, Álvaro Fernández, and one blacksmith, and neither man possessed the necessary tools of his trade. The only cutting instruments available were their swords and a few knives. Necessity forced them to improvise. The nonessential iron found in the crossbows, stirrups and spurs was gathered up and melted down; it was then forged into rudimentary axes and saws for cutting down trees, and hammers and nails to be used to secure the finished slabs of wood. The efforts of these two principal designers to build boats that would enable all to escape this godforsaken land was further hindered by the weakened condition of so many fever stricken soldiers.

With their food supply nearly exhausted, the soldiers were forced to kill and butcher a horse every third day in order to nourish themselves while they attempted to complete the difficult task of building rafts sturdy enough to carry them across the water to a Spanish port in Mexico. Narváez believed, as did most of the others, that the port at Panuco, which they had been seeking ever since they set sail, was much closer than the island of Cuba. What they did not know was that Panuco was slightly more than one thousand miles away, while Cuba was but a third of that distance.

Fibers from the plentiful palmettos were twisted into a caulking material similar to oakum and also to make lines for rigging. The resin extracted from pine trees was made into pitch, an adhesive substance used to waterproof the boats. Many of the body parts of the slain horses were utilized in the making of these five barges. The hides were used to cover the sides of the boats and also to make vessels that were to store freshwater. Horsehair was woven into rope and cord for additional rigging. The men contributed the shirts off their backs to make sails. Oars were carved from wood and stones were collected to serve as ballast.

A band of soldiers returned to the Aute village to pillage corn and any other food items that could help nourish them during their quest to leave this region. After several such incursions, the Spaniards managed to procure more than six hundred bushels of corn, which was deemed sufficient to keep them fed while building the boats and to sustain them during the upcoming voyage. The Aute warriors reciprocated by launching raids against Narváez and his men while they were feverishly working to complete their boats. Ten soldiers were killed in two separate ambushes while attempting to collect shellfish along the shore to feed their comrades back at camp.

The five boats were finally ready to set sail on September 22, 1528. These flat bottom vessels, each of which were approximately thirty-three feet in length, were a combination of raft and boat, and designed primarily for sailing close to shore. The Spaniards boarded their makeshift boats shortly after the last horse was killed, butchered, and distributed. Since most of the clothing had to be used to make sails that were large and strong enough to propel their vessels, every man was naked except for a breechclout that modestly covered his privates. The men were almost equally divided among the officers placed in command of the boats. Pánfilo de Narváez had a crew of forty-nine aboard his craft, as did Comptroller Alonso Enríquez. Captains Alonso del Castillo and Andrés Dorantes were joint masters of a boat carrying forty-eight men. Captains Téllez and Peñalosa were joint commanders of a raft with forty-seven soldiers, the same number that shared a boat with Cabeza de Vaca and Inspector Alonso de Solís.

Once all the men and provisions were on board, the Spaniards cast off in hopes of finding Río de Palmas, where they hoped the other ships would be found waiting for them. Before leaving, they christened the region Bahia de Caballos (Bay of Horses), to honor the many horses who were sacrificed in order that they might live. Many surely took a moment to remember the numerous comrades who fell victim to fever, starvation, and native attacks. Staying close to one another and within sight of the shore, Narváez and his men sailed on a course guided by little more than the heavens above, the currents below, and the shoreline before them.

These inexperienced seafarers spent seven days wandering inlets in search of a passage that would lead to the ocean. Along the way they confiscated five canoes from some local fishermen, which were used to buoy their badly waterlogged boats. Once the coast was located, the Spaniards went ashore just long enough to make necessary repairs to their rafts and to gather as much food and water as they could before heading out to sea. The horsehides used for storing freshwater were quick to rot and the Spaniards now found themselves in a desperate search for drinking water. They happened upon an islet where they hoped to find freshwater but none was to be found. Their situation worsened with the sudden onset of a storm, the violence of which forced them to remain anchored for six days. Overcome with thirst, several soldiers ignored the advice of their comrades and drank the readily available saltwater. Five of these six poor souls paid with their lives for having made such a foolish mistake. When the weather finally cleared, the feeble surviving soldiers sailed away on leaky vessels that were on the verge of sinking.

It took Narváez and his men nearly a month to sail from Aute, now known as St. Marks Bay, to Pensacola Bay, where they hoped to find relief from the terrible hunger and thirst that plagued one and all. The mariners happened upon a number of canoes carrying unarmed natives who, after seeing the pitiful condition of the Spaniards, guided them to their nearby village. Here the weary explorers were treated to a satisfying amount of food and drink. Narváez was invited to the house of the chief and at this meeting the commander gave his gracious host some of the trinkets and corn he still possessed as an offering of appreciation for the comfort and aid rendered by both him and his people. That night the slumbering Spaniards were caught off guard by many warriors wielding rocks. Three soldiers camped on the beach died after their skulls were cracked open while they were sound asleep. Narváez was wounded in the face by the chief he had looked upon as his friend. He was saved from certain death by the timely intervention of Cabeza de Vaca and several others who rushed to his rescue. The chief was captured but was released after the Spaniards saw that the warriors were massing in great numbers. It was hoped that such a gesture would diffuse the escalating tension.

The majority of the Spaniards, including the wounded Narváez, made a hasty retreat back to the boats anchored along the shore. Roughly fifty soldiers, including Cabeza de Vaca, stayed behind to defend the retreat of their comrades. Cabeza de Vaca and his men also wanted to prevent the natives from chasing after the Spanish boats with their much faster and more maneuverable canoes. Those who remained behind soon had to shield themselves from a torrent of spears and rocks, an assault that forced the Spaniards to fall back until they were out of range. While these warriors were proving to be every bit as tenacious as those of Apalachee, the Spaniards were relieved that this enemy was not as well armed, for they had few bows and arrows. The natives continued their advance and once in range they launched another volley of lethal projectiles. Once again, the Spaniards were forced to fall back in order to make another stand. While the warriors were preparing for a third assault, a group of soldiers laid in wait and once the enemy had passed their way they leapt out with swords drawn and attacked them from behind. So startled were the natives that not only did they retreat at once but they chose not to mount another attack. To make sure that they did not attempt to follow them on the water, Cabeza de Vaca ordered the destruction of nearly thirty canoes.

Cabeza de Vaca and the rest of the defenders rejoined their comrades, who were anxiously waiting along the shore. A gathering storm delayed their plans for an immediate departure. This time was put to use making temporary shelters, patching up the numerous leaks in their boats, and gathering whatever food and water they could find. All of this was done while maintaining a watchful eye for hostile natives who, much to the relief of Narváez and his men, never reappeared. The wary Spaniards set sail the moment the storm had passed.

The five boats followed the westward trend of the coast, a course that brought them to Mobile Bay after three days. There they came upon a canoe carrying several natives and through the use of sign language the Spaniards were able to convey their urgent need for water. These Indians indicated they would take some of the Spaniards to where water could be found but they would have to supply their own means for carrying it. Doroteo Teodor, a soldier of Greek descent, volunteered himself and one of the African men in the company to go with the Indians to retrieve water. Narváez and most of the other officers were skeptical about such an offer. Sensing their concern, the natives suggested that two of their own would remain with the Spaniards until their two comrades had returned with water.

The concern of everyone aboard the boats turned fearful when the same canoe soon returned without Doroteo Teodor, the African servant, or any water. Suspicions of native treachery seemed to be confirmed when the two hostages attempted to escape. Their effort was thwarted by Narváez's men and the natives aboard the canoe had to return to shore without them. The next morning an armada of canoes appeared with many armed warriors and several lords who demanded the release of their two comrades. Pánfilo de Narváez made it clear that he would not comply with their request until his two men had been returned. The five or six lords in attendance stepped forward and attempted to persuade the Spaniards to come to their village where they would be reunited with the two Christians and rewarded with food and water. While they spoke, a great number of canoes maneuvered into position to bar the conquistadors' only means of escape from the estuary. When Narváez refused to release the hostages, the Indians began hurling spears and flinging stones from their slings. The Spaniards broke through the blockade and sailed away as fast as they could, leaving behind their two companions.

The Spaniards continued to hug the coast, clinging to the faint hope of finding either a Spanish port or the ships that had been dispatched earlier. On occasion they were able to make landfall in order to gather food and water. But in each instance they left empty handed, which was probably due either to their terrible fear of an impending Indian attack or to their inability to locate the items they so desperately required. At the mercy of the sea, the boats were slowly but steadily pulled from shore. Narváez and his men soon found themselves caught up in the doldrums, where, without the benefit of a breeze and a lack of strength to row themselves, the barges simply floundered upon calm waters while an unrelenting sun scorched the naked bodies and sapped the strength of men already weakened by thirst and hunger. Their ordeal grew ever more grim with each moment they remained adrift. When the water ran out several men drank from the ocean to quench their thirst and, just like those who previously made the same mistake, they soon became delirious and died.

Fortunately, a returning gust of wind finally sped them along, but unfortunately its forceful nature tore away at their already tattered sails while the surge of the sea steadily wore down their makeshift vessels. Up to this point, the five barges had managed to remain together as a group; but by the end of October they found that this was no longer possible. It was then that Narváez and his men reached a bay where they could taste the freshwater that gushed from the mighty Mississippi River that emptied near there. Realizing that they must be close to land, the Spaniards frantically rowed toward where the river meets the sea. Try as the might, they were not strong enough to overcome the powerful current that pushed the rafts farther out into the Gulf of Mexico and farther away from one another.

Discovering it was becoming increasingly difficult to stay together, Cabeza de Vaca called out across the water to ask his commander what they should do next. Realizing that he no longer had control of the situation, Narváez relinquished his command by replying: "It was no longer time for one man to rule another, that each should do whatever seemed best to him in order to save his own life."[4] Shortly thereafter, a sudden storm, which claimed the lives of several men, scattered the fragile boats even farther apart. Two of the barges managed to remain together, while the others drifted off in various directions. A sense of hopelessness pervaded the thoughts of all: they had now lost sight of land and their sense of direction, their supply of water was exhausted, rations of food had dwindled to just handfuls of raw maize, and most were too weak to even make an effort to help themselves. While many were resigned to the belief that death was near and certain, there were a few who still possessed the will to survive.

The Ordeal of Juan Ortiz

Unbeknownst to Pánfilo de Narváez and his men, the three ships under the command of Caravallo and the one piloted by Miruelo had returned to Tampa Bay shortly after they turned inland to begin their search for Apalachee. Unable to locate the Spanish settlement he had been sent to find, Miruello returned to Cuba, as he had been instructed by Narváez, and loaded his brigantine with provisions to aid in the conquest and settlement of Florida. However, once back at the harbor where he had parted company with his commander, Miruello was able to find only Captain Caravallo and the crew aboard his three ships. Caravallo had also been unable to find either the Río de las Palmas or the settlement of Santisteban del Puerto and eventually he doubled back in an effort to rejoin Narváez. The reunited ships spent several months sailing up and down the coast in an exhaustive search for their missing comrades but their efforts proved to be of no avail. Most suspected that Narváez and his men had met with an unfortunate end in the forests of Florida. The search was abandoned and all the ships returned to the safety of a known Spanish port, and once there the company officially disbanded.

María de Valenzuela, the devoted wife of Pánfilo de Narváez, was not yet ready to give up hope of finding her beloved husband. She organized a small expedition, which consisted of many of the men who had just sailed back to Cuba, to return to Florida to resume the search for Narváez and the rest of the troops. Juan Ortiz, a young hidalgo whose noble family hailed from Seville, was among those who signed on for this rescue mission. Juan was a member of the original Narváez expedition to Florida but now counted his blessings at being included among the group who had safely made it back to Cuba. Ortiz sailed aboard a brigantine that hoped to save their fellow Spaniards or, at the very least, bring a sense of closure by learning of their fate.

The brigantine sent by María de Valenzuela soon reached the Florida coast, where it happened upon a stretch of shoreline that had escaped the notice of those who had recently searched for the missing expedition. According to a conquistador who was familiar with this event, the men aboard the boat were lured toward land by the sight of a "a cane sticking in the ground with its top split and holding a letter."[5] Believing that this dangling piece of paper was a note left by their commander, the Spaniards steered their vessel close to shore for a better look. They were surprised by the sudden appearance of several natives.

The Spaniards were unaware of the fact that they had stumbled upon Ocita (aka Ucita), which was the domain of Hirrihigua, the Timucuan chief who had suffered greatly at the hands of Pánfilo de Narváez. An opportunity for exacting revenge presented itself when some of Hirrihigua's warriors spied this Spanish ship sailing along the coast. The chief sent emissaries to meet those aboard the ship to extend an invitation for all to come visit his village and to tell them that he had previously befriended Narváez. Wary of such a claim, the Spaniards politely declined the chief's offer. Hirrihigua gained their trust by sending out a canoe carrying four of his subjects, each of whom were to serve as hostages aboard the boat while an equal number of Spaniards went ashore to see that it was safe. Trusting to the sincerity of this overture, Juan Ortiz and three others swapped places with the natives. The four hostages jumped overboard and swam back to shore the moment the canoe carrying the Spaniards reached land. Realizing they had been lured into a trap, the men aboard the brigantine raised anchor and quickly sailed away, leaving behind Juan Ortiz and his three comrades.

As for the four who had gone ashore, they were escorted by warriors to the nearby Timucuan village where they were presented before Chief Hirrihigua. Juan Ortiz and his comrades were horrified by the ghastly sight of the ruler, who was missing his nose and a noticeable portion of his lips. The captive Spaniards began to tremble once they learned that it was Narváez who was responsible for the terrible disfigurement to the chief's face. The concern for their own safety grew bleak once they realized that their shipmates were not going to return for them and turned grave when they were informed that Narváez was also responsible for the brutal death of Hirrihigua's mother.

The four captives were forced to wallow in their growing fear for several days while they awaited their fate. A grand feast was planned at which Juan Ortiz and his comrades were slated to be the main entertainment. The Spaniards were to serve as target practice for warriors eager to prove their prowess with the bow and arrow. They were stripped naked and forced one by one to run across an open plaza while attempting to dodge the steady stream of projectiles that descended upon them. Hirrihigua was pleased that his warriors proved so skillful at inflicting wounds that prolonged the suffering of the victims before unleashing the final fatal blow. Juan Ortiz waited his turn while being forced to watch as his fellow shipmates fell to their deaths before a wildly cheering crowd. Luckily for Juan, he was spared a similar fate thanks to the timely intervention of the chief's wife, who felt compassion for this young man who was barely eighteen years old.

Though permitted to live, Ortiz was compelled to endure life as Hirrihigua's slave. Forced to do whatever he was told, Juan filled his days performing such menial tasks as fetching wood and water. His reprieve did not mean that he had entirely escaped the vengeful wrath of Hirrihigua, who constantly found ways to torture and humiliate him. Ortiz was subjected to regular and often brutal beatings. The physical and mental tortures were so abusive that Juan often harbored thoughts of taking his own life in order to bring an end to his suffering. He was, on several occasions, forced to run from sunrise to sunset along the plaza where his comrades were slaughtered, and should he pause at any point, he was to be put to death by the warriors who watched over him. The chief, who still had designs on killing his white slave, had Juan roasted over coals resting in a pit normally used for cooking wild game. His unrestrained screams of anguish were so loud that they were heard by the wife and daughters of Hirrihigua, who rushed to rescue the helpless lad, but not before half his body was disfigured with blisters caused by the searing flames. The women nursed him back to health but the scars would forever remain as a reminder of this horrific ordeal.

Once his strength had returned, Juan Ortiz was sent to keep watch over the sacred burial grounds of the tribe's ancestors, which had been frequently disturbed by a panther that freely roamed the region. The charnel house where the dead temporarily rested before their ceremonial interment was easy prey for carnivorous creatures who caught the scent of blood and rotting flesh. Juan managed to win a brief reprieve from Chief Hirrihigua's hatred by skillfully killing with one blow of a dart the beast that had been feasting upon the bodies of the dead.

However, a grateful Hirrihigua soon had a change of heart and proclaimed that the Spanish slave was to be sacrificed at an upcoming festival. He also declared that this time he would not tolerate any interference from

The capture of Juan Ortiz and his three comrades.

either his wife or his daughters. Uleleh, the eldest daughter of the aggrieved chief, told Ortiz of his impending doom and offered to help him escape the vindictive wrath of her father. A trusted native was to guide Juan to a neighboring village where Mucozo, a young tribal chief who was betrothed to the princess, would honor her request to provide him a safe haven. Uleleh saved Ortiz for humane reasons and not, as some have intimated, because she was hopelessly infatuated with him.

Upon learning of Ortiz's escape and that he was being sheltered by a chief to whom Uleleh was promised, an infuriated Hirrihigua demanded that Mucozo return the fugitive slave at once or he would never consent to the marriage of his daughter. The young chief sympathized with the plight of the young Spaniard. Mucozo knew that if he turned over Ortiz he would condemn him to additional rounds of torture, an ordeal that would end with his sacrificial death. By refusing to comply with Hirrihigua's demand, Mucozo remained true to the promise he made to his beloved Uleleh to protect Ortiz from harm. After having lived for a year and a half under the constant threat of a hateful Chief Hirrihigua, Juan Ortiz would enjoy the next eight and a half years under the kindly protection of Chief Mucozo, during which time he resigned himself to the thought that he would never leave this land. As for Uleleh and her true love Mucozo, three years would pass before Hirrihigua yielded to the gentle persuasion of his daughter, as well as the native priests who interceded on her behalf, and consented to their marriage.

3
___

THE SPIRITUAL PATH
OF CABEZA DE VACA

The Isle of Misfortune

Unable to keep up with the barge that carried his commander, Cabeza de Vaca paired his boat with another raft led by Captains Peñalosa and Téllez. Battered by the elements and weakened by a lack of food and water, there were few who possessed enough strength to steer the boats. Several of those who collapsed from exhaustion soon lapsed into an unconscious state, which for many was a prelude to death. Left to the mercy of the sea below and God above, the two boats drifted aimlessly atop an ocean that charted their course. After four days adrift, the two barges became entangled in a terrible storm. The weary Spaniards fought desperately against a raging sea that steadily pushed their vessels westward. Too tired and weak to continue the battle, those aboard the boats cast their fate to the wind and simply let the sea carry them wherever it chose. Lying down to get some much needed rest, they could not help but think that the end was close at hand.

According to his own recollection, Cabeza de Vaca awoke on the morning of November 6, 1528, to the sensation of his boat being pulled toward land. He soon heard the sound of waves crashing against a not too distant shore, and before he could awaken his companions the ocean hurled the barge on to a desolate beach. By now they were all awake and each man frantically summoned enough strength to crawl out of the boat before the powerful undertow pulled it back into the water. Cabeza and his comrades dragged themselves to a nearby bluff where they collected enough wood to make a fire to warm themselves and to roast some of the maize they still possessed. They were also fortunate to locate some fresh water to quench their thirst. While satisfying their basic needs and giving thanks for being alive, their thoughts turned to the fate of those aboard the other boats, the silence of this solemn moment interrupted only by the rhythmic breaking of the surf against the shore. Their own moans and groans soon returned everyone's thoughts to their desperate situation.

To get a sense of the land that they had been thrust upon, Cabeza de Vaca instructed Lope de Oviedo to climb to the top of a nearby tall tree. From such a vantage point, Oviedo saw that they were stranded upon an island. The boat that carried Cabeza de Vaca and his crew had washed ashore on an isle near the coast of Texas, which many historians seem to agree was Galveston Island. Roughly two miles wide and twenty miles long, Galveston Island at the time of their landing was much further from the mainland than it is today. A second look revealed a native trail, which Lope de Oviedo was asked to explore. He discovered that the path led to a village that, at the moment, was uninhabited. Lope took a dog and several other items to bring back to Cabeza de Vaca and the others as evidence of what he had discovered.

While Cabeza de Vaca and his weary castaways sat along the barren shore pondering what to do next, they noticed that they now had company. Three Indians armed with bows and arrows had suddenly appeared but kept a safe distance from the Spaniards, as if they were spying on them. Within a half hour another one hundred natives arrived, all carrying bows and arrows. The band of Indians who stood before them were without clothes and each had a round shell ornament running through his pierced lip, a menacing sight to the nearly naked Spaniards. The huddled soldiers feared that their grand adventure was about to come to a brutal end, for they had few weapons and little strength to defend themselves.

Cabeza de Vaca and Alonso de Solís, who was the inspector and co-commander of the raft, approached the natives with an offering of the few beads and bells they still had on hand. Much to the relief of the anxious Spaniards, each Indian responded to their friendly gesture with the offering of a single arrow as a token of their friendship. Through the use of sign language, the two groups managed to initiate a dialogue, which the Spaniards used to recount the terrible ordeal they had been through. The natives made it understood that they would return the following day with food for Cabeza de Vaca and his men.

As promised, the natives returned at sunrise with a bountiful offering of fish, roots, and nuts, which the famished Spaniards consumed in one sitting. A similar array of edible items was brought again in the afternoon. Besides sharing their food and company, these island inhabitants built fires for the castaways. The grateful Spaniards showed their appreciation with another offering of trinkets. This routine, which continued for several days, helped to restore the health of Cabeza de Vaca and his comrades. Finding that their strength had returned, the Spaniards decided to attempt another trip by sea. The grounded raft was dug out and after necessary repairs were made they once again set sail. Their escape was foiled by a powerful wave that overturned the raft and drowned three who were aboard, including Alonso de

Solís. A subsequent series of waves hurled the survivors back on shore, where they lay as naked as the day they were born. The force of the sea had claimed their boat, their clothes, their comrades, and what few worldly items they still owned.

Before they all passed out from exhaustion, the surviving Spaniards managed to muster enough strength to revive a fire the natives had previously made for them. It was now November, a time when the north winds blew in the chill of winter. Cabeza and his men awoke near dusk to the sight of several Indians staring down at them. Seeing how pitiful the Spaniards looked, the natives sat down among them and began to weep for the troubles of those they considered their friends. Cabeza de Vaca remembered: "And this lasted more than half an hour, and truly, to see these men, so lacking in reason and so crude in the manner of brutes, grieved so much for us, increased in me and others of our company even more the magnitude of our suffering and the estimation of our misfortune."[1] These compassionate natives left but returned the next day with additional food.

Seeking shelter from the cold winter winds, Cabeza de Vaca asked the natives if they would take him and his men to their village. The kindly natives consented to his request. There were, however, several hesitant Spaniards who were all too familiar with the stories of ritual sacrifices practiced by the Aztecs and Maya and feared they were about to be led to their own death at the altar of some heathen god. All finally agreed to be taken to the village after being reminded that if it were not for the help of these natives few would still be alive, and to stay where they were was tantamount to suicide. The Spaniards made every effort to keep up with their guides, but when their strength and feet began to falter the Indians carried them on their backs and in their arms. The natives transported the feeble soldiers for a great distance before stopping to rest at a bonfire, a series of which had been built along the way so the Spaniards could warm themselves for the next leg of the journey.

They all eventually reached a small village where the fatigued Spaniards were housed and well fed, even though their hosts barely had enough food to feed their own people. The Indians who rescued Cabeza de Vaca and his companions were the Karankawas, one of many coastal tribes that inhabited this region. The Karankawas were a tribe of hunter-gatherers who, due to their lean surroundings, were forced to live a rather primitive existence This migrant tribe chose to live on the island from October through February — the oyster season, which provided them far more sustenance than the stark terrain of the neighboring mainland could offer during those bleak months. The Karankawas used dugout canoes to travel between the mainland and the island.

The Karankawas depended on shellfish, fish, roots, and small game for sustenance. The surrounding waters yielded an adequate supply of oysters, fish, turtles, mollusks, and alligator. The mainland provided an opportunity to feast upon white-tailed deer, ducks, and smaller mammals, all of which they hunted with their long bows. Toads, snakes, and prickly pear (cactus fruit) were also an important part of their diet. They planted no crops but did eat whatever edible roots they could dig up. The Karankawas supplemented their intake with harvested berries, nuts, and edible plants. One of their favorite foods was something known as "swamp potatoes," which are edible roots pulled from the water that look very similar to nuts. It was a harsh life, but the Karankawas endured by making the best use of what was available.

The name Karankawa is believed to mean "dog-lover," which is probably derived from the fact that they had many domesticated canines. The men were lean, muscular, and tall — often six feet and above, which meant that many were taller than the average Spanish soldier. The men and women wore very little clothing. The only common coverings about their bodies were etched tattoos and designs applied with paint. To ward off the swarms of mosquitoes that took delight in their nakedness, the Karankawas covered their bodies with dirt or grease obtained from sharks or alligators. They were known to make an hallucinogenic concoction known as the "black drink," which was consumed during religious ceremonies. The Karankawas were to suffer the same fate that befell so many native American tribes in the wake of European exploration and expansion — they became extinct. The last of their tribe died off sometime during the 19th century.

Thanks to the attentive care of the Karankawas. the stranded Spaniards quickly regained their strength. One day Cabeza de Vaca noticed that some of their hosts were exchanging between themselves items similar to but not quite the same as the trinkets they had given them. When he inquired as to where they had obtained such articles the natives responded that there were others just like them on the island who were being sheltered by a different tribe that lived a short distance to the east. A message was immediately dispatched to the other village and soon Cabeza de Vaca and his crew were reunited with Captains Andrés Dorantes, Alonso del Castillo and their surviving crew.

The boat that carried Dorantes, Castillo, Esteban, and the other survivors had come ashore a day earlier and approximately five miles up the coast at Matagorda Bay. They were met and cared for by the tribe that lived on that part of the island. These castaways also attempted to escape the island but were to suffer the same misfortune of having their vessel capsized by turbulent waters. They had, however, weathered the storm better than Cabeza de Vaca and his comrades: they managed to retain most of their possessions, including their clothes. As for the fate of their commander, some of the survivors would later learn that the barge that carried Pánfilo de Narváez had been swept out to sea.

The joyful reunion also revived their hopes of getting off the island. Repairs were made to the salvaged raft that belonged to Dorantes and Castillo but all were disappointed to see their means of escape sink before they even had a chance to cast off. While they resigned themselves to the thought of having to spend the duration of the winter on the island, the Spaniards were not prepared to give up hope of being rescued. Believing that the visible but distant mainland just might be Panuco, the Spaniards decided to send Álvaro Fernández and three soldiers remembered only by their last names—Méndez, Figueroa, and Estudillo—to see if they could locate a Spanish settlement. Those chosen for this task were considered the best swimmers, a skill everyone felt they would need to get across other bodies of water in order to reach a Spanish outpost that could render aid to those still stranded on the island. They were accompanied on this journey by an Indian who, besides also being a strong swimmer, was to serve as their guide and interpreter.

Since eighty Spaniards was simply too many for any one tribe to feed and shelter, the natives decided the strangers would be split into smaller groups and distributed among the various tribes of the island. There they would wait out the winter and come spring they could hopefully resume their homeward journey. Unfortunately, the Spaniards were not prepared for the bitter cold and severe storms that descended upon the region. One terrible tempest lasted for six long days. The winter season brought an abrupt halt to the supply of food from the sea and made it difficult to find edible roots. Food became so scarce during this time that many Spaniards died of starvation. This was an accepted part of the cycle of life for the natives—the strong survived while the weak did not. The Karankawas, who were accustomed to such deprivations, suffered through this ordeal with quiet dignity. The same could not be said of the Spaniards. Winter proved so harsh on the island that the Spaniards named it Malhado (Misfortune Island).

Many of the Spaniards waited out the harsh winter while housed in huts just outside of the main village, where they were periodically checked on by the natives. One group of five men chose to live close to the beach, a choice that led to an even greater degree of suffering from cold and hunger. When a member of this group passed away from extreme hardship, the remaining Spaniards satisfied their ravenous hunger by feasting upon the lifeless body of their comrade. When the natives finally had a chance to check on those who were camped so far from the village they were shocked to find five corpses, four of which had been stripped of their flesh. The last had apparently starved after there was no one left to eat. The natives were horrified to discover that the Spaniards had resorted to cannibalism and from that point on they kept a constant vigil over the others to make sure that such a barbarous act was not repeated.

While the surviving soldiers were terribly ashamed of the actions of their dead comrades, they were even more disappointed to discover that the Karankawas had lost all respect for them following this gruesome discovery. Having grown weary of the constant bickering and complaining of the Spaniards, the natives forced their guests to perform chores normally assigned to the women. From this point on the survivors were treated as if they were slaves. Cabeza de Vaca and his comrades had no choice but to shed their European ways and adopt the practices of the natives in order to survive. They had to dig up roots for food, collect wood for fueling fires, and fetch water to drink for themselves as well as for the tribe. It was a lesson in humility for the proud Spaniards.

A mysterious illness contributed to the demise of many Spaniards and Karankawas who were already weakened by the grave effects of such a harsh winter. The scarce supply of food, the severe weather, and illness all took their toll and by spring of 1529 there were only fifteen of the eighty survivors of the two rafts still left alive. Nearly half of the natives perished for the same reasons. The passage of time also caused those stranded on the island to lose hope of ever hearing from the five men who had been sent to the mainland, fearing that they had fallen victim either to a hostile native tribe or the harsh winter.

The five men who left the island in search of a Spanish settlement did reach the mainland but were unable to find any signs of civilization. Estudillo, Fernández and the native guide soon perished from an accumulation of hardships related to their adventure. Figueroa and Méndez would happen upon the Quevenes, a wandering tribe who permitted them to share their food and shelter. However, Figueroa realized that he was a prisoner of this tribe when Méndez, after having set out on his own to resume the search for a Spanish outpost, was hunted down and brutally executed by the Quevenes. During his travels with this tribe, Figueroa met up with Hernando de Esquivel, a survivor of the boat under the command of Father Juan Suárez. It was from Esquivel that he learned the fate of their former commander. The boat that carried Pánfilo de Narváez and his crew reached land and the men immediately went ashore. However, a despondent Narváez remained on board, as did the pilot and a page who had taken ill. A sudden storm swept the three out to sea, and they were never heard from again.

Mainland Separation

The long-awaited arrival of spring meant it was time for the Karankawas to return to the mainland of present-day Texas to take advantage of the more abundant supply of fish and game. They were accompanied by several of the Spaniards, while the rest, who were mostly those too weak to travel, remained at the island. Captains Dorantes and Castillo soon returned to gather those left behind so they could accompany them on an inland search for a Spanish settlement. Jerónimo de Alaniz and Lope de Oviedo, both of whom were too ill and weak to make the journey, remained on the island of Malhado. Shortly after reaching the mainland, Cabeza de Vaca was stricken with the mysterious ailment that had already claimed so many lives. All, including Cabeza de Vaca himself, believed that the hand of death was very near. Too weak to accompany his comrades, the royal treasurer remained with the tribe that had cared for the Spaniards throughout the long winter.

Those who were strong enough struck out on their own to resume the search for either the ships dispatched by Pánfilo de Narváez or the ever-elusive province of Panuco. Unfortunately, these Spaniards fared no better in this quest than the five brave souls who had gone before them. All ended up being captured by natives and were either forced into slavery or offered up in sacrifice to the gods of the tribe. Their numbers would soon dwindle down to a mere three.

Thanks to the efforts of those who cared for him, Cabeza de Vaca gradually recovered and regained his strength just in time to follow the natives on an inland hunting expedition. He lived with a tribe that numbered between four and five hundred, and as a member of the group he was expected to earn his keep. There were many days that Cabeza de Vaca's fingers were bled raw from having to perform the backbreaking chore of digging up roots for food. He also had to collect bundles of wood to build bonfires, the smoke of which helped to repel the swarms of mosquitoes that constantly plagued everyone. It was a rather humbling experience for a man who took pride in being a hidalgo, a son of someone considered to be part of the Spanish gentry. Through it all, though, Cabeza de Vaca came to appreciate these primitive people who showed so much kindness to each other as well as to the Christians who had placed such a burden on the tribe. He was especially touched by the loving care they displayed toward their children.

Once the Karankawa were finished with their hunting expedition they began making preparations for a return to their island home. A fully recovered Cabeza de Vaca, however, chose to stay at the mainland. He joined up with the Charruco, one of the many different Coahuiltecan Indian tribes who inhabited a large area of southern Texas and northwestern Mexico. While the tribes of the mainland were not much more advanced than the tribes of Malhado Island, they did, however, benefit from a wider variety of food. A lack of big game meant that the various Coahuiltecan tribes had to hunt rabbits, small rodents, birds, armadillo, lizards, snakes, and salamanders. These wandering natives also had to resort to collecting ant eggs, snails, spiders, worms, termites, and deer dung for sustenance. A delicacy was the prickly pear, a seasonal type of cactus that yields a delectable fruit with a savory juice that was greatly prized by the natives.

It was as a member of the seminomadic Charruco that Cabeza de Vaca found his niche in tribal life by discovering he had a knack for conducting trade. He soon earned his keep by traveling from one village to another to trade a variety of goods. Cabeza de Vaca would carry on his back a pack filled with items from the coast, an inventory that included seashells, conches, pearls, mesquite beans, and shark oil, which were swapped for animal skins and red ochre (a dye) owned by the inland tribes. He also peddled the "black drink," a native beverage concocted from the leaves of the yaupon plant. The yaupon leaves were boiled until they turned black, at which point they formed a dose of caffeine so strong that it not only caused the imbiber to become hyperactive but, in excessive quantities, could produce hallucinogenic visions. The emetic "black drink" also induced vomiting and therefore was viewed as a sacred beverage that cleansed both body and soul.

Because of the many splendid items he brought, Cabeza de Vaca was warmly received at the villages he visited, where he enjoyed generous offerings of food and shelter. The freedom to travel about while plying his trade was certainly better than remaining a slave to the many menial tasks he was previously forced to perform. Cabeza de Vaca learned the native sign language, a skill that enabled him to communicate with the various tribes, and over time he began to acquire knowledge of their spoken language. He even began to hone his abilities as a healer. The only thing that seemed to offend Cabeza de Vaca on these journeys between villages was the occasional sight of a man dressed as a woman while living as the wife of another man. While homosexuality was viewed by the Catholic Church as a sin against both nature and God, the natives saw those inclined to such behavior as simply colorful members of their tribe.

Cabeza de Vaca would return every year to Malhado in the hope of convincing a reluctant Lope de Oviedo to leave the island and join him in search of a Spanish settlement. Jerónimo de Alaniz, the other Spaniard who stayed behind with Oviedo, had long ago succumbed to his terrible illness. Three times he crossed over to the island to try to persuade his comrade to leave. But because Oviedo lacked the courage for another adventure, Cabeza de Vaca always returned to the mainland alone. He returned once again toward the end of 1532, this time with news that finally convinced Lope de Oviedo to leave Malhado.

On his recent travels among the Coahuiltecan tribes, Cabeza de Vaca encountered some visiting Quevenes tribesmen who told him they knew of three other Spaniards living as members of another tribe. They even provided him with their names: Dorantes, Castillo, and Esteban. They went on to say that these three were being treated harshly by a tribe that held them as their slaves. When Cabeza de Vaca inquired about the others, the Quevenes replied that they were all dead, some having passed away from cold and hunger while others died unmercifully at the hands of their Indian masters. The Quevenes offered to lead him to the place where the cruel Indians and his surviving comrades could be found. Cabeza de Vaca decided he would leave with the Quevenes but first, he had to return to the island to try to coax Lope de Oviedo to leave with him. Oviedo did leave the island but he was terribly frightened by the appearance and manner of the Quevenes. Having lost what little courage he had managed to summon from the encouraging words of Cabeza de Vaca, Lope de Oviedo returned to the familiar terrain of Malhado where he lived out his remaining days with the Karankawas. A deeply disappointed Cabeza de Vaca set off alone with the Quevenes Indians.

The native guides led Cabeza de Vaca to the place where the tribe they spoke of had gathered to collect the ripened nuts of large trees that flourished at a place later remembered as the "river of nuts"—most likely where the Guadeloupe and San Antonio rivers meet. These Quevenes, like most of the tribes of the region, were small bands of hunter-gatherers who wandered in search of lands that could provide adequate food and water. At given times, the various tribes would converge upon and congregate at a place where a natural harvest was known to occur, as was now the case at the "river of nuts." It was here that Cabeza de Vaca found Andrés Dorantes, and the reunited soldiers embraced while shedding tears of joy. Dorantes, who had long given up all hope of ever seeing Cabeza de Vaca after leaving him in the care of the Karankawas, was surprised to see that the treasurer had recovered and was still alive. Alonso del Castillo and Esteban, the enslaved Moor who belonged to Dorantes, soon joined the joyous reunion.

Besides being updated about the fatal end of those who accompanied Dorantes, Castillo, and Esteban from Malhado, Cabeza de Vaca learned of the fate of the five skilled swimmers who were the first to leave the island. The wandering Spaniards had crossed paths with Figueroa, one of the chosen swimmers, in the spring of 1529. Figueroa told them that three of his companions, including the Indian guide, fell victim to the harsh winter, while another was killed during an unfriendly native encounter. He also told them that he learned from a chance encounter with Hernando de Esquivel, a survivor from another raft, that Pánfilo de Narváez, their former commander had perished at sea. Figueroa soon joined the ranks of his fallen comrades.

Believing that divine intervention had played a hand in their finding one another, Cabeza de Vaca urged his comrades to flee with him to resume the search for Panuco. Dorantes convinced him that it was best to wait another six months, a time when the tribes that had enslaved them would venture to another region in search of tuna, the tasty fruit of the prickly pear cactus. This was a period when wandering tribes from all over converged on the vast fields of cactus that grew in and around present day San Antonio to consume the juice and fruit of the prickly pear and to carry on trade with one other. To leave now, Dorantes told him, would be an act of suicide, for the natives would surely hunt them down. To keep from being separated again, Cabeza de Vaca permitted himself to become a slave to the Mariames, a brutal tribe that owned Dorantes. He became a slave of an Indian who was blind in one eye, an affliction that appeared to trouble a number of people of this tribe. Castillo and Esteban, meanwhile, remained slaves of the Yguaze Indians. It was in this manner that the last four survivors of the Narváez expedition were able to stay close to one another for six months, a period that covered April to September of 1533.

In order to stay alive, the four Spanish slaves performed whatever tasks their native masters required. They were subjected to severe beatings when they failed to perform what was asked of them, and the threat of a painful death made them work hard to keep their owners pleased. Esteban surely must have taken some pleasure in knowing that his master finally understood what it felt like to be the slave of another man. In seeking new ways to make the Spaniards more useful to the needs of the tribe, the natives insisted that they become medicine men. They showed them how to cure the ill by simply blowing on the victim and to cast away sickness for good with the guiding motions of their hands. When Cabeza de Vaca refused to comply with their request to cure an afflicted person with what he believed were heathen rituals the tribe stopped giving him food. This was motivation enough for all four Spaniards to learn and perform the rites of the shaman. However, they added a Christian twist to their healing routine by making the sign of the cross while saying the Pater Noster and an Ave María blessing. It also helped that Dorantes, who was the son of a doctor, had a basic knowledge of medicine.

Native medicine men were responsible for healing the soul as well as the body. Mescal beans, a hallucinogenic seed often employed in shaman rituals of tribes of southwest America, were a widely traded item during the time of Cabeza de Vaca's odyssey. In Texas there have been finds of such beans in caves that date back more than ten thousand years. Shamans used hallucinogenic substances as a gateway to the spiritual realm. The Spaniards were most likely exposed to such rituals and probably used them in their own healing procedures. However, this is a practice they surely would have wanted to remain silent about, fearing that Christian authorities would consider such medicinal magic as the work of the devil.

Wandering Shaman

The four Christian captives bided their time until September, at which point they found an opportunity to elude their Indian masters in order to resume their search for Panuco, the region where the Spanish settlement of Santisteban del Puerto had been founded in 1523 by Hernán Cortés. They followed along the Texas shore for a brief distance before heading inland toward the vast expanse of the dry Texas plains. This was the beginning of a two year odyssey that witnessed a growing multitude of natives who came to view the four Christians as savior shamans. At each village encountered, they offered their services to heal the sick in exchange for food and temporary shelter. Cabeza de Vaca and his comrades put on a splendid show for the natives, combining elements of Christian ceremony and native practices they had learned into a ritual that both dazzled and inspired the spectators. Most of these Indians had little to offer but were generous with what they did possess. Cabeza de Vaca, who was becoming ever more attuned to the native way of life, remembered that "These people see and hear better, and have keener senses than any other in the world. They are great in hunger, thirst and cold, as if they were made for the endurance of these more than other men, by habit and nature."[2]

Historians still wrangle over the route followed by Cabeza de Vaca and his three comrades and, given the vague descriptions left by these intrepid wayfarers, it is unlikely that their precise route will ever be mapped without some shadow of doubt hovering over such an endeavor. A great many Texas towns claim that the Spanish adventurers passed their way, a list that includes the city of Austin. It appears that by following the beaten paths of the natives, the four men crossed the Colorado River where the capital of Texas now stands and from there they followed a southwesterly route toward the San Antonio River.

We do know that the first tribe the four Spaniards fell in with were the nomadic Avavares, who were kind enough to shelter them for the winter. Though suspicious at first of these strangers, Cabeza de Vaca managed to allay the concerns of the Avavares by healing a warrior who complained of being plagued with terrible headaches. The Spanish shaman cured his ailment by making the blessing sign of the cross before rubbing the head and blowing upon the painful area of the victim. After this the man was pronounced cured. The Spaniards were treated to a bountiful feast once the patient agreed with this diagnosis. Neighboring tribes heard about the Christian healers living with the Avavares and began bringing their sick to be cured. Once finished making the signs of the cross and reciting the proper prayers, Cabeza de Vaca remembers "praying with all earnestness to God our Lord that He would give health and influence them to make us some good return."[3] The power of belief certainly was a rewarding experience for all concerned parties. Recovered warriors paid the powerful shaman with their prized bows and arrows, while others rendered an offering of gathered nuts or animal hides.

There was one seemingly miraculous feat that led to Cabeza de Vaca's being revered by all as a great healer. After having been brought to another village, where he saw many were weeping over the passing of a male member of the tribe, the natives asked him to work his magic on the dead. His concern that a refusal might be construed as an insult to the tribe was accompanied by a fear that if he failed at this task the natives might think he was a sorcerer and therefore punish him with extreme prejudice. Cabeza de Vaca was able to surmise, probably after having checked his patient's pulse, that the man was simply unconscious, most likely a victim of sleeping sickness. The Spanish shaman proceeded to perform his standard ritual: he made the sign of the cross, recited several Christian incantations, and silently prayed for a miracle. Those prayers were answered that night when the man suddenly awoke from his temporary coma. News of Cabeza de Vaca having raised the dead spread throughout the land, and the people now saw him as someone greater than a shaman — a new native Messiah.

Natives from near and far came in great numbers to be healed of their various ailments and afflictions by the man they believed had the power to resurrect the dead. So great were their numbers that Cabeza de Vaca had to anoint his comrades, who also came to be viewed as sacred beings, as disciple shamans. The four Christians had become so revered that many dreaded the day they would leave, fearing their departure would permit a return of the many maladies they had cast away, including the specter of death.

Cabeza de Vaca and his comrades found the life of the Avavares even harder to stomach than that of the previous tribes they had encountered. During lean periods, which were often, the Avavares subsisted on a diet of deer dung, rotten wood, lizards, worms, ant eggs, and spiders, none of which appealed to the Spaniards. This was a stark contrast to the berries, mesquite beans, nuts, seeds, and cacti consumed by the Coahuiltecan tribes during hard times. Forced to endure another winter season with little to protect their bodies, the four shamans found it difficult to heal their own skin ulcers brought on by constant exposure to the sun and wind.

The first hint of spring revived the desire of the Spaniards to resume their search for civilization. Avavare guides led them and a few loyal followers to the Rio Grande, one of the longest rivers in North America. They crossed the river but instead of heading toward the east, which would have led them to their intended destination that was but a mere three hundred miles away, they continued westward. The natives tried to steer the Spaniards toward the coast, where they would find tribes who had more food to offer. Cabeza de Vaca and his companions, however, preferred the inland natives to those who inhabited the coast. They remembered all too well that the poor coastal tribes treated them like slaves, expecting them to toil for the needs of their masters, while the natives of the interior, who revered them as sacred holy men, were kind enough to share their food and surroundings.

The Christian wayfarers and their faithful followers soon arrived at a relatively large Indian town where they were well received. Cabeza de Vaca left us with this observation of his gracious hosts: "They carried pierced gourds with stones inside, which is the item of highest celebration, and they do not take them out except to dance or to cure, nor does anyone but they dare to use them. And they say that those gourds have virtue and that they come from the sky, because throughout that land there are none nor do they know where they might be, but only that the rivers bring them when they flood."[4] As they had done so many times before, the wandering Spaniards offered their service as healers, curing just enough to convert many more as their eternally grateful followers.

The Avavare guides relinquished their services to natives of this region who now assumed the responsibility of guiding the Spaniards and their growing entourage to the next tribe that would become accountable for the travelers. Once again the Spanish healers were able to cure a number of people who had complete faith in their abilities. News of their miraculous deeds preceded them at each village along the way. These wandering shamans, whose feats of healing the sick had become legendary, came to be thought of as "Children of the Sun" by the natives who revered them. Upon entering a new village these four medicine men were carried on the shoulders of Indian escorts and paraded before a large gathering that eagerly awaited their arrival. The crowd of natives who wished to remain in the company of the Spaniards grew larger at each village along the way and soon the holy men supposedly had several thousand natives following them.

Encountering so many friendly natives proved to be both a blessing and a curse. The progress of the Spaniards was slowed by the fact that several hours of each day had to be spent administering cures. Cabeza de Vaca and his comrades were called upon to heal the sick, raise the dead, and cause the clouds to release the rains they had stored for far too long. Children born along the way were brought to the Spaniards so they could be blessed with the sign of the cross. The multitude of faithful followers even brought their food to the Spaniards so that it could be blessed by their breath and the sacred sign of the cross. Feeding so many followers also became a problem and led to the uncontrollable ransacking of many villages along their route.

Besides the kindness of the local natives, the Spaniards were the recipients of several gifts on this leg of their journey. In one such instance, two appreciative medicine men presented the Christian shamans with their ceremonial gourds. These gourds, which contained pebbles that rattled when shaken, were elegantly decorated with mystical symbols that conveyed the religious convictions of the tribe. The grateful Christians accepted these offerings of medicine rattles imbued with magical powers and incorporated them into their healing ritual. Esteban would cherish such a gift until the day he died.

These four holy men were further distinguished by their beards, which by now had grown quite long. Their bodies had become lean and they generally wore garments that merely covered their privates. The constant exposure to the sun had darkened the skins of the three white Spaniards to a shade close to that of the natives. Cabeza de Vaca and his comrades wore hand carved crosses around their necks and their long hair was braided. The Spaniards learned as many as six native dialects but found there was a language barrier at many places they stopped. Their knowledge of sign language proved useful during such occasions. Esteban did most of the speaking for the group. One of the reasons for this is that many of the Indians thought the three fair skinned men were returning gods and the Spaniards reinforced this belief by keeping their distance while they ate and slept. Another reason is that the Moor had a better ear for the native languages and therefore was the more fluent of the four men. The Spaniards were considered to be natives and the four had come to think of themselves in this way. Cabeza de Vaca accumulated many tattoos about his body during his days as a wandering medicine man.

Their travels took them to a village of forty houses where the people gave Andrés Dorantes "a large, thick, copper bell, and on it was outlined a face, and they showed that they valued it greatly."[5] They told the Spaniards that this metal rattle came from a place up north where many more items of similar quality could be found. The delighted Spaniards concluded that such a piece derived from an advanced civilization, one that knew how to use molds for casting metal into intricate shapes and designs. They may have even deluded themselves into believing that it came from the elusive native kingdom that the Pánfilo de Narváez expedition had originally set out to find.

The route of the Spaniards passed along the Sierra Madre Oriental mountain range and eventually deposited them along the edge of the Coahuila Desert — a hot, dry, and desolate region of Northern Mexico punctuated with broken plateaus. Fortunately, the Spaniards were conditioned for the arduous trek across this desolate land. Their circuitous route led them to a farther stretch of the Río Grande. It was near the Río Nadadores that the wandering shamans met up with a small tribe that presented them with margaxita, which are crystallized iron pyrites that have the look of silver. The Christians partook of the tribe's abundant harvest of prickly pears and pine nuts. It was in this region that Cabeza de Vaca's reputation as a great healer was once again put to the test. A tribesman presented before him complained of a pain directly over his heart. The man had been struck in the shoulder by an arrow a long time before, and the tip, which remained imbedded in his torso, had slowly shifted to an area that now caused him much discomfort.

The entire tribe gathered around to watch Cabeza de Vaca perform another miracle. The patient pointed to the spot where his pain was occurring and once the general location of the tip could be felt, the white shaman used a sharp knife to carefully cut open the surrounding area and then began to probe for the lodged arrowhead. Once located, Cabeza de Vaca stuck his finger into the opening and succeeded, though after much difficulty, in removing the arrow point that had come to rest close to the heart of the man. The Indian, who endured the operation without complaint, watched as the Christian healer closed up his wound with two stitches, after which he returned to his hut. There was cause for much celebration when Cabeza de Vaca showed the arrow point to the members of the tribe. The stitches were removed after two days and the recuperating patient was pleased that he no longer felt any pain. The Spaniards' reputation as great medicine men remained intact.

After having been shown the copper bell that Dorantes had received, the local natives told them that the place where metals were unearthed could be found at a village not too far away. The grateful Indians supplied the Spaniards with guides to show them the way to the next village, which Cabeza de Vaca and his comrades hoped would prove more rewarding. Each of the four Christian shamans had a specific group of Indian men and women who followed them. Even though the Christian shamans were revered as great religious leaders wherever they went, the natives, however, still obeyed the commands of their tribal leaders. As they headed along a southwesterly course toward the foothills of the Sierra Madre Oriental, the throng of followers, much to the chagrin of the Spaniards, took to pilfering items at each village they happened upon.

The guides led the Spaniards and their followers into the barren mountain region of the Sierra Madre, where jagged peaks soar to heights as high as twelve thousand feet. The harsh landscape offered many magnificent views but little in the way of food, which led to much suffering during this difficult leg of the journey. Their efforts were eventually rewarded with the discovery of more verdant lands. They wandered onto the plains known as the Stockton plateau, where the Spaniards were met by a tribe that supplied them with two women who would serve as their guides. Cabeza de Vaca and his entourage traveled along an ancient shell trail, a path that had been followed for thousands of years by pueblo peddlers from the north and native merchants from Mexico and Central America who plied their trade in shells, feathers, and other commodities.

The Spaniards were determined to head toward the direction of the setting sun, but those who followed them did not want to go that way because such a path led to lands inhabited by tribes that were their enemies. The women guides were sent to scout the land ahead. While debating over which route to follow, a mysterious malady suddenly swept through the flock of native followers, claiming eight lives and leaving many too ill to continue. Cabeza de Vaca believed that the people had simply worried themselves sick over the forbidden route they followed and he sought to cure their illness with prayers to the Almighty. Their sudden recovery was attributed to divine intervention but the return of the women guides may have played a greater role in their recuperation. They returned with news that the lands where the people feared to tread were abandoned, most of the tribes having left to follow the migration of the bison.

The Spanish shamans and their faithful flock now proceeded at a more lively pace, but the scarcity of food along this route was becoming a major concern. Alonso del Castillo, Esteban and the women guides were sent down a different path in search of sustenance for the entire group. They returned after three days to report they had found a permanent settlement inhabited by a people who dined on beans, squash, and maize, the latter being a crop that the Spaniards had not seen since setting sail from the Bay of Horses and one that they considered a prime indicator of more advanced native societies. It was at La Junta de los Ríos that they met with a settled tribe they referred to as the Jumanos, the people of the cows, because they periodically went off to hunt bison. Though not a tribe friendly to those who followed the Spaniards, the Jumanos were kind enough to provide food and water for the weary travelers for the next couple of days. When the Spaniards inquired about where they could find tribes that raised corn they were told to head west.

The Christian shamans and their devoted followers continued in the direction where maize was said to grow, confident that such a course would lead them to the native civilizations of Mexico that were familiar with the whereabouts of a Spanish settlement. Unfortunately for all, the path they followed for the next seventeen days had little to offer in the way of food and they managed to stave off starvation thanks only to the generous supply of deer fat provided by the Jumanos. They crossed the Río Grande for the third and last time in the vicinity of El Paso and headed across the desert highlands of northern Chihuahua. Fortunately, the exhausted and famished wayfarers stumbled upon a native settlement where they were welcomed with a bountiful offering of food that included corn.

Convinced they were finally on the right path to salvation, the Spaniards had an understandable desire to resume their quest. They came across several permanent settlements along this route that were inhabited by people who lived quite comfortably off the fruits of their labor. Besides cultivating sufficient quantities of beans, maize, and a variety of gourds, the natives of this region feasted on the deer and wild turkey they regularly hunted. These friendly inhabitants of Mexico, who were far better attired than the wandering natives of Texas, gave the Spaniards shawls they had woven to cover their nakedness.

The people of this land showered the Spaniards with gifts and honors normally reserved for the upper echelon of their society. At one of these settlements Dorantes was the recipient of five ceremonial arrowheads he believed were made of emeralds, though most likely these precious stones were either turquoise or malachite. When the Spaniards inquired as to their origin the natives said they had acquired them in trade with people from the north who swapped their plentiful supply of precious stones for the colorful feathers of the parrots indigenous to the forest regions of central Mexico. The natives also told the shamans that these northern tribes lived in large cities containing stones houses that were carved into the mountains. To the Spaniards it sounded as if the natives were describing a magnificent city like the Aztec capital of Tenochtitlan. The natives, however, were speaking of the pueblo tribes of Arizona and New Mexico, tribes that Cabeza de Vaca and his comrades never encountered on their odyssey.

One of the reasons why the Mexican tribes showed such reverence toward the Spaniards was that they had come from the east, a direction from which Quetzalcoatl, one of the Mesoamerican gods of creation, had promised to return to earth. Since such beliefs elevated Cabeza de Vaca and the others to the status of deified healers who were entitled to many earthly rewards, the Spaniards made no effort to discourage such thoughts. Andrés Dorantes, who seemed to always receive the more lavish gifts offered to the group, was given six hundred sun dried deer hearts, which provided sustenance for the Spaniards and their many followers, at the same village where he received the ceremonial arrowheads. The appreciative Spaniards called this place "Pueblo de los Corazones," the "Village of Hearts."

4

RUMORS OF MAGNIFICENT REALMS

A Spanish Reunion

The Spaniards and their followers remained at the Village of Corazones for three days before resuming their journey. Their first day out was marred by the sudden onset of a powerful storm that caused the Yaqui River to overflow its banks. They had little choice but to remain where they were for a fortnight and a day, which was how long it took for the floodwaters to subside to a depth where the river was passable. It was during this time of waiting that Alonso del Castillo came upon an Indian who wore around his neck a Spanish sword belt buckle with a nail, the same type of tapered metal used for shoeing horses, attached to it. An excited Castillo called for his companions, and after all had a chance to examine this intriguing article they began to question the owner as to how he came into possession of this peculiar amulet. The native told them that it was left by men who came from the sea, all of whom wore beards much like the four who were cross-examining him. He went on to say that these men rode on mighty beasts while carrying lances and swords used to harass the people of this land. Even though they knew he was probably speaking of a slaving expedition in search of natives to work the fields and mines of the Spanish colonies, Cabeza de Vaca and the others could barely contain their joy over such a discovery and the prospect that they might soon be reunited with fellow Spaniards.

Encouraged by this news, the four Spaniards and their large entourage headed southward, in the direction where they were told that the men from the sea had landed. They walked at a steady pace from dawn till dusk. Cabeza de Vaca and his comrades observed that much of the countryside had been abandoned, the residents having fled out of fear of those who had invaded their land. They soon saw more ominous signs that other Spaniards had recently passed through these lands: smoldering villages that had been plundered and the lifeless bodies of natives hanging from trees.

While most of the people had left the fertile lands near the river in order to escape the grasp of the Spanish slavers, Cabeza de Vaca and his group encountered a great many emaciated and frightened souls who refused to abandon their homeland entirely by seeking shelter in the neighboring highlands. They learned from these displaced people that Spanish slave raiders had been coming to this region for several years, and with each visit they carried off any healthy natives they could capture and killed anyone who dared to resist their efforts. Elaborating on these Spanish atrocities, the Indians spoke of how their people were whipped and shackled with heavy chains before being marched to a place from which they would never return.

While Cabeza de Vaca, Alonso del Castillo, Andrés Dorantes, and Esteban were elated by the thought of being reunited with their fellow Spaniards, they surely must have felt a great sense of shame over the harmful acts that their countrymen had inflicted on these peaceful people. Fearing that the natives might vent their anger at them, the four chose not to reveal that they shared a heritage with these cruel Spaniards. They were relieved to see that these people who had suffered so terribly brought them gifts and offered them food and shelter at their highland village that was too difficult for Spanish horses to reach. Those who had escaped the carnage made it clear that they feared to return to their sacked and burned villages. But Cabeza de Vaca convinced them that he would shield them from harm if they guided him and his followers to the place where these Spaniards could be found. Seeing the four shamans as their saviors, these natives chose to join those who already flocked around these holy men with beards.

It was late January of 1536 when Cabeza de Vaca and his comrades reached the Río Sinaloa, a time that even then was unbearably hot. As they followed the river on its course toward the ocean, they saw evidence of Spanish camps that had been recently deserted. Fearing for the safety of those who accompanied them, Cabeza de Vaca and his three companions tried to convince the natives to return to their homelands, but all had placed too much faith in the four Christians to abandon them at this point. Feeding so many in a land that had been raped by marauding conquistadors was a difficult task and most suffered terribly from the pangs of hunger during this long and arduous trek.

When it was noticed that the tracks of the horses they followed appeared to be relatively fresh, Cabeza de Vaca decided to go on ahead with just Esteban and eleven Indians to try to catch up with the Spaniards. A two day march brought the thirteen men to a recently vacated Spanish campsite. On the following day, which was March 14, they were rewarded with the sight of four soldiers on horseback. An ecstatic Cabeza de Vaca and Esteban ran toward the Spanish cavaliers, frantically waving their arms and shouting that they too were Spaniards. The four horsemen quickly surrounded the two who were on foot and kept them at bay with the point of their lances. Captain

Lázaro de Cárdenas and his three cavaliers, who were members of a slave raiding party under the command of Diego de Alcaraz, were caught off guard by the sight of two nearly naked men, one black and one brown, with numerous tattoos, who spoke proper Castilian. Cabeza de Vaca later remembered: "They remained looking at me a long time, so astonished that they neither spoke to me nor managed to ask me anything."[1]

Once Cabeza de Vaca was able to convince Captain Cárdenas that he was who he claimed to be — the treasurer and one of the few survivors of the ill-fated Pánfilo de Narváez expedition — he and his comrades were escorted to the nearby Spanish camp. There they were met by Diego de Alcaraz, an officer who had served under Nuño de Guzmán during the bloody conquest of northwestern Mexico to establish the province of Neuva Galicia, and who was now the commander of a slaving mission that answered to Melchior Díaz, the alcalde mayor of the Spanish settlement of Culiácan. Diego de Alcaraz, who was more interested in enslaving than saving souls, doubted the veracity of Cabeza de Vaca's story but was extremely interested in the part of the tale about the hundreds of natives who had followed him. Alcaraz had fifty foot soldiers, three horsemen, and several native porters accompany Esteban when the Moor set out to retrieve Andrés Dorantes, Alonso del Castillo, and the other natives who had been left behind.

Dorantes, Castillo, and nearly six hundred men, women, and children followed Esteban and the soldiers to the Spanish camp where Cabeza de Vaca anxiously awaited their arrival. The natives of the land celebrated this suspension of hostilities by bringing forth numerous clay pots filled with a generous offering of corn, a staple they had kept hidden from their Spanish oppressors. Unfortunately, the joyous reunion was abruptly shattered when Spanish soldiers, who were simply following the orders of their commander, began rounding up the many natives who had faithfully followed Cabeza de Vaca and his three comrades, so they could be added to the current inventory of slaves. Diego de Alcaraz, who was salivating over the prospect of such a large haul of human chattel, intended to enslave every native who entered his camp, but Cabeza de Vaca interceded on behalf of his Indian companions. A verbal battle ensued as Cabeza de Vaca and Diego de Alcaraz debated over the rights of the natives.

After having firmly stood his ground long enough to gain a concession from Alcaraz not to enslave his followers, an ashamed Cabeza de Vaca returned to the multitude of natives who had stayed by his side and pleaded with them to leave this place and return to the safety of their homes before the Spanish commander had a change of heart. When the natives refused to leave, Cabeza de Vaca tried his best to convince them that he was not a deity but merely a mortal who hailed from the same race of men who had committed so many atrocities across this land. Refusing to believe that the four shamans were related to those who were so cruel, one Indian responded, "You heal the sick while the others murder the healthy. You are not greedy and you desire nothing for yourself, while the others only rob and give nothing. You came to us naked and barefoot, while others came in armor, galloping on their horses. How can you say you are of the same people as the slave-raiders and gold-seekers?"[2]

After he was finally able to convince the reluctant natives to return to their homelands, Cabeza de Vaca and his three companions began making preparations for their journey to Culiácan, where they were to meet with Melchior Díaz, the vice governor of the region. In their haste to depart, the four Christians left behind with their former followers many of the gifts, including the five emerald arrowheads and the molded copper bell, they had received for the various services they rendered during their travels. They did, however, remember to bring the ceremonial gourds that had pebbles inside and sacred etchings on the outside. Diego de Alcaraz provided four horsemen to escort the four survivors of the Pánfilo de Narváez expedition to the Spanish settlement where Melchior Díaz resided.

Unbeknownst to Cabeza de Vaca, Alonso del Castillo, Andrés Dorantes, and Esteban, their Spanish guide, Lázaro de Cebreros, was purposely leading them astray. The unscrupulous Diego de Alcaraz had instructed Lázaro to lead the four survivors of the Narváez expedition to a remote region of the desert, where they were to be left without food and water after being abandoned by their mounted escorts. Lázaro was to return to the company of Alcaraz once this dastardly deed was done. The murderous plot seemed foolproof, for who would miss men who had been presumed dead for many years?

Meanwhile, back at the Spanish camp, Diego de Alcaraz ordered his soldiers to round up the six hundred natives who previously enjoyed the protection of Cabeza de Vaca. Now that they knew where the local natives were hiding, the Spanish slavers went after the scores of Indians who sought refuge in the hills. The Requerimiento was read aloud, the legal document that legitimized the Spaniards' right to wage war and enslave heathens who did not freely submit to their will.

Shortly after having trekked out to the middle of nowhere, the four horsemen charged with escorting the four survivors of the Narváez expedition suddenly turned tail and galloped away. It was then that Cabeza de Vaca and the others realized they had been duped by the cunning Diego de Alcaraz. Without food, water, or a sense of direction, the four on foot must have wondered if they had endured so many travails only to die in the desert because of the treachery of a fellow countrymen. Fortunately for them, Lázaro de Cebreros had a change of heart and, instead of returning to Alcaraz as instructed, rode straight to Culiácan. Once there, the guilt ridden soldier confessed to Melchior Díaz the terrible crime he had committed by order of his commanding officer. The vice governor of the region immediately sent a rescue party to the place where Cebreros had stranded the four men.

With a renewed faith in their fellow man, Cabeza de Vaca, Alonso del Castillo, Andrés Dorantes, and Esteban followed their rescuers back to San Miguel Culiácan where they were warmly received by Melchior Díaz. After hearing the impassioned appeal of Cabeza de Vaca, the vice governor sent a company of soldiers to compel Diego de Alcaraz to release the numerous natives he had unjustly enslaved and to give an account of his unseemly actions. Melchior Díaz showed great respect toward the four survivors of the ill-fated Narváez expedition as well as the natives who had followed them.

A Warm Reception at Mexico City

After several days of rest, during which time the four were fed, bathed, shorn, and dressed, Cabeza de Vaca and his fellow survivors left Culiácan on May 15. They were escorted to the town of Compostela, a distance of nearly one hundred leagues, to meet with Governor Nuño de Guzmán. The four men were well received by the governor, who made sure they were provided with whatever they required, including the finest accommodations. However, after having lived for so many years among the wandering tribes of North America it took the Christian shamans quite some time to get used to the comforts they once took for granted. Cabeza de Vaca wrote that "For many days I could bear no clothing, nor could we sleep, except on the bare floor."[3]

The next stop for Cabeza de Vaca and his companions was Mexico City, which they reached on July 24, 1536. It was here, where the Aztec capital of Tenochtitlan once stood, that the four wayfarers were hailed as heroes while being officially greeted by a delegation that included Viceroy Antonio de Mendoza and Hernán Cortés, the conqueror of Mexico who now had to settle for the title of Marques del Valle. Cabeza de Vaca was a guest at the home of Viceroy Mendoza where the conversation focused on the most memorable moments of his amazing journey. A grateful guest regaled his gracious host with colorful stories of the astounding things he had seen during his days as a wandering shaman and trader of goods. He spoke of villages that housed large collections of animal hides, colorful feathers, seashells, emeralds, and turquoise. Even though much of the vast region they traversed was an arid wasteland, Cabeza de Vaca emphasized that there were large tracts of fertile land where corn, beans, squash and cotton were grown.

Cabeza de Vaca also boasted of the many magnificent gifts that the natives had bestowed upon them, especially the large copper bell and the five emerald arrowheads. While he regretted having left behind such precious offerings, Cabeza de Vaca hinted that these items were evidence of precious metals and stones just waiting to be mined from these unexplored regions of the New World. Viceroy Mendoza's curiosity was piqued by his report of native tales pertaining to cities north of the Village of Hearts that were said to be great in both size and splendor. Even though his guest never claimed to have seen such cities and had failed to bring back evidence that could support such an account, the viceroy had little reason to doubt such places existed. After all, it wasn't all that long ago that Hernán Cortés had laid claim to the rich city of Tenochtitlan, and that find had recently been eclipsed by Francisco Pizarro's conquest of Cuzco, the capital of the vast and wealthy empire lorded over by the Incas. Mendoza was eager to learn if there was any truth to these tales of magnificent native cities to the north but decided to proceed cautiously with his investigation. The viceroy did not wish to risk Spanish lives in pursuit of an elusive and impossible dream.

In addition to these informal talks, Cabeza de Vaca was instructed to put to paper an account of his many adventures over the last eight years and perhaps a rough map to chart the route he followed. Alonso del Castillo and Andrés Dorantes, the two other Castilian survivors, were also ordered to recount their adventures on paper, all of which were to be included in the official report to the Spanish authorities. The three Castilians spent the next few weeks recuperating and reacquainting themselves with the comforts they had been denied for many years, while penning their recollections for a "Joint Report" to be presented to the Audencia of Santo Domingo, the governing body charged with supervision of Spanish expeditions in the New World. Their testimony was collected between the latter part of July and the beginning of October 1536. Some of what they wrote was merely a retelling of native claims that had never been verified by the wandering Spaniards and some exploits may have been embellished in order to gain a sympathetic ear. Cabeza de Vaca and his comrades reported that the natives they encountered did not commit sacrifices nor were they idolators. Unfortunately, the official report was, at some point, lost and only a portion has survived, which seems to have been paraphrased in the historical account written by Gonzalo Fernández de Oviedo y Valdez. Posterity has been deprived of many of the more intimate details of this epic journey, a fact that has forced historians to rely on the sanitized account written by Cabeza de Vaca several years after his return to Spain.

The private talks between Cabeza de Vaca and Viceroy Mendoza, as well as the written accounts of all three Castilians, were supposed to be done in secret, but tidbits of these discussions and reports inevitably found their way to a curious public. Rumors of the four survivors' exploits grew grander with each retelling. Soon there were stories circulating that they had wandered across lands and over mountains teeming with gold, silver, emeralds, and various other precious materials. Cabeza de Vaca's statement that in the mountains they had seen "undeniable indications of gold, antimony, iron, and other metals"[4] lent credence to such gossip. Some even began to speculate that the native cities to the north were the legendary Seven Cities of Antillia. The rapidly spreading stories of wondrous lands filled with roaming bison and native towns of great wealth produced calls for an expedition to find the cities that were equal to the magnificence of Tenochtitlan or Cuzco.

5

RIVALS FOR THE RIGHTS TO FLORIDA

A Disappointing Return to Spain

Viceroy Antonio de Mendoza offered Cabeza de Vaca an opportunity to lead a reconnaissance expedition to explore the northern regions where the rich native cities were said to exist, but he politely declined such an appointment. Mendoza then made a similar offer to Andrés Dorantes, but he also gracefully declined the viceroy's offer. Unbeknownst to Viceroy Mendoza, these two surviving officers of the Narváez expedition had already entered into their own pact, one that had a far grander design. Cabeza de Vaca, who had no intention of serving under another Spanish officer, had already made plans to return to Spain, where he hoped to parlay his new found celebrity into a grant from Emperor Charles V to lead his own expedition to the Florida region. Andrés Dorantes, who had agreed to join Cabeza de Vaca in this venture, also planned to return to Spain. Dorantes booked passage aboard a different ship, one that was part of a convoy returning to the Old World with the many riches harvested from the New World.

Carrying with him little more than the hope of being granted the governorship of all Florida, Cabeza de Vaca boarded a ship at Vera Cruz in April of 1537 that was destined for Spain. He believed that his being the highest ranking survivor of the Pánfilo de Narváez expedition, combined with his knowledge of the land and its people, would carry enough weight for him to inherit this vacant and coveted title. The ship that carried Cabeza de Vaca across the Atlantic made an unscheduled stop at Lisbon on August 9, 1537. His ship had been guided to the capital of Portugal after having been rescued by a Portuguese armada from a close encounter with marauding French corsairs eager to get their hands on gold from the New World. Andrés Dorantes, however, found himself stranded at Vera Cruz when the vessel he sailed aboard was forced to return to port after it quickly proved too weather worn for such a lengthy crossing.

Cabeza de Vaca proceeded to the Spanish court at Valladolid to offer an official report on the ill-fated Pánfilo de Narváez expedition and to promote himself as the logical choice to lead the next expedition to explore, conquer, and settle Florida "from one sea to the other." Here he might have been guilty of enhancing some of his exploits in an effort to get his own command. Cabeza de Vaca was disappointed to learn that his return to Spain had not been soon enough. The Narváez grant to Florida, which had remained in force for more than a decade, had been ceded to Hernando de Soto, one of the richest and most celebrated of all the New World conquistadors. Besides being appointed governor of Cuba, Hernando had greased enough palms at the royal court to be named adelantado of Florida in April of 1537 — just ten days after Cabeza de Vaca had departed Vera Cruz.

An Illustrious Career

There were few Spaniards of this era who possessed as many of the romantic characteristics associated with the title of conquistador as did Hernando de Soto. His undoubted valor in combat, his remarkable equestrian skills, and the loyalty he inspired among the men he led in battle were admirable traits honed while serving with great distinction in the conquests of Panama, Nicaragua, and Peru. He was one of the few conquistadors who seemed to have the good sense to retire while he was still in possession of both his health and wealth, returning to Spain while in his mid-thirties with a fortune that was the envy of all. De Soto was also afflicted with many of the base motives inherent to the brutal era of the conquistadors: he was exceptionally ruthless toward his enemies and often exhibited unrestrained cruelty toward those who were his prisoners.

Very little is known of Hernando de Soto's early years in Spain and even the date of his birth is somewhat of a mystery, though many historians seem to agree that he was born in or just prior to the year 1500. We do know that his father was Francisco Méndez de Soto, a respected hidalgo, and his mother was Leonor Arias Tinoco, who was descended from a "line of hidalgos in the city of Badajoz."[1] Hernando was probably born at Jerez de los Caballeros, the hometown of his father and also the birthplace of Vasco Nuñez de Balboa. This "son of someone" spent his formative years in this relatively large town located in the province of Estremadura, which was one of the poorest regions in all of Spain.

When he reached the age of fourteen — a time in Spanish circles when a boy was considered to be a man — Hernando de Soto signed on as one of more than two thousand colonists headed to Panama under the command of Pedro Arias Davila, an infamous governor often referred to simply as Pedrarias. The Pedrarias expedition was the Spanish Crown's response to a message received from Vasco Nuñez de Balboa, a stowaway conquistador who had assumed command of a poorly led rescue mission organized by Martin Fernández de Enciso, in which he claimed to have learned of a region rich with gold. Balboa also wrote of having settled upon fertile lands inhabited by peaceful natives willing to carry on commerce, an idyllic scenario for founding a Spanish colony of which, of course, he hoped to be appointed governor. He also made mention of a "Southern Sea," which the natives said was a short trek from where they were presently settled, and once found, this other sea would lead them to lands that overflowed with precious gold and lustrous pearls.

King Ferdinand heeded Balboa's call for the founding of a Spanish settlement, which was to be called Castilla del Oro (Golden Castle). However, the king was disinclined to award the governorship of such a potentially prosperous colony to a man charged by Martin de Enciso before the royal court with being a stowaway, a usurper of his rightful command, and having wrongfully expelled Diego Nicuesa, the lawful governor of the region. Ferdinand instead gave the appointment to the politically connected Pedrarias.

The king of Spain was also disturbed by reports that had recently come to his attention concerning Spanish atrocities committed against his New World subjects and therefore instructed the newly appointed governor to treat the natives in a more humane manner. Pedrarias brought with him the just issued "El Requerimiento," an official document that was to be read to the natives of the New World before compelling them to submit to Spanish authority. No Indians were to be killed or branded as slaves unless they refused to recognize the terms of El Requerimiento. This act, which combined Christian orthodoxy and Spanish objectives, was intended to protect the natives from unnecessary harm, but all too often it was artfully employed as a means to legitimize the enslavement of the indigenous people. Such was the case with Pedrarias, who is said to have owned nearly nine thousand native slaves when he became governor of Nicaragua.

Hernando de Soto faithfully attached his star to the cause of Governor Pedrarias and his mettle in military campaigns against the natives was steadily rewarded with a rise in rank. By the age of twenty Hernando was already a captain, and four years later he was leading a battalion of men in the conquest of Nicaragua. In 1527, an appreciative Pedrarias appointed de Soto as his captain of the guards. The historian Garcilaso de la Vega described the fully matured Captain Hernando de Soto as "slightly above medium height with dark and cheerful countenance."

Hernando had an opportunity to learn from both Pedrarias and Vasco Nuñez de Balboa during his stint at Panama. Besides offering the young Spaniard an opportunity to earn fame and fortune, Pedrarias encouraged him to be ruthless in battle and demonstrated how to extract useful information through the use of torture. In contrast, Balboa showed him the benefits of commanding the respect of his men and the advantages of using diplomacy in dealing with the natives. Hernando surely must have admired the adventurous spirit of the charismatic Balboa, a veteran conquistador who hailed from his hometown. He also served alongside Francisco Pizarro, a seasoned officer who was Balboa's lieutenant but who was quick to ingratiate himself within the inner circle of Pedrarias. De Soto was attached to the command of Balboa when the Spanish discoverer of El Mar del Sur prepared for a second expedition across the isthmus of Panama in what proved to be another failed attempt to locate the native lands to the south said to be rich with gold. Hernando was stationed at Acla awaiting the return of his commanding officer when he learned that Balboa had been beheaded by the elderly and envious Pedrarias. The arresting officer was Francisco Pizarro.

During his time spent at Panama, Hernando de Soto formed a partnership with Hernán Ponce de León and Francisco Compañón whereby the three agreed to pool their earnings and divide them into equal shares. When this pact was forged, the three young conquistadors possessed little more than their good names, but that soon changed as earnings accumulated from campaigns of plunder and a lucrative trade in native slaves made them all men of respectable wealth. The partnership had to be restructured after the death of Francisco Compañón sometime between late 1527 and early 1528. Compañón's share was dissolved and shipped to his grieving mother in Spain.

Hernando de Soto also served under Gasper de Espinosa in campaigns that subjugated and plundered a great number of tribes along the western region of Panama. Espinosa would later become a silent partner in Francisco Pizarro's expeditions to find the rich kingdoms to the south of Panama that had proved beyond the reach of Balboa. The attention of most Spaniards stationed at Panama was, for the moment, diverted toward the north after it was learned that Hernán Cortés had discovered and conquered the Aztec capital of Tenochtitlan, a city that exceeded the splendor and wealth of any contemporary city of Europe. Everyone was convinced that there must be other such opulent native kingdoms just waiting to be conquered. Before long, the Spaniards of Panama, led by Pedrarias, were waging war with the Spanish conquistadors of Mexico for the right to exploit the native tribes of Nicaragua. Hernando de Soto was among the many soldiers who fought under the banner of Pedrarias, and the great service he rendered to the governor's cause was rewarded with an appointment as alcalde mayor of the town of León.

Hernando de Soto's fortune further improved with the arrival of Bartolomé Ruiz and Nicolás de Ribera at La Posesion in June of 1529. These Spanish officers, both of whom were members of the Francisco Pizarro and Diego de Almagro expedition in search of a place called Biru, had come to

Nicaragua to find recruits and obtain native slaves to aid in this promising venture. Their need for slaves brought them into contact with Hernando de Soto and Hernán Ponce de León, two ambitious officers who supplemented their income by trafficking in human chattel. Both were intrigued by Ruiz's eyewitness account of having finally found evidence that supported the rumors of wealthy native kingdoms to the south of Panama. Having grown weary of his role as an administrator, Hernando was receptive to the idea of joining the expedition of Francisco Pizarro, an officer he was already acquainted with. To avoid any interference from Pedrarias, Hernando and Hernán entered into a secret pact with these agents in which they pledged to provide more recruits and provisions in exchange for the promise of appointments of substantial rank in Pizarro's regime.

Hernando de Soto left Nicaragua shortly after Pedrarias passed away at the advanced age of ninety-one. He managed to join up with the third expedition of Francisco Pizarro in 1532 at the island of Puna, near the coast of Peru. He arrived with his recruits just in time to help Pizarro and his beleaguered troops fend off a fierce native assault. Hernando was disappointed to learn that instead of being given command of the army, as he had been promised, he was to lead only a unit of horse soldiers. De Soto surely must have considered returning to Nicaragua after seeing that the coastal town of Tumbes, which Pizarro had bragged was a city of great wealth, lay in utter ruins, a consequence of the bloody civil war between Atahualpa and Huascar, the sons of the deceased Inca ruler Huayna Capac, for control of the empire. Thoughts of abandoning this quest slowly abated with native testimony that the capital city of Cuzco was endowed with vast quantities of gold, and were finally quelled with the later news that Atahualpa, who was the victor of this conflict, was camped at the highland town of Cajamarca.

After several grueling days climbing over mountainous terrain, Francisco Pizarro and his army of just one hundred sixty-eight soldiers reached the town of Cajamarca, which had been abandoned for their benefit by order of Lord Atahualpa. Pizarro sent Hernando de Soto as his emissary to Atahualpa, who was camped nearby with an intimidating army estimated at eighty thousand strong. After instructing those who were to accompany him to show absolutely no sign of fear, de Soto and his small band of cavaliers rode through a host of armed Inca warriors who keenly watched their every move. Shortly after appearing before the Inca ruler, Hernando was unexpectedly joined by Hernando Pizarro, the commander's brother, and together they made greetings and salutations on behalf of Francisco Pizarro. De Soto noticed that many of the Incas could not take their eyes off the horses, the likes of which they had never seen before, and decided to foster their sense of awe over this beast with a show of his renowned equestrian skill. After Atahualpa agreed to meet with the Spaniards at Cajamarca, Hernando put his steed through a series of intricate maneuvers before charging toward the seated Atahualpa. De Soto brought his horse to an abrupt halt within a breath of Atahualpa's face. The Inca ruler never flinched. However, several members of the royal retinue recoiled in fright. It is reputed that after the Spaniards left, Lord Atahualpa ordered the execution of all who were unable to control their fear, a toll that supposedly numbered forty.

Hernando de Soto was a pivotal participant in the surprise attack at Cajamarca that ended with the capture of Atahualpa and the massacre of thousands who were members of the ruler's large entourage. De Soto struck up a genuine friendship with the imprisoned Atahualpa and looked forward to their conversations while enjoying a game of chess, in which the emperor proved himself a worthy adversary by occasionally besting his Spanish teacher. Hernando had been away on a reconnaissance mission when Atahualpa was executed. When he learned what had happened, Hernando immediately confronted Francisco Pizarro and proceeded to chastise his commander for committing such a brazen and brutal act. De Soto's cruel nature also came to the forefront during the conquest of Peru. He personally tortured the captured Chalcuchima, severely burning the Inca general's legs until he told him what he wanted to hear.

Hernán Ponce de León, who had remained behind to liquidate the partnership holdings in Nicaragua, finally joined up with Hernando de Soto at Peru during the winter of 1534–35. Like so many other conquistadors, de Soto took a native mistress while stationed at the Inca capital of Cuzco. His Peruvian paramour was Tocto Chimpu, the young and strikingly beautiful daughter of Huayna Capac, the former Sapa Inca. Their two year relationship produced a daughter, Leonor de Soto, named after the conquistador's mother. Hernando also had a daughter by a native mistress in Nicaragua, who was named María de Soto. Both mother and daughter were left behind when the conquistador sailed for Peru.

De Soto made the mistake of siding with Diego de Almagro in the bitter dispute with the Pizarro brothers over which conquistador was, according to the recent decree of a grateful Spanish Crown, entitled to claim the city of Cuzco as his own. Hernando expected that his alliance with Francisco Pizarro's disgruntled partner would lead to an appointment as second-in-command of Almagro's planned expedition to Chile. De Soto even sought to assure this commission with an offer to contribute two hundred thousand of his own pesos toward the campaign. He was taken aback by Diego de Almagro's decision to appoint Rodrigo de Orgóñez as his second-in-command, a slight that left the ambitious Hernando de Soto without a future in Peru.

Hernando de Soto decided the time had come to return to Spain, where he would have an opportunity to enjoy his new found wealth and seek royal approval to lead his own expedition to search for other rich native kingdoms in the New World. The vast horde of treasure he had accumulated at Panama, Nicaragua, and especially Peru was loaded on a caravan of several hundred llamas and transported back to the coast where it was loaded onto a ship. De Soto departed Cuzco during the latter part of 1535, leaving behind both his Peruvian mistress and their young daughter.

Preparations for a Return to the New World

De Soto's return to Spain in the spring of 1536 was cause for much celebration, during which time he permitted himself to bask in the glory of being hailed as a conquering hero. While at Seville, Hernando was a guest at the home of Pedro Cataño, a fellow conquistador who had sailed back to Spain the previous year. Hernando stayed at Cataño's residence until he found a palatial abode that was to his liking. During his time at Seville, Hernando furthered his already esteemed status at the royal court by taking Isabel de Bobadilla, a daughter of Pedrarias, as his wife. Their wedding took place at Valladolid in November of 1536. Isabel de Bobadilla y Peñalosa, Hernando's mother-in-law and once Queen Isabella's lady-in-waiting, took an interest in the officer who had faithfully served her husband in the New World and helped press the ambitious plans of her new son-in-law at the Spanish Court.

Don Hernando de Soto had earned for himself the fame and fortune that every conquistador who ever sailed to the New World dreamed of acquiring but few ever realized. In spite of all that he had already achieved, Hernando still felt overshadowed by the accomplishments of Hernán Cortés and Francisco Pizarro. Not content to sit back and reflect upon his past glories, the young and restless conquistador proposed to lead his own expedition to conquer other New World native empires that would further enrich and enlarge the emerging empire of Spain. Only then would he be recognized as a conqueror equal in stature to Cortés and Pizarro.

Hernando petitioned the royal court for the governorship of Quito and the right to lead an expedition to conquer the unexplored regions to the north of Ecuador, where an empire like the one forged by the Incas was sure to be found. After this request was denied, de Soto sought the governorship of Guatemala, where he hoped to uncover a native kingdom similar to the one founded by the Aztecs. Unfortunately, this request was also declined. Undeterred by these rejections, Hernando continued to seek an appointment to a prominent position in the New World, particularly where there was the possibility of making a discovery that would further his fame and fortune. After meeting personally with Emperor Charles V, Hernando was finally granted a governorship and the right to lead his own expedition. Since he had previously borrowed a considerable sum of money from Hernando de Soto to defray some of his mounting administrative expenses, the emperor was obligated to find a way to express his gratitude to the veteran conquistador.

On April 20, 1537, the Spanish Crown officially granted Hernando de Soto the governorship of Cuba along with the added incentive of being appointed adelantado (advancer) of Florida, a region that had already seen several Spanish expeditions end in failure. De Soto was granted the right to explore, conquer, and colonize lands from the province of Río de las Palmas in northern Mexico to the Florida region where Juan Ponce de León had landed. In other words, he inherited the vast realm that had been granted to Pánfilo de Narváez more than a decade ago. In addition to being entitled to all lands north of these two coastal points, Hernando was given the rights to Tierra Neuva, the region that was originally assigned to Lucás Vázquez de Ayllón. It was a loosely designed boundary assumed to stretch from sea to shining sea. In addition to the obligatory royal fifth share owed to the Royal Court for all confiscated treasure, it was further stipulated that on this expedition the Crown was entitled to half of all the precious items obtained from native graves or temples. Covetous Spanish officials, having learned from the testimony of conquistadors who had participated in the conquest of the Aztec and Inca empires, knew that these were often the most rewarding sites. A very grateful Emperor Charles V made Hernando de Soto a knight of the prestigious Military Order of Santiago, an honorary title befitting his many past deeds.

Hernando's commission to "conquer, pacify, and people" the Florida region was executed at Valladolid. The conquistador was expected to find what he was looking for and to complete the conquest in four years' time. Since his claim to Florida had no inheritable rights, all of Hernando's discoveries were to revert to the possession of the Crown upon his passing. Realizing the importance of this mission, Hernando de Soto would spend the next two years making sure his expedition was better prepared to explore the unknown lands of North America — where he expected to find great civilizations like those discovered in Mexico and Peru — than were the ill-fated campaigns of Juan Ponce de León, Lucás Vázquez de Ayllón, and Pánfilo de Narváez.

Interest in this expedition to the New World was heightened by the return to Spain of Álvar Núñez Cabeza de Vaca, one of the few survivors of the disastrous Narváez expedition. Rumors of his amazing adventures had preceded his arrival and the gossip that surrounded Cabeza de Vaca's visit with the emperor fueled much speculation about native empires that existed in the lands to which Hernando de Soto was soon headed. When Hernando learned of de Vaca's return, he immediately arranged a meeting with him. De Soto and his officers met for several days with Cabeza de Vaca, taking note of every detail the intrepid Spaniard was willing to reveal about his incredible odyssey. Hernando was particularly interested in the tales about the fierce Apalachen warriors of Florida and the stores of wealth they apparently were trying to conceal from the Spaniards. Cabeza de Vaca was often evasive about what he had actually seen or heard on his journey, especially when it came to the topic of wealth. De Soto offered him a prominent position in his command, but the proud Spaniard, who had no interest in serving in an expedition he believed should have been his to lead, graciously declined this offer.

Hernando felt that the meeting with Cabeza de Vaca had yielded a great deal of useful information for his upcoming expedition. Believing that the Florida region was home to more wealth than either Mexico or Peru, de Soto and his officers were convinced that this was clearly an expedition worthy of their best effort. Cabeza de Vaca's continued silence on the rumored rich kingdoms cast an aura of mystery over the lands he had explored, which many interpreted as confirmation that this was indeed a region of untold riches. Others viewed his silence as nothing more than petty jealousy, convinced that Cabeza de Vaca felt slighted by not having been appointed commander of this expedition.

While there is no written record of what Cabeza de Vaca told Hernando de Soto, what was said, or what was believed to have been said at their meeting, it was evidently enough to encourage many a hidalgo and commoner to liquidate his assets in order to join the expedition. The initial reports of the surviving members of the Narváez expedition combined with the rumors that circulated after Cabeza de Vaca met with Hernando convinced a number of already fortunate men to sell their estates and other worldly possessions to fund the purchase of armor, weapons, clothes and other essential items that would help them obtain even greater rewards in the New World. Even though he could not be coaxed into joining the upcoming expedition, Cabeza de Vaca did not hesitate to encourage friends and relatives to sail to the Americas. When two of his cousins asked his advice about joining the ambitious undertaking that was underway, the veteran soldier told them that, because of his prior agreement with Andrés Dorantes, he was sworn to secrecy. But his recommendation to them was to sell all of their belongings and join up with Hernando de Soto. So many adventurous Spaniards heeded this call of untold riches that de Soto found himself in the enviable position of having to turn away able-bodied recruits simply because there was no more room on the ships.

Volunteers for the Florida expedition were also encouraged by the fact that Hernando de Soto, a renowned soldier who had already earned a significant amount of fame and wealth, was willing to risk everything he owned in order to finance this venture. Many Spaniards speculated that the famed conquistador must have in his possession undisclosed knowledge so compelling and favorable that he was willing to gamble his entire fortune and reputation on an expedition where so many others had failed. Like all other Spanish explorers seeking to lead an expedition to the New World, de Soto had to incur all the costs associated with such a speculative venture. However, unlike other commanders, Hernando possessed the financial means that freed him from having to sell off shares of his expected profits to investing partners.

Hernando de Soto spared no expense when it came to purchasing the supplies and weapons he felt would ensure the success of his mission. The inventory of food items included a large quantity of cured meats, olive oil, wine, and hardtack. Besides the weapons that each man was required to bring for his own use, there was an additional arsenal of swords, crossbows, arquebuses, and gunpowder. Hernando's intentions toward the native population was clearly stated by the inclusion of chains like those he used at Nicaragua to enslave Indians. Other items of importance were to be acquired after reaching the island of Cuba. However, while de Soto took care of the financing for the expedition, those who signed on were responsible for bringing their own supplies and weaponry. Like all prior expeditions, these recruits received no salary. They expected to be remunerated with a share of the wealth that was to be discovered and an allotment of land, as well as slaves to work the land.

Nuño de Tobar, an officer who had served with Hernando de Soto at Peru and hailed from the same town as the commander, was appointed second-in-command of the expedition. Baltasar de Gallegos was named chief constable and Diego Tinoco, a maternal relative of Hernando's and an excellent horseman, was made captain of the horse. Luís de Moscoso, a relative of Pedro de Alvarado and also a veteran of the Inca conquest, was appointed "maestro de campo," which meant he was in charge of the camps and the duty roster. Francisco Maldonado and Juan Ruiz Lobillo were put in command of the infantry units. The cavalry commands were divided between Pedro Calderon, André de Vasconcelos, and Alonso Romo, all of whom reported to Diego Tinoco. Juan de Añasco, who served with de Soto at Peru, was appointed comptroller of the expedition and given the rank of captain. Pedro Carrion was another veteran soldier who signed on for the Florida expedition, having served with Hernando at both Nicaragua and Peru.

Probably after hearing about the desperate effort of Narváez's soldiers to build boats while stranded at Bahia de Caballos, Hernando de Soto made sure an experienced shipbuilder was aboard, which he succeeded in doing by signing a Genoan named Maestro Francisco. Twelve priests committed to saving heathen souls also joined the expedition. Also on board were three men, and perhaps a fourth, who wrote of their adventures while members of the expedition. Luís Hernández de Biedma, an appointed royal factor, wrote a brief but succinct account of the expedition from the moment it left the shores of Cuba until it ended at Panuco in New Spain. Rodrigo Rangel, who was de Soto's personal secretary and is best remembered as simply Rangel, also wrote his own account of this journey. Another report was written by a mysterious individual known as simply Elvas or the Gentleman of Elvas. While the true identity of Elvas is uncertain, a gentleman named André de Burgos has been mentioned as a possible candidate. A fourth individual is mentioned because Garcilaso de la Vega, the contemporary historian and Peruvian mestizo who wrote what still stands as the most insightful and entertaining account of Hernando de Soto's adventure in the New World, relied on information provided by an unidentified member of the expedition. Many historians believe that Gonzalo Silvestre, a cavalier from Herrera de Alcántara, is Vega's unmentioned source.

On April 7, 1538, following mass and a celebratory feast that centered around a great deal of fanfare, Hernando de Soto and his men boarded the ships to begin their voyage to Cuba. According to Garcilaso de la Vega's account, de Soto's fleet consisted of seven large ships and three smaller vessels, the latter group consisting of one caravel and two brigantines. Depending on which eyewitness account a historian subscribes to, there were anywhere from six hundred to nine hundred fifty eager adventurers who sailed from the port of San Lucar de Barrameda. Hernando de Soto sailed aboard the flagship *San Cristóbal* (sometimes called the *Magdalena*) while Nuño de Tobar, the second-in command, sailed on the *Concepción*.

Hernando's fleet was accompanied on the voyage across the Atlantic by an armada of twenty ships which were headed for New Spain under the command of Gonzalo de Salazar. The expedition docked for eight days at Gomera, one of the Canary Islands, to gather additional provisions for the long voyage to Cuba. The ships destined for Mexico departed the company of Hernando de Soto shortly before the island of Cuba was sighted.

De Soto's ships had the misfortune of arriving at Cuba during a time when the island was coming under attack from French corsairs. As the fleet drew near the island, a man was seen along the shore who appeared to be directing them toward the best spot to drop anchor. Prior to their arrival, a Spanish ship had engaged a French vessel and when the townsfolk saw Hernando's approaching fleet they feared that the enemy had returned with an armada to exact revenge. One of the colonists was sent out to try to direct the ships toward the rocks and shoals that served as the island's best means of defense. Once this individual realized these were Spanish ships he was misdirecting, the man frantically tried to steer the fleet away from danger. The helmsmen aboard the ships complied but not soon enough for the flagship, which struck a rock. Luckily, the only damage was a few broken jugs. Once he was safely ashore, a forgiving Hernando de Soto assumed his role as governor of Cuba, though his primary concern was preparing for his quest to locate the elusive riches of Florida.

Unfortunately for Hernando de Soto, his plans to advance on Florida were abruptly delayed by the duties of his new office. An urgent message arrived at Santiago, where de Soto and his men were busy procuring provisions for the planned expedition, informing the governor that French corsairs had launched a raid that left the port city of Havana in charred ruins. Hernando was compelled to devote a great deal of time and energy to rebuilding the city he had planned on using as a base to support his conquest and colonization of Florida.

Vasco Porcallo de Figuero, the wealthy landowner and slave trader who had previously supplied Pánfilo de Narváez with horses and supplies, met with the new governor and offered to join the upcoming expedition to Florida. In return for Figuero's pledge to provide horses and native porters for the mission, de Soto appointed Vasco Porcallo as captain-general of the army, replacing Nuño Tobar, who apparently was demoted for having an improper affair with a lady-in-waiting to Hernando's wife, a young woman who was also a relative of Isabel de Bobadilla.

In late 1538, while still overseeing repairs at Havana, Hernando sent two ships under the command of Juan de Añasco, the comptroller and an experienced mariner, to probe and map the Florida shores in order to determine a suitable harbor for the fleet to dock. The Spaniards were already aware of Charlotte Harbor, where Juan Ponce de León had gone ashore, and Tampa Bay, where Pánfilo de Narváez had dropped anchor. It was hoped that this reconnaissance expedition would be able to locate a site that would prevent an encounter with the hostile natives known to reside along those shores. The signs seem to indicate that Añasco anchored his two ships at Tampa Bay, where he went ashore to capture natives who could be trained as guides and interpreters for the expedition. Añasco and his shore party soon came upon a group of Indians who, through sign language, communicated there was much gold to be found in these lands. Conquistadors frequently used the gold rings on their fingers to elicit a response from the natives regarding the existence of this prized metal. The comptroller repaid the natives for this valuable information by taking four of them back to Cuba.

After an absence of two months, Juan de Añasco returned to Cuba to report on his findings. According to Garcilaso de la Vega, the governor, who was greatly encouraged by the news of gold just waiting to be claimed, promptly sent Añasco back to Florida to plot an accurate course for the best harbor to dock the fleet. He returned after three months with two more natives and a place in mind along the vast shoreline of Tampa Bay to begin the conquest of Florida.

Hernando de Soto felt confident that he was fated to succeed where so many others had failed. Besides the benefit of Cabeza de Vaca's report on the lay of the land and his own experience in dealing with the natives of the New World, the governor had amassed an army of conquistadors that was larger and better equipped than any of the previous Spanish forays to Florida. Now that Añasco had provided him with the news he wanted to hear, all that was left for Hernando to do was to set sail. There was, however, the small matter of news coming from New Spain that Hernando found somewhat disconcerting.

Mendoza Mounts an Expedition of His Own

Antonio de Mendoza, the viceroy of New Spain, had taken a keen interest in the travels of Cabeza de Vaca and his three comrades, especially the rumored tale of native cities to the north that just might prove even grander than the Aztec city of Tenochtitlan. The viceroy was eager to commence with his own expedition after meeting with the survivors of the Narváez campaign but was greatly disappointed to learn that neither Cabeza de Vaca, Alonso del Castillo, or Andrés Dorantes shared the same interest. Without an experienced guide, Mendoza felt compelled, though only briefly, to put his ambitious plan on hold.

Mendoza came from a renowned Spanish family that could trace its noble lineage as far back as the days of the Roman occupation. His distinguished military career did not go unnoticed by Emperor Charles V, who rewarded him with an appointment as the first viceroy of New Spain. Antonio de Mendoza assumed his new post shortly after landing at Vera Cruz, in October of 1535, the same region where sixteen years earlier Hernán Cortés had begun his epic march that culminated in the conquest of the Aztec empire. Perhaps the most difficult task Mendoza had to face was to take over the reigns of a government that owed its very existence to the determined effort of Hernán Cortés, a popular conquistador who found himself having to relinquish much of his power after settling for the lesser title of Marquis of the Valley of Oaxaca. The viceroy was able to balance this delicate situation by making Cortés welcome at court and occasionally seeking his counsel on affairs of state.

Ever since Cabeza de Vaca and his comrades had arrived at Mexico City, the viceroy had worried that the ambitious Hernán Cortés would attempt to lead his own expedition to find the native kingdoms of the north, even though the conqueror of Mexico had been restricted by royal decree to confine his explorations to the coastal regions of northern Mexico. Mendoza feared that his window of opportunity was beginning to close after he learned that Hernando de Soto was preparing an expedition that was to land at Florida, and Hernán Cortés was planning to explore an arm of the Pacific Ocean now called the Gulf of California, but which was once known as the Sea of Cortés. Concerned that either one or both of these expeditions might reach the rich native kingdoms of the north before him, the viceroy enlisted the aid of Francisco Vásquez de Coronado.

Just twenty-five when he sailed to New Spain as an officer accompanying Antonio de Mendoza, the newly appointed viceroy, Francisco Vázquez de Coronado, was the son of a prominent and influential family from Salamanca. Handsome, intelligent, and ambitious, the young Coronado rose quickly through the military ranks. It also helped that he became a good friend of the viceroy, who in turn became Coronado's mentor. Mendoza sent his protégé to the mines of Amatepeque to investigate and punish those involved in a slave uprising. After obtaining a full confession, Coronado had the guilty parties drawn and quartered. His swift and decisive action greatly impressed Viceroy Mendoza, who later rewarded Coronado with an appointment on the influential city council at Mexico City.

In 1537, Coronado furthered his good standing by taking as his wife the beautiful Dona Beatríz de Estrada, daughter of the deceased Alonso de Estrada, the former treasurer of New Spain who was reputedly an illegitimate son of King Ferdinand. She brought to the marriage a large dowry that greatly enriched the pockets of the young and aspiring officer. Coronado had certainly become the brightest star on the vast horizon of New Spain.

Viceroy Mendoza appointed Coronado as acting governor of the province of Neuva Galicia in August of 1538. He was to replace Perez de la Torre, who had died quite unexpectedly that same year. Torre had recently been appointed to replace governor Nuño Beltrán de Guzmán, who had been imprisoned for his harsh treatment of the natives. Coronado was confirmed as the governor of Neuva Galicia the following year.

Gonzalo de Salazar and the fleet under his command reached New Spain shortly after parting ways with Hernando de Soto. In keeping with protocol, the commander would have met with the viceroy to discuss his mission and to deliver any official documents from Spain. Salazar would have surely reported on de Soto's return to the New World and perhaps added his own conclusions about the celebrated conquistador's plans. At the very least, he would have presented Mendoza with the royal document that announced Hernando's appointment as both governor of Cuba and adelantado of Florida. This news put a damper on the viceroy's plans to search for the rich native cities of the north, which could arguably be considered part of the vast land grant ceded to Hernando de Soto. Mendoza feared that Cabeza de Vaca had divulged information to de Soto that he had not told him. Perhaps the survivors of the Narváez expedition had actually come across the seven cities that another Indian had mentioned and maybe Cabeza de Vaca had revealed this information to the newly appointed adelantado of Florida.

Nuño Beltrán de Guzmán, a lawyer who came to New Spain after the fall of Tenochtitlan, was possibly the first Spaniard to hear the story that was to become the basis for the legendary tale of the Seven Cities of Cibola. In 1529, one of Guzmán's slaves, an Indian by the name of Tejo, told him that to the north there were seven heavily populated cities, each of which were equal to or exceeded the wealth and magnificence of the city once known as Tenochtitlan. Tejo claimed that when he was a but a lad he ventured north of Panuco with his father to carry on trade with the people of these seven cities. This intriguing story captured the imagination of Guzmán and others who saw a connection to the oft-told Iberian tale concerning the Seven Cities of Antillia. According to this popular legend, seven Portuguese bishops had sailed westward with their Christian flock to escape the wrath of an invading Muslim army. To pay homage to God for having delivered them to a safe land, each bishop built a city that was glorious in every conceivable way. Now, after nearly eight centuries of searching the world over, it seemed to Guzmán and other hopeful Spaniards that the Seven Cities of Antillia had finally been found. While Guzmán failed to discover the exact whereabouts of these magnificent cities, the stories heard by Cabeza de Vaca and his comrades during their wanderings seemed to lend credence to the story told by Tejo.

Mendoza decided the time had come to take matters into his own hands. The viceroy made his intentions official with the appointment of Francisco Vázquez de Coronado, his good friend and favorite officer, as leader of an expedition to search for the native cities to the north. Even though there was a sense of urgency to this mission, both Mendoza and Coronado knew that success hinged on careful preparation and planning. It was decided to first send out a small expeditionary force that would chart the best possible course to these magnificent cities deemed worthy of a Spanish conquest.

6

A CLERICAL ERROR

An Odd Pair

Before risking the lives of the many men already recruited for his costly expedition to conquer lands of untold wealth, the cautious Antonio de Mendoza decided to send out a small scouting party to reconnoiter the path followed by the four survivors of the Narváez expedition. The viceroy tried once again to recruit the surviving Spaniards whom were still at New Spain, but neither Andrés Dorantes or Alonso del Castillo, both of who were now quite comfortable with their new surroundings, were eager to return to the rugged lands they had only recently left behind. Mendoza was fortunate to obtain the services of Esteban but he was not about to entrust this Moor with the command of such an important expedition. The viceroy needed a leader that not only he could trust but also one the natives would as well. The name of Fray Marcos de Niza was submitted to the viceroy as a candidate for this post.

Marcos de Niza was a Franciscan friar of Italian descent who grew up in France's port city of Nice. He came to the New World in 1531, first serving in the priesthood at Santo Domingo and then at Guatemala, where Pedro de Alvarado was governor. Fray Marcos followed Alvarado to South America when the renowned conquistador sought to lay claim to Quito, a northern province of the recently conquered Inca Empire. When the governor returned to Guatemala, Marcos remained at Ecuador with the troops who had been part of a negotiated settlement in which Pedro de Alvarado forfeited all claims to the region to Diego de Almagro, the partner of Francisco Pizarro, after being paid one hundred thousand pesos. During his brief stay in the service of Almagro and Pizarro, Fray Marcos had an opportunity to witness the enormous treasure trove that the Spaniards had collected at the city of Cuzco. Fray Marcos returned to Guatemala and in April of 1537 he was transferred to New Spain. Marcos served at the Spanish settlement of Culiácan, where he helped to free many natives who had been forced into slavery by Nuño Beltrán de Guzmán and his soldiers.

According to Father Antonio de Ciudad-Rodrigo, Fray Marcos de Niza was qualified to lead such an expedition because he was "skilled in cosmography and in the arts of the sea, as well as in theology."[1] The viceroy had come to believe that a friar just might be the logical choice to lead his small expeditionary force. After all, the natives encountered by Cabeza de Vaca and his comrades had looked to the Christians as healers and shamans, and there were few Spaniards who could exude such admirable qualities as well as a man of the cloth. It was also hoped that the presence of a priest would help to assuage the concerns of natives who had good reason to equate armed soldiers with cruel slavers. Viceroy Mendoza placed his faith in the hands of Fray Marcos de Niza, who he chose to lead the expedition that was to be guided by Esteban.

Esteban, the dark-skinned Moor who had endured as much pain and suffering as his Anglo comrades, viewed this reconnaissance mission as an opportunity to gain the favor of the viceroy and to earn for himself a status equal to that of every other free Spaniard. Mendoza wanted him to retrace the route he had followed with his comrades in the hope that it would lead directly to the legendary seven cities. Mendoza let both Fray Marcos and Esteban know exactly what he expected to be learned on this quest: confirm the existence of the seven native cities; determine if the trade routes of the Indians led to the coast (Hernán Cortés had already sent his own expedition by sea to make the same determination); report on the typography and the people; and find evidence of precious minerals that were waiting to be unearthed. If the priest and the guide returned with a favorable report, then the viceroy would promptly send a much larger armed force to claim the region for Spain.

The African Moor and the French-Italian priest in the service of Christ, Spain, and Mendoza set out on their quest shortly before the spring of 1539. Esteban and Fray Marcos traveled to Culiácan, a distance of roughly six hundred miles from Mexico City, in the company of Francisco Vázquez de Coronado, the newly appointed governor of New Galicia and the supervisor of their reconnaissance mission. The entourage also included Fray Onorato, a company of soldiers, and a number of Indians, some of whom were among the many faithful who had previously followed Cabeza de Vaca and his companions. Once at Culiácan, Coronado found himself having to put down a native insurrection by capturing Ayapin, a chief who led the rebellion. The prisoner was summarily tried, convicted and sentenced to death. Coronado ordered that the rebel leader was to be quartered.

The Trek Northward

After a brief stay at Culiácan, Fray Marcos, Esteban, Fray Onorato, and several native companions parted company with Coronado. They set out on the Camino Real on March 7, 1539, following a northern route that would take them through the Sonora Valley and into the unexplored region of Arizona. The expedition was slowed by the fact that Franciscan friars were forbidden to ride horses, an animal that St. Francis of Assisi, the founder of the order, believed was an ostentatious symbol of wealth. Coronado recalled that the natives "carried the padre on the palms of their hands, pleasing him in everything they could."[2] Fray Marcos carried with him samples of the metals and stones that were considered precious to the Spaniards. These specimens were to be shown to natives along the way so there would be no misunderstanding over where items of similar value could be located.

The plain and solemn garb of the priests stood in stark contrast to the outlandish dress of their guide. Esteban chose to adorn himself in a most peculiar manner, combining garish elements of Spanish and Indian attire. He wore armbands fitted with brightly colored feathers and around his ankles he strapped small bells, known as cascabeles, that jingled every time he moved. Esteban also carried with him at least one of the medicine rattles he received during his wanderings in the company of Cabeza de Vaca. Two magnificent greyhounds accompanied the Moor on this journey as did a bevy of nubile native maidens who were brought along to satisfy his every demand and desire.

After only a few days into their journey, Fray Marcos sent a message back to Culiácan informing Coronado that the natives of these lands were both friendly and helpful toward their cause. An elated Coronado forwarded this encouraging letter to Viceroy Mendoza. Shortly thereafter the expedition had its first setback. Fray Onorato became ill after reaching the Sinaloa River at Petatlán and had to be carried back to Culiácan on a litter.

Continuing on with their mission, Fray Marcos and Esteban soon came upon some Indians who claimed they came from a place where there were many pearls to be found, though they did not have any on hand to support such a claim. Even more encouraging news was obtained from natives along the Río Fuerte, who told them that a march of just a few more days would bring them to a region near the Río Mayo where people used gold to make jewelry and goblets. On March 21, the explorers reached the Indian settlement of Vacapa situated along the Río Mayo, which was not quite as rewarding as they had been led to believe.

It was decided after reaching the village of Vacapa that it might be in the best interest of the expedition if Esteban went on ahead by horse. Besides his regular entourage, the Moor was to be accompanied by Bartolomé, a native who had joined the expedition at Petatlán. Marcos instructed Esteban to keep him apprised of the significance of his findings by sending back crosses of varying size. A white cross the length of a palm would indicate that the region was of minor interest while a cross twice that size meant that it was a land of great promise, "and if it were something greater and better than New Spain, he should send a large cross."[3] Another reason for the use of crosses was the fact that the Moor, who was fluent in Spanish, could neither read nor write the words of his adopted homeland. Esteban left Vacapa on the 23rd of March.

While Fray Marcos realized that his sauntering pace was slowing down their efforts to reach the seven cities, the priest probably had a far more personal reason for sending the Moor on ahead. Tasting for the first time the many delights that his Spanish overlords had flaunted before him, Esteban clearly reveled in the importance of his role as a guide. The Moor took to dressing and acting as if he was of noble birth. Esteban entered each village with the proclamation that he was a returning child of the sun and therefore should be honored with an offering of many gifts. The priest surely would have been offended by the bevy of beautiful native girls that the guide collected for his personal harem. There is little doubt that the pious priest was relieved to be momentarily rid of such offensive behavior.

Even though he was familiar with many of the native dialects, Esteban made sure that he brought with him several samples of precious metals and stones to avoid any misunderstandings about what he was eager to find. After an absence of just four days, a messenger sent by the Moor returned to Vacapa urging Fray Marcos to come at once, a request punctuated by the presentation of a cross nearly as tall as the priest. The courier said that the natives up ahead claimed that the seven cities they sought were a thirty day march from where Esteban was presently located. The messenger went on to say that these cities, which the natives called Cibola, contained many buildings made of stone, most of which were several stories high. To Fray Marcos this tale of the Seven Cities of Cibola sounded as if it were the legendary Seven Cities of Antillia, the magnificent cities founded by Christian priests who had been forced to flee Portugal. Fray Marcos certainly would have offered up thanks to almighty God for having received such rewarding news.

Fray Marcos did not leave Vacapa until the eighth of April, a delay due in part to a sacred observance of Easter and a desire to wait for the return of natives he had sent to reconnoiter the coast. It was during this time that the priest met with several other Indians who testified to the existence of the Seven Cities of Cibola. Encouraged by this news, Fray Marcos quickened his pace and was able to reach in just three days the town where Esteban had sent his message. He was disappointed to learn that the impatient Moor had already gone on ahead but was comforted by further confirmation from these natives, as they gladly showed off the turquoise and hides acquired in trade from that region, that the Seven Cities of Cibola were indeed real places.

An enlivened Fray Marcos continued on to the next native settlement where, he received another large cross and a message from Esteban stating that he had set off in search of the first of these seven cities. After five more days of travel, a trek that took the priest and his entourage through a number of native towns, Fray Marcos received yet another message from the Moor. This dispatch claimed that the guide would wait for the priest at Corazones, the village where Andrés Dorantes had been awarded six hundred dried deer hearts. Marcos rushed to this "town of hearts" only to discover that Esteban had once again gone on ahead.

As he followed the trail of the restless Moor, Fray Marcos entered a lush valley that was home to a great many towns. He continued to hear tales of the multistoried homes found at Cibola and how the residents of these structures used ladders to get in and out of their upper apartments. It was at one of these local villages of the valley that the priest was fortunate to meet up with an Indian who said he was from Cibola. The native promised he would guide them to his homeland on the condition that once there the padre would use his influence to get him back in the good graces of the tribe. The troubled Indian sought forgiveness for an offense that had forced him to flee Cibola.

Though encouraged by the prospect that he would soon reach one of the Seven Cities of Cibola, Fray Marcos was somewhat perturbed by Esteban's habit of not waiting where he said he would. His annoyance turned to concern when the messages from the Moor suddenly stopped. The priest and his followers came to the Despoblado, a vast and desolate region that took fifteen days to cross. Shortly afterwards, the solitude of their hastily prepared camp was interrupted by the arrival of one of the Indians who had accompanied Esteban. He carried with him the disturbing news that the Moor was most likely dead. Learning that they were but three days from Cibola, Fray Marcos set out to learn what had become of Esteban. Two days later they encountered two other natives from the Moor's entourage, both of whom were bloodied from numerous wounds about their bodies.

A Fateful Discovery

The sluggish pace of Fray Marcos wasn't the only reason Esteban chose not to remain for very long at any one location. The Moor was eager to lay claim to fame and fortune for himself by being the first to discover the Seven Cities of Cibola. The ambitious Esteban ventured into the Sonora Valley, at which point he veered toward the northeast. It was near the present site of the Arizona and New Mexico border that the Moor and the Mexican Indians who accompanied him caught a glimpse of the Zuni pueblo of Hawikuh, one of the multistoried stone cities that the natives had told them about.

Convinced that this was one of the Seven Cities of Cibola, Esteban sent a messenger back to alert Fray Marcos of his discovery and then dispatched several natives to Hawikuh to announce his arrival. The Moor gave one of his envoys a gourd rattle he had received from an Indian tribe during his travels with Cabeza de Vaca. In addition to unique ritualistic markings, this particular gourd rattle was adorned with small bells and two feathers, one white and the other red. Esteban felt confident that such a sacred symbol would make the Zuni leaders understand that he was a wise and powerful medicine man who deserved their respect and adoration.

The chief of the Zuni pueblo received the messengers sent by Esteban but was greatly disturbed by the gourd rattle they presented to him, which he recognized from its markings as being crafted by a tribe that was an enemy of his people. One of the displeased Zuni elders defiantly threw the gourd to the ground, whereupon it shattered into many pieces. The angered chief made it clear that he wished them to leave his land at once or they all would suffer a terrible consequence for their disobedience.

The frightened Mexican emissaries quickly returned to Esteban to tell him of their unfriendly meeting with the Zunis and the ominous warning uttered by their chief. Believing these were simply idle threats and that the Zuni people would submit to his will once he stood before them, the Moor proceeded to chastise his envoys for their ignorance. The arrogant Esteban then took matters into his own hands. Shortly before sunset, the Moor rode up to the Zuni pueblo and announced that he was one of the "Children of the Sun." The horse that he sat upon was truly a strange sight to the natives, a beast that was bigger than a dog but smaller than a buffalo. It was Esteban himself who was perhaps the most peculiar sight to the Zunis. While they were intrigued by the darkness of the Moor's skin, they were, however, somewhat offended by the strange manner of his attire. Esteban believed he could scare the Zunis into submission by dressing and acting as if he were a god. Bright feathers were placed about his body and he attached small bells around his wrists and ankles. He proceeded to make outrageous demands. Besides requesting food and shelter for him and his entourage, the Moor ordered the Zunis to bring him women and gifts, preferably items made of gold. Finding himself whisked off by many natives to a hut, Esteban believed the Zunis finally understood that he was a man to be reckoned with.

The ambassadors of the Hawikuh chief relieved the Moor and his followers of most of their possessions and then housed them in a hut just outside their pueblo. There they languished without food or water while the Zuni elders attended a council to debate over the best way to handle this dark skinned man who had trespassed upon their land and who was most likely a spy sent by an enemy tribe. Unaware that his fate was being decided by the tribal council, Esteban made the best of the situation by getting some much needed rest.

Esteban and his retinue awoke to the disturbing sight of a great many armed Zuni warriors approaching their shelter. Those encamped outside the pueblo took flight the moment they saw that the warriors had stopped and were beginning to pull back on their bowstrings. Unfortunately, few were able to outdistance the skillful aim of the Hawikuh archers. One wounded native escaped and returned to inform Fray Marcos of this terrible turn of events. The two bloodied natives that the padre later met up with had managed to save themselves by hiding under the bodies of the dead. As they prepared to make their escape, the two Mexicans saw that the people of Hawikuh were wildly cheering from the tops of their roofs, not realizing they were celebrating the execution of Esteban. The Moor faced a brutal death, after which his body was chopped into many small pieces. His flesh was stripped and dried, pieces of which were sent to other towns as proof that this dark-skinned intruder was not a "Child of the Sun" or any other deity known to man. Esteban's personal porters were also killed. The Zunis retained some of the survivors but permitted nearly sixty captured natives to return to their homelands. The Hawikuh natives kept the feathers and bells worn by the Moor as well as the greyhounds that accompanied him.

The Return of Fray Marcos

The woeful tale told by the few battered and bruised Mexicans who escaped the carnage at Hawikuh greatly frightened the natives in the company of Fray Marcos, and many chose then and there not to carry on with this quest. Father Marcos, however, refused to abandon the mission and continued on in the company of just two native guides. Many historians have questioned whether Marcos still possessed the fortitude to venture into such a dangerous territory, but given how much was at stake it seems unlikely that the padre would have passed on an opportunity to catch a glimpse of one of the seven cities that just might have been founded long ago by seven Christian priests.

Fray Marcos continued on to Hawikuh and was soon rewarded by the sight of a city, which he judged from the safety of an overlooking hill, that looked to be much larger than Mexico City. His mind became filled with visions of magnificent earthly rewards after being told by his guides that he was gazing upon the smallest of the Seven Cities of Cibola. He saw with his own eyes a large and towering settlement that appeared as if it were made of gold, not realizing that his eyes had been fooled by a setting sun that had cast a gilded glow off the stone structures of the pueblo—a mirage that lent credence to Esteban's claim that he had found one of the seven golden cities. Fray Marcos laid claim to the land for Spain by planting a cross, which was held in place by a pile of rocks, and christening the region El Neuvo Reino de San Francisco (New Kingdom of San Francisco).

Having no desire to recklessly risk his neck the way that Esteban had, Fray Marcos made a hasty retreat back to where those who feared to venture any further anxiously awaited his return. After all, he reasoned, this mission could not be deemed a success unless someone returned to report on what had been discovered. Fray Marcos and his entourage passed by the province of Abra, where the priest reportedly saw off in the distance seven native settlements nestled in the valley that also seemed full of promise.

Fray Marcos arrived at Culiácan only to learn that Coronado was currently at Compestela. Marcos proceeded at once to this Spanish post to issue his official report. Even though he had returned to New Spain without any physical evidence to support the native stories of northern towns that held vast stores of precious metals and gems, the priest's claim of having seen one of the Seven Cities of Cibola was treated as gospel. Eager to inform Viceroy Mendoza of this wondrous discovery, Coronado immediately dispatched a message to Mexico City. He then escorted Fray Marcos to the capital of New Spain so that the friar could provide the viceroy with a firsthand account of all that both he and the deceased Esteban had discovered.

Father Marcos returned to Mexico City where, on September 2, 1539, he made an official report before a spellbound Viceroy Mendoza. The intrepid priest boasted that he ignored the advice of those in his company who had told him to turn back and braved his way to Cibola so that he could see the magnificent city with his own eyes. Fray Marcos reported: "The settlement is larger than the city of Mexico. At times I was tempted to go to it, because I knew that I risked only my life, and this I had offered to God the day I began the expedition. But the fact is that I was afraid, realizing my peril, and that if I should die it would not be possible to have an account of this land, which, in my opinion, is the largest and best of all those discovered." Marcos went on: "When I told the head men with me how good Cibola appeared to me, they said it was the least of the Seven Cities, and that Totonteac is much larger and better than all the Seven Cities put together, and that it has so many houses and people that it has no end."[4]

Besides staking a claim to the vast wealth that Cibola surely housed, Fray Marcos de Niza said he had learned of the equally rich kingdoms of Totonteac, Acus, and Marata. This tale of additional golden realms contributed to a growing belief that native lands to the north were far richer than first thought. Marcos also pointed out that the hostile nature of the natives certainly indicated the need to send a large army in order to enforce a Spanish claim to the province of Cibola. The aggressive behavior of the Zunis was construed by many as evidence that Hawikuh was a town of immense wealth, for clearly they must possess something that was worth protecting from outsiders.

The contents of the confidential report issued by Fray Marcos proved difficult to suppress. Stories of the Seven Cities of Cibola became the talk of the entire town and even found its way into the sermons preached from the pulpit. While he never specifically mentioned gold in his report, Marcos did, however, imply that Cibola was home to many precious items. The padre said the natives told him that the seven cities were centers of trade for precious minerals such as turquoise, which the Cibolans used to decorate many of their doors. The tale of Cibola became fodder for gossip mongers, with each managing to put an even grander spin on an already incredible story. It wasn't long before people began saying that every door at every city was encrusted with every jewel known to man. The province was also said to be heavily populated with people who all wore elegant jewelry made of gold and spoke Nahuatl, the language of the Aztecs. Some individuals familiar with the legends of the Aztecs speculated that these cities might be Aztlan, their celebrated ancestral home.

Fray Marcos firmly believed in what he had seen with his own eyes and his persuasive words convinced others that there were a great many rich native cities just waiting to be claimed for Spain. The good friar's tale certainly lent credence to the rounds of gossip that had been circulating ever since Cabeza de Vaca and his comrades wandered into Mexico City. After all, Hernán Cortés and Francisco Pizarro had each found native cities of incredible wealth, therefore it was reasonable to conclude that similarly rich kingdoms were sure to be found up north.

There were, however, some who doubted the veracity of the padre's tale. Hernán Cortés, the conqueror of Mexico, was among those who thought Fray Marcos to be less than truthful. Even Viceroy Mendoza had lingering doubts about the priest's assertion of having found the Seven Cities of Cibola and decided to send another scouting party up north to verify this claim. Mendoza instructed Melchior Díaz, the alcalde mayor of Culiácan, to follow the route paved by Esteban and Fray Marcos. Melchior and a small company of horsemen left Culiácan on November 17, 1539.

So great was the speculation over the wealth that awaited at the province of Cibola that Viceroy Mendoza felt compelled to publicly announce his plan to launch a major expedition before others, such as Hernán Cortés or Pedro de Alvarado, attempted to mount campaigns of their own. The viceroy was also concerned that the Florida expedition of Hernando de Soto, which was already underway, would happen upon a route that led to the Seven Cities of Cibola. Evidence of Mendoza's sense of urgency is confirmed by his order to Francisco Vásquez de Coronado to lead an army of conquistadors to Cibola without bothering to wait for confirmation from the scouting party led by Melchior Díaz.

The Old Conquistadors Seek a Share of the Prize

Even though his youth and authority had waned significantly since the glory days when he masterminded the campaign that toppled the Aztec Empire, Hernán Cortés was still a presence to be reckoned with. No one in Mexico was more aware of this fact than Viceroy Mendoza. The ambitious Marquis of the Valley of Oaxaca possessed the wherewithal to finance his own expedition, and that is exactly what he did. Cortés had been busy preparing an expedition that would search by sea for the cities that Cabeza de Vaca had alluded to and Fray Marcos and Esteban had been sent to find. When the legendary conquistador learned of the initial reports sent back to Mexico City by the reconnaissance mission, he immediately offered his services to the viceroy, hoping to seal the deal with an offer to finance the entire expedition. Not wanting to provide Hernán Cortés with another opportunity to further his already considerable fame and fortune, Mendoza summarily declined his generous offer.

Finding himself unable to persuade Viceroy Mendoza to allow him to join in the search for the Seven Cities of Cibola, Hernán Cortés decided to enlist the aid of Francisco Vásquez de Coronado to help make the viceroy see things his way. Besides finding Mendoza adamant in his refusal to let Cortés participate in the upcoming expedition, Coronado found himself being chastised by the viceroy for having offered the elder conquistador an opportunity to seduce him with his persuasive charm. A frustrated but determined Hernán Cortés decided during the summer of 1539 to proceed with his planned nautical expedition. Three ships set sail under the command of Francisco de Ulloa, a relative of the marquis. Ulloa sailed during the time when Fray Marcos was headed back to Mexico City and Hernando de Soto had already landed along the shores of Florida. The race to find the native cities of the north was now officially underway.

The Ulloa expedition was the second seafaring venture orchestrated by Hernán Cortés to probe the unknown lands to the north of New Spain. Before Cabeza de Vaca found his way back to civilization, the conqueror of Mexico set sail from Acapulco in 1535 with three ships to explore, conquer, and settle regions that he hoped would replicate his success at Tenochtitlan. The flotilla hugged the Pacific coast and eventually established two settlements along the Baja Peninsula. These two colonies were founded for the express purpose of locating the rich pearl beds the natives had told him he was sure to find in this remote region. Unfortunately for Cortés, nothing panned out as he had planned. The intense heat and lack of freshwater simply added to the mounting frustrations of those who toiled long and hard without any reward. An already dire situation worsened with the unwelcome introduction of a mysterious fever that claimed the lives of twenty-three of the three hundred twenty colonists. After considering the numerous complaints of his men, Cortés decided to abandon the ill-fated settlements that had nearly bankrupted him. He returned to New Spain in 1536 in time to hear of the incredible journey of Cabeza de Vaca and his three comrades.

Cortés decided that this time he would leave the exploring to Francisco de Ulloa, whom he instructed to search for a strait that might be the long sought passage to the true Indies and to seek out the location of the rumored native kingdoms of the north. Cortés would, however, assume a more active role once Ulloa returned with news that justified the launching of a much larger expedition. The three ships probed northward along the western shore of Mexico, a course that led to the Gulf of California — the body of water that Ulloa christened El Mar Vermejo (the Vermilion Sea), later known as the Sea of Cortés. After sighting the mouth of the Colorado River, the flotilla sailed southward along the eastern coast of the Baja Peninsula, which many believed was an island. The tip of the peninsula was rounded and the ships followed the northern trek of the western coast until the journey came to an abrupt halt. The expedition had been hampered by severe weather and turbulent waters, but it was the loss of a ship and the alleged death of Ulloa that brought an end to this quest. One story states that Francisco de Ulloa was stabbed to death by a soldier, while another account claims he returned to Acapulco with the crew aboard the two remaining ships. The enormous expense of this failed expedition nearly drained what remained in Cortés' coffers, thereby forcing the most famous of all the conquistadors to drop out of the race to find Cibola.

Adding to Viceroy Mendoza's growing list of worries related to being the first Spanish official to lay full claim to the Seven Cities of Cibola was the news that Pedro de Alvarado, the renowned conquistador who played an instrumental role in the conquest of Mexico, had returned to the New World with a royal grant to explore the northern regions that everyone in New Spain was now interested in. The former governor of Guatemala had recently sought to add to his already considerable reputation and fortune by leading an army of conquistadors and a priest by the name of Marcos de Niza over the towering peaks of the Andes to stake a claim to the city of Quito in Ecuador, once part of the Inca empire and a region that later was part of a boundary dispute between several conquistadors. Francisco Pizarro and Diego de Almagro, partners in the conquest of the Inca Empire, managed to end this threat to their claim to Quito by offering to pay Alvarado one hundred thousand pesos for the rights to his troops and supplies. Ironically, it was Hernando de Soto who was dispatched to Cuzco to gather the gold that the veteran conquistador had agreed to accept.

After his aborted adventure in Ecuador, Pedro de Alvarado returned to Spain to renew his contract of 1527 to locate a passage to the Spice Islands. In addition to this request, Alvarado was granted the right to explore lands that rested to the north of New Spain, the very region to which Viceroy Mendoza was preparing to send an expedition. A series of intense negotiations between Mendoza, Alvarado, and representatives of the Spanish court concluded in November of 1540 with an agreement that a partnership was to be formed between the viceroy and the celebrated conquistador. The arrangement called for the two to share in both the costs and the anticipated rewards of this grand venture. The expedition under the command of Francisco Vásquez de Coronado was already underway by the time this accord was reached.

Viceroy Mendoza viewed Hernando de Soto as the greater threat to his planned expedition. What with so many ships sailing between ports, secrets rarely remained secret for very long in the New World. The governor of Cuba had learned of the viceroy's plan to send a small expeditionary force to search for native cities to the north of New Spain while he himself was still busy preparing for his expedition to Florida. De Soto surely must have thought that Mendoza had information he was not privy to—perhaps a tidbit that Cabeza de Vaca had neglected to reveal to him. When the first reports of the expedition of Fray Marcos and Esteban seemed to confirm the existence of the Seven Cities of Cibola, Mendoza attempted to keep news of this magnificent find from Hernando de Soto by ordering that no one was permitted to leave Mexico without his approval.

Despite the best efforts of the viceroy, news of the discoveries made by Fray Marcos and Esteban still managed to reach Havana. Some sailors testified they heard that the cities of Cibola were grander in size and greater in wealth than any that had been found in Mexico or Peru, the latter, of course, being the region that was the principal source of Hernando de Soto's vast wealth. Just as they did in New Spain, these wondrous stories grew greater with each telling. Concerned that Mendoza might try to lead a large expedition into lands that would interfere with his campaign, de Soto sent Alvaro de San Jorge to New Spain to find out what Mendoza was up to and to present the viceroy with a message reminding him that the vast region of La Florida had been granted to him.

Viceroy Mendoza responded to Hernando de Soto's concerns by stating that the expedition he was planning to send was headed in a direction contrary to that of the governor's and added "that the land of La Florida was so large and broad that there was room for all."[5] Mendoza hoped to put to rest all of Hernando's lingering suspicions by concluding with a pledge to render any assistance the governor might require for his upcoming expedition. The viceroy was not quite as magnanimous as he pretended. He had already been instructed by the Crown to keep away from lands that were granted to the governor of Cuba. Hernando was not pleased with Mendoza's brusque reply but chose to let the matter pass. After taking into account that the distance between the two expeditions was great and their intended destinations was even farther apart, Hernando de Soto had good reason to believe that their paths would never cross.

7

THE CORONADO EXPEDITION

Ambitious Plans

It was the report issued by Fray Marcos de Niza of the existence of many splendid native cities to the north that prompted Viceroy Mendoza's formation of a large expeditionary force that was expected to lay claim to the Seven Cities of Cibola. Elated by the prospect of finding cities that exceeded the wealth of Tenochtitlan or Cuzco, Mendoza had initially planned on leading the expedition himself, but he was talked out of such a decision by advisors who reminded him that his presence was required at Mexico City. After all, the duties of his office were much too important to be merely relegated to someone who had not been sanctioned by the Crown. Francisco Vásquez de Coronado, a soldier who had served Mendoza so well in the past and whom the viceroy knew as an officer he could count on to complete a mission of such importance, was the logical choice to lead the expedition. Cristóbal de Oñate was named acting governor of Neuva Galicia to serve while Coronado was leading his army of conquistadors to Cibola.

In the hope of avoiding any further royal intervention, Mendoza decided that all funding for this epic expedition would be provided solely by the principal partners, with each sharing a significant and nearly equal stake in the success of the venture. The viceroy contributed upwards of fifty thousand ducats to the cause, while Coronado pledged exactly fifty thousand ducats, most of which came from his wife's dowry. Dona Beatríz de Estrada had to mortgage much of her inherited property in order to help her husband raise his required share of funds. Once he agreed to become a partner in this venture, Pedro de Alvarado was compelled to ante up a sum equal to that of the other investors. Such a large contribution by each partner seems to indicate that each investor expected to reap the rewards of a discovery that was to eclipse any previous New World find.

Enlistment for the expedition to the province of Cibola took place at Mexico City. Most of those who signed up for a chance at finding fortune and glory were only in their twenties, and several were still in their teens. This was a youthful army led by a young commander who was barely thirty years old. The expeditionary force quickly grew to three hundred well equipped soldiers and nearly one thousand natives who were prepared to follow the path blazed by Fray Marcos and Esteban.

Viceroy Mendoza appointed Lope de Samaniego, an experienced officer who had once served under Nuño de Guzmán, as second-in-command of the Cibola expedition. At the time of his appointment, Samaniego was in charge of the royal arsenal at Mexico City. Hernando de Alvarado was named captain of the artillery and Pablos de Melgosa was made captain of the infantry. The ensign rank of standard-bearer was awarded to Pedro de Tovar. The cavalry captains were Diego Gutiérrez, Diego López, Rodrigo Maldonado, Tristán de Arellano, Diego de Guevara, and García López de Cárdenas. The latter was a seasoned officer who had seen much service in South America and Cuba before coming to Mexico.

Fray Marcos, who had been elevated to provincial of the Franciscan Order in New Spain by an appreciative Bishop Juan de Zumárraga, was urged to join the expedition. After all, who else was better qualified to lead the way than this man of the cloth who had seen with his own eyes the glory of Cibola? Marcos de Niza was accompanied by four friars who were to assist him in attending to the spiritual needs of the troops and spreading the word of God among the heathens.

The viceroy made sure that Coronado's expeditionary force was sufficiently supplied with provisions, weapons, horses, and livestock to meet the needs of the campaign. More than a thousand horses and mules were rounded up to carry the essential supplies and to haul back the hoard of treasure that everyone expected to find at Cibola. A multitude of pigs, cattle, goats, and sheep accompanied the expedition to ensure that the soldiers would not have to march on empty stomachs. The Spaniards also traveled in the company of a large number of dogs, canines trained to hunt animals and to keep the natives in line.

Unlike previous Spanish campaigns in the New World, this expedition made a conscious effort to protect the rights of the natives. Viceroy Mendoza issued directives that stipulated any Indian who served in this quest must be a volunteer and must be shown the same consideration accorded any other free man, which was understood to mean that they were not to be mistreated in any manner. Indians could carry items that served the good of all but not solely for the good of an individual Spaniard. Soldiers were expected to carry their own belongings. Several hundred Mexicans, most of whom came from the Michoacán province, signed on as servants, cooks, porters, scouts, interpreters, and herdsmen. Many of these Mexicans joined for the opportunity to see if the legends of Cibola were true.

Coronado and his men were forbidden to forcefully take food or any other items, regardless of how necessary or valuable they were deemed, from natives encountered along the way. But should any tribe dare to challenge the Spaniards then Coronado and his troops were well within their rights to claim as spoils of war whatever the hostile natives possessed. Coronado would make every effort to comply with the instructions of the viceroy, taking care to make sure the natives were well compensated for any services or goods they rendered. The Spanish mules carried numerous trinkets that were to be used to barter for food and goods from the tribes. The commander was later accused by some of being too generous in his dealings with the natives, an accusation that was never leveled at Pánfilo de Narváez or Hernando de Soto.

On January 6, 1540, Viceroy Antonio de Mendoza finally received royal approval for his expedition to search for the Seven Cities of Cibola and confirmation of Francisco Vásquez de Coronado's appointment as governor of Neuva Galicia. Neither Mendoza nor Coronado had sat by idly while waiting for approvals that were undoubtedly forthcoming. The newly recruited army marched on ahead to Compostela where they were to await the arrival of Governor Coronado and Viceroy Mendoza, both of whom were still busy attending to the many duties of their office and making last minute preparations for this historic expedition.

A grand review of the troops was overseen by Viceroy Mendoza at the town square of Compostela on February 22, 1540. Coronado stood at the head of an army that totaled three hundred thirty-six soldiers, two hundred twenty-five of whom were cavaliers. Also joining the assembly were eight hundred Mexican retainers and Fray Marcos and his fellow priests. There were three women who were to travel in the company of the men: María Maldonada, who was to serve as a nurse; Francisca de Hozes, the wife of the shoemaker on the expedition; and the native wife of Lope Caballero. A mass that was attended by all was heard after the review. Afterwards, the viceroy addressed the troops with a speech that reminded them of their expected loyalty to their commander during this quest to lay claim to the Seven Cities of Cibola. This was followed by Coronado swearing with his hand on the Bible that he would do his best to fulfill the duties of his command and make every effort to see that the objectives of this mission were reached. The troops then followed suit by pledging their allegiance to both the captain-general and the mission.

Since these ceremonies took up most of the day, it was decided to delay the start of the march toward Cibola until the next morning. As a show of support, Viceroy Mendoza rode alongside the troops for the first two days, probably traveling as far as Tepic, which at the time was simply a small village, before making his return to Mexico City. Mendoza used this time to provide Coronado with additional instructions and encouragement. The viceroy also hoped that during this brief journey he would hear some good news from the scouting mission he had previously dispatched, but Melchior Díaz and his men had still not returned by the time they reached Tepic. After parting ways with Mendoza, Coronado and his troops marched to Culiácan, where they would make last minute preparations before setting off on their quest.

An Inauspicious Start

As the expedition proceeded toward the Río Santiago, Fray Marcos and the other priests went ahead on foot to announce to the various tribes along their route that Christian soldiers who meant them no harm were coming their way. Besides hoping that they would ease the fears of the natives, Coronado had decided to send the priests in advance of the troops because of their inability to keep pace with the others. The commander, who of course was concerned for the safety of Fray Marcos and his fellow friars, made sure they were accompanied by armed soldiers.

Spurred on by rumors that the streets of the Seven Cities of Cibola were paved with gold and every home was bedecked with a vast array of precious stones, the soldiers managed to average a pace of ten miles per day at the start of the march. After crossing the Río Santiago, a distance of approximately thirty-three miles from Tepic, Coronado picked up the path that Melchior Díaz had followed, which was the same route traveled beforehand by both Cabeza de Vaca and Fray Marcos. No new ground was being broken during this stage of the expedition. The conquistadors were merely following old and well established Indian trails that led to water holes where both man and beast could quench their thirst.

After crossing the Río Santiago, the pace of the Coronado expedition slowed considerably for the next three hundred miles, due in part to the thick overgrowth of trees and brush that had to be hacked away from the path. Another contributing factor was the edict that the Indians who had freely joined this expedition were not permitted to serve as personal porters for the Spaniards, which meant that the soldiers had to shoulder the burden of their own supplies. Many a proud cavalier was forced to walk alongside their horse that bore the extreme weight of their provisions. Most of the officers, however, were fortunate to own more than one horse. In this manner, the Spaniards had now entered the Sinaloa region of Mexico.

The conquistadors proceeded to Tuxpan, where they had to cross the San Pedro River, and from there they marched northward to Chiametla. Coronado had his men set up camp near the mouth of the Río Chiametla, where he planned to spend the next few days gathering additional items needed for the campaign. Lope de Samaniego, the mastre de campo, and several soldiers went in search of neighboring villages where they could barter for provisions. These Spaniards soon encountered a band of natives who showed their hostile side by capturing a soldier who had carelessly strayed from the group. His cry for help was heard by Samaniego. The officer rushed to his rescue and then dragged the frightened soldier to the safety of a nearby brush. Believing they were both out of harm's way, Samaniego raised his protective visor just high enough to provide an opening for an arrow that ripped through his eye socket, a blow that instantly ended the life of this hero. Lope de Samaniego, the second-in-command and the first to die on the expedition, was buried at the very spot where he was slain.

Angered by this unprovoked attack, Coronado dispatched a group of soldiers to find the natives who had so callously killed his deputy commander and wounded several other men. Eight men and women from Chiametla who were judged responsible for the death of Lope de Samaniego were rounded up and summarily executed, their necks stretched from the limbs of nearby trees. García López de Cárdenas was promoted by Coronado to fill the position once held by Samaniego.

In the meantime, Melchior Díaz and his scouts were returning from their mission and they met up with Coronado while the commander and his men were still at Chiametla. Díaz reported to Coronado that they had traveled as far as Chichilticale, near the Gila River and at the foot of the Great Despoblado, and said they saw or heard little that could corroborate Fray Marcos' claims of cities that were teeming with gold and gems. The captain stated that they were well received by the various tribes encountered on their journey. Díaz said he questioned the Indians at Chichilticale about the place called Cibola and they confirmed that such a place did exist. They told him that there were seven cities, each of which contained many multistoried structures, known collectively as Cibola. The encouraging news was that the Cibolans raised crops and had many domesticated animals. Unfortunately, except for turquoise, these natives knew nothing about the precious stones or metals that reportedly could be found at Cibola. Diaz also learned that there was little water and no fruit bearing trees to be found in the province the Spaniards wished to claim as their own. Perhaps the most disturbing news was that the natives at Chichilticale knew of the death of Esteban at Hawikuh and that word had been sent to the neighboring towns to resist the advance of the Spaniards. Knowledge of this report was confined to just a few of Coronado's officers, but some of the disconcerting details managed to filter down through the rank and file.

Immediately following the meeting with Melchior Díaz, Coronado sent

The Coronado expedition in search of the Seven Cities of Cibola.

Juan de Zaldívar and three other soldiers to Mexico City to report to Viceroy Mendoza on the findings, or the lack thereof, of this reconnaissance mission. Meanwhile, Coronado, Díaz and the rest of the army continued on to Culiácan. Since Melchior had reported that there were very few villages along the route they intended to follow and few, if any, of these settlements were large enough to feed and house an army as large as the one that Coronado was leading, the Spaniards were forced to spend several days at Culiácan gathering additional provisions for the long journey ahead.

Coronado decided that the best way to pick up the pace was to divide his army. While the rest of the troops trudged behind with the bulk of the provisions, livestock, and beasts of burden, the commander would lead an advance force of approximately one hundred soldiers that was to be accompanied by Fray Marcos and the other friars in an expedited search for the Seven Cities of Cibola. Coronado and his select troops carried enough rations to last eighty days, which was deemed sufficient to see them through to Cibola. As per Coronado's instructions, the main army did not leave Culiácan until twenty days after the departure of his advance party.

After leaving Culiácan, Coronado and his company of soldiers marched at a steady clip to the Sinaloa River, where they were well received by a tribe that provided them with additional supplies. From there the Spaniards marched another three days to the Fuerte River. The previous peaceful pilgrimages of Cabeza de Vaca and Fray Marcos had helped soothe the ill feelings of the natives who had suffered greatly from the unrestrained hostilities inflicted by previous incursions of Spanish slavers. With the good friar by his side, Coronado was warmly received wherever he stopped. The captain-general made sure that the natives were well paid for whatever they offered, generously bartering with a supply of trinkets that included colorful glass beads and inexpensive knives.

Melchior Díaz and fifteen cavaliers were sent by Coronado to scout the province of Abra, an area located in the Mayo Valley where Fray Marcos said he had sighted several settlements, all of which, the natives told him, were rich in many ways. After having ventured over several mountains to find the valley that the priest had spoken of, Díaz and his men returned to report that they had come to "two or three poor villages with twenty or thirty huts each."[1] This hardly fit the glowing description offered by Fray Marcos.

At this point, the commander decided to send another message back to Viceroy Mendoza, to inform him of Díaz's latest disappointing discovery. In this report, Coronado informed the viceroy that he was doing the best he could to assuage the mounting concerns of his troops: "I tried to encourage them as well as I could, telling them your Lordship has always thought this part of the journey would be a waste of effort; that we ought to devote our attention to the Seven Cities and the other provinces about which we had information; and that these should be the objective of our enterprise."[2]

Refusing to wallow in disappointment, Coronado led his men to the native village known to the Spaniards as Corazones. The road proved much more difficult than Fray Marcos had described, which simply accentuated the fact that nothing seemed to correspond with what the priest had told them about this land. They had lost roughly a dozen horses and several Indians and Negroes in their retinue by the time they reached the village that had previously welcomed Andrés Dorantes with a generous offering of dried deer hearts. Coronado and his men spent four restful days at Corazones.

During the latter days of May 1540, Coronado and his troops crossed over the portion of the Sonoran Desert that is now part of Yuma, Arizona. At that time, this was a desolate region punctuated with bleached bones and towering saguaro cacti, the latter now recognized as the state flower of Arizona. The scorching heat of the day was a stark contrast to the bone-chilling cold that set in once the sun went down. The expedition followed an old Indian trail that led to the San Pedro River, where the weary soldiers and horses had an opportunity to quench their thirst and bathe their bodies. The men also found time to fish for the rainbow trout that inhabit this river. Coronado and his men also encountered Indians who were more primitive than the Ópata tribes they had previously met.

The expeditionary force continued on to Chichilticale, a Yaqui term used to denote a house made of red earth. This was a place where Fray Marcos had said an elegant native town existed. Even though this fabricated tale had already been exposed by Melchior Díaz during his scouting expedition, the conquistadors were still shocked to see just how little this village compared with the extremely favorable report provided by the padre. Pedro de Casteñeda, a soldier who later wrote his own account of the expedition, recorded that "The men were all disgusted on seeing that the famous Chicilticale turned out to be a roofless ruined house."[3] Many soldiers now wondered if Fray Marcos had spoken the truth about anything he had seen in this godforsaken land.

García López de Cárdenas was sent on ahead with fifteen cavaliers to reconnoiter the land while Coronado and the rest of the troops followed close behind. They passed through the final stretch of the vast and bleak desert and were rewarded with a view of splendid forests and spectacular mountains. The Spaniards crossed the Pinaleño Mountains and entered the lush valley where the Gila River flows. The adventure was finally beginning to look promising. The trek soon led to the White River, which at that moment had spilled over its banks. The soldiers had to build rafts in order to transport themselves and their supplies to the other side. The Spaniards remembered their effort to cross this river by christening it the Río de las Balsas.

Further up the path, the weary members of the expedition reached a pine forest where they set up camp near Lake Mountain. Three Spaniards, two Negroes, some Indian allies, and several horses made the fatal mistake of indulging in some plants they thought would relieve their hunger. It is believed that they died after partaking of a poisonous parsnip, a root later known as "water hemlock" (cicuta douglassi), that grows along the marshes of this region. Those who had to bury their fallen comrades remembered this place as "the Camp of Death."

The entire company of soldiers was now suffering from a lack of food. Coronado had counted on receiving additional supplies from ships that were to be dispatched by Viceroy Mendoza. Hernando de Alarcón had, indeed, sailed up the Gulf of California with two well provisioned ships but was unsuccessful in his effort to link up with those who had ventured forth by land. Coronado and his men were driven onward by the thought that they were getting close to the province of Cibola, a place where their bellies would be filled with food and their pockets would be lined with gold, silver, and precious stones.

8

Bitter Disappointment

The Battle of Hawikuh

Shortly after leaving the pine forest, Coronado and his men came to a river that ran red from all the mud it carried downstream. They followed the path of the river they called the Río Bermejo (and now known as the Little Colorado) until it intersected with the Zuni River. A two day march along the banks of the Zuni River brought the Spaniards to the fringe of the legendary realm of Cibola. They soon arrived at the place where the survivors of the Hawikuh massacre had met with Fray Marcos to tell of Esteban's sudden demise. Coronado's troops remained one day behind the pace of Cárdenas and his fifteen horsemen, who had on gone ahead to make sure that the natives of Cibola were not laying a trap. There was good reason to expect a confrontation. They were, after all, in the region where Esteban had been killed and it was already known that natives of Hawikuh had sent out messages urging the other tribes to forcefully oppose the Spaniards.

Soon after having entered the province of Cibola, Cárdenas and his soldiers encountered four natives from Hawikuh who greeted them in a seemingly friendly manner. Through interpreters, the four envoys made it known that they would return the following day with a bountiful offering of food and drink for the Spaniards. Cárdenas thanked the natives for their generosity and permitted two of them to return to Hawikuh in order that they might fulfill their promise and to tell the others that the Spaniards would soon come in peace to their fair city. To shield against some unforeseen treachery, the two other emissaries were retained as hostages. Hernando de Alvarado was sent back to report to Coronado the news that was sure to lift the spirits of the tired and hungry troops. The expectation of finally reaching their goal certainly inspired Coronado's men to step up their pace, but even their already accelerated stride was further quickened by the sudden arrival of ominous news.

Instead of waiting for Coronado, Cárdenas and his men proceeded toward Hawikuh, the first of the legendary Seven Cities of Cibola. Along the way, the captain decided to investigate a pass that seemed to be an ideal spot for warriors to stage an ambush. There on a hill he saw several Zunis who apparently were on a reconnaissance mission of their own. Cárdenas went to meet with them under a sign of peace. He handed the natives several trinkets and a cross to carry home as a symbol of his friendly intentions toward the citizens of Hawikuh. Convinced that this meeting had gone well, Cárdenas had his men pitch camp for the night. The slumbering soldiers found themselves suddenly awakened by a frantic call to arms sounded by their two posted sentries. The silence that had prevailed was broken by the terrifying yelps of Zuni warriors as they shot a steady stream of arrows at the Spaniards. Cárdenas and his men barely managed to escape with their lives.

Coronado and his troops were approximately four leagues from Hawikuh when they were met by a messenger sent by Cárdenas who, besides reporting of the surprise attack, urged the commander to rush to the aid of his beleaguered comrades. Coronado's first sighting of the hostile Indians was from afar. He saw the smoke from the bonfires of Zuni priests performing a religious ceremony, which the commander interpreted as signals to warn of his approach. Coronado later remarked that this was "a method of communication as good as we could have devised ourselves. Thus they both give warning of our approach and revealed our whereabouts."[1]

Once reunited with Cárdenas, Coronado and his troops proceeded with extreme caution toward Hawikuh, the westernmost of the Seven Cities of Cibola, which supposedly had been viewed from a distance by Fray Marcos and where Esteban was known to have died. Smoke signals became more prevalent the closer they came to Hawikuh. Along the way, they encountered a small party of Zunis who quickly fled when they saw the approach of the many armored and mounted conquistadors. Coronado had his men prepare for the possibility of an engagement before they reached the city. While there was a heightened sense of concern among the troops, many soldiers saw these threatening signs as an indication that the natives truly did have something of great value to protect.

The Spaniards caught their first glimpse of Hawikuh shortly after the Zunis had fled their presence. The date was July 7, 1540. The sight of the adobe structures that housed the Zuni people hardly matched the magnificent image that Fray Marcos had conjured up in the minds of all who signed on for this mission. There were no fortified walls or sacred temples, the Spanish measure of what constituted a New World city of great importance. Instead of a city as large and splendid as either Tenochtitlan or Cuzco, the Spaniards saw a small pueblo comprised of a few buildings made of mud and rock. After seeing the disappointment on the faces of those in his company, Pedro de Castenada says he became very concerned for the safety of the padre because "such were the curses some of them hurled at Fray Marcos that I pray God to protect him from them."[2]

As the disappointed Spaniards pressed on to Hawikuh, there slowly came into view the menacing sight of several hundred armed warriors who were waiting for them outside the pueblo. Alerted by the smoke signals of the priests, which now warned of the enemy's approach, the women and children were sent to the safety of Corn Mountain while the men remained behind to defend their homes. The Zuni warriors armed themselves with clubs, spears, stones, and bows and arrows when they saw the approach of Coronado and his men. A group of medicine men stepped forward and laid down a line drawn with consecrated cornmeal, a sacred food scattered to elicit favor from the spirits they revered. Anyone who dared to cross such a boundary risked incurring the full wrath of the Zunis.

Coronado decided to send out emissaries bearing gifts and kind words that he hoped would diffuse this tense situation. Captain Cárdenas rode out with several soldiers and two of the priests to confer with the Zunis. Cárdenas sought to further emphasize the peaceful intentions of the Spaniards toward the people of Hawikuh by having his men lay down their weapons in full view of the warriors. But none of these tactics achieved their desired result. The very moment Cárdenas and his soldiers crossed the line of cornmeal the Zunis let loose a volley of well aimed arrows. Juan Bermejo, the notary, suffered a wound, as did the horse he rode. As soon as he saw what was occurring, Coronado rushed forward with several cavaliers to render aid to his endangered emissaries. Clinging to the hope that a peaceful resolution was still possible, the general made sure to bring additional trinkets with him, but the Zunis simply responded by taking aim at him. Angered by this hostile reception, Coronado took the fight to the Zunis by ordering his men to attack in full force. The warriors fled behind the safety of their walls, but not before losing between a dozen and a score who were slain by the furious charge of the mounted conquistadors.

General Coronado believed it was still possible to negotiate a settlement that would avoid further bloodshed, but he found himself facing stiff resistance from within his own ranks. The soldiers, all of whom had been deprived of food and sleep for far too long, were not in a position to mount a long siege. Now was the time for action. Even Fray Marcos urged Coronado to attack, thereby absolving the general and his troops of any transgressions they were about to commit. The commander took the precaution to legitimize his actions by ordering one of his men to read aloud to the Zunis the Requiermento, which was required reading before any conquest of the natives was to take place. An additional offering of gifts was presented to tempt the Zunis to submit to his will. These gestures were rebuffed with the unleashing of yet another volley of arrows. Coronado issued the order to attack by sounding the battle cry of Santiago-y-a-ellos (For Saint James and at them), but the cavalry was abruptly stopped in its tracks by another torrential shower of arrows.

Coronado decided to deploy the soldiers armed with crossbows and arquebuses to a position where they could pin down the Zuni archers while he personally led a group of soldiers in a daring assault that was to scale the wall that stood at the entrance of Hawikuh. Nothing went according to plan. The strings of the crossbows broke and the arquebusiers were simply too weak to wield their cumbersome weapons. Such a breakdown allowed the warriors to concentrate their efforts on the offensive undertaken by Coronado and his troops, whom they were able to pelt with arrows and rocks with near impunity.

The suit of armor donned by Coronado could not fully shield him from the steady barrage of projectiles that rained down on him. The general was knocked to the ground twice, the second instance occurring while he was attempting to scale a ladder that led to a flat roof of the besieged pueblo. The commander was struck down by the blow of a stone slab that landed flush on his head. While his helmet absorbed much of the impact, the force of the blow was great enough to leave him at the mercy of warriors who were preparing to drop another large stone on him. The Zunis surely would have ended the life of the Spanish commander then and there had it not been for the timely intervention of García López de Cárdenas and Hernando de Alvarado. The two officers saw that Coronado was in trouble and rushed over to shield him with their armored bodies from the torrent of rocks and arrows. The devoted officers dragged their wounded commander back to a tent where he lay unconscious from his many injuries, one of which was an arrow wound to the leg. Coronado would later testify that he had received "three wounds in the face, an arrow wound in one leg, and bruises all over his body."[3]

The bruised and battered Spaniards kept up their assault on Hawikuh until the Zuni warriors were forced to submit. The battle had lasted for nearly an hour before the natives finally sued for peace. The fight surely would have gone on longer had the Zuni defenders not exhausted their arsenal of rocks and arrows. While no Spaniards died during this conflict, several were temporarily incapacitated by the severity of their wounds, and nearly all had significant dents in their armor from the pummeling inflicted by the determined enemy. The Zunis, however, suffered an estimated fifteen casualties during this encounter. As part of the condition of their surrender, the Zunis asked Cárdenas, who had momentarily assumed command, for permission to leave Hawikuh. The captain replied that they were welcome to stay and promised that no further harm would come to them. Cárdenas felt compelled to grant the Zunis their leave when they persisted with their request. The conquistadors were delighted to see that the natives left behind plenty of food. The famished conquistadors feasted on corn, beans, and turkeys. Coronado awoke shortly thereafter, his spirits buoyed by the news that his men had succeeded in capturing Hawikuh.

A Seemingly Fortuitous Encounter

Once they had finished filling their bellies and tending to their wounds, the Spaniards looked around and saw that their victory was of little consolation. They had been forced to risk their lives for a town that, besides being much smaller than what Fray Marcos had reported, had no manner of material wealth to fulfill their dreams of finding fame and fortune. What was supposed to have been one of the magnificent Seven Cities of Cibola was little more than a few adobes built into a rock plateau. One Spanish soldier described Hawikuh as a "little, unattractive village, looking as if it had been crumpled up all together."[4]

Coronado and his men were even more disappointed to learn that the other cities of Cibola were just as bereft of precious metals and gems as was Hawikuh. To many, this was hardly a place worth even laying claim to. All around, for as far as they could see, there was nothing but a baked land that was devoid of trees and grass. Fray Marcos, the priest who had guided them to this place with his wondrous stories, saw the bitter disappointment on the faces of the soldiers and soon found himself becoming the focal point of their disdain. Many began to openly mock the padre after he found it impossible to offer a satisfactory explanation for his poor judgment.

The Spaniards made camp at Hawikuh, where they would spend several days resting their weary bones and feasting on the stores of food left behind. Once he regained his composure, Coronado realized that everything Fray Marcos had described was merely a fanciful tale that blended native rumors with Iberian legends of the Seven Cities of Antillia. The only items of value collected so far were but a token amount of turquoise and the return of Bartolomé, the baptized Mexican who was in the company of Esteban at the time of the Moor's execution.

In an effort to make the best of this disappointing situation, Coronado sent messages to the Zunis who had left Hawikuh inviting them to come meet with him. Several of the chiefs responded to this request. The general told them that they were free to return to their homes and pledged that all of their belongings, with the exception of the food, would be restored to them. The grateful Zuni elders promised they would soon return with the rulers of the other pueblos, who also wished to pay their respects to the Spaniards. Several days later the chiefs of Mácaque and neighboring pueblos came bearing gifts of blankets, turquoise, and bows and arrows. Coronado gave them a warm reception and reiterated his desire for peace. Convinced that he had finally gained the trust of all the chiefs, Coronado was shocked to see that on the following day the natives had gathered all of their belongings and retired to the mesa of Towayálane, better known as Corn Mountain.

Once he felt strong enough, Coronado ventured to Mácaque, where he was received by an elderly Zuni chief who presented him with a blanket made of remnants. The chief promised to return in three days from Corn Mountain with other nobles from his tribe. True to his word, the Zuni lord returned with the chiefs, each of whom brought an offering of beggarly looking blankets and a few pieces of turquoise. After much discussion and many assurances, the Zunis agreed to become Christians and vassals of Emperor Charles V. Several days passed before all the tribes felt it was safe to return to their homes.

While at Hawikuh, Coronado drafted a letter addressed to Antonio de Mendoza in which he informed the viceroy that his findings failed to correspond with the spellbinding tale spun by Fray Marcos: the cities were neither grand nor large, the people were somewhat primitive in both manner and attire, and besides turquoise there were no precious stones and certainly no precious metals to be found. Coronado wrote, "So far as I can judge, it does not appear to me there is any hope of finding either gold or silver, but I trust in God that if there is any to be had we shall get our share of it, and it shall not escape us through any lack of diligence in the search."[5]

By stressing that this was an oppressively hot region absent of any fruit bearing trees or bushes, the captain-general made it clear in his report that Cibola seemed an unsuitable site to sustain a Spanish settlement. Coronado stated that the Zuni people survived on a steady diet of maize, legumes, and wild game such as rabbits and deer, the latter he judged from the number of animal skins in their possession to be rather plentiful. He closed his report to the viceroy with a request for additional supplies. This letter was sent back to Mendoza along with a small sample of Zuni craftsmanship, an inventory that included some fragments of turquoise, a few pieces of jewelry, two baskets, an animal hide, and examples of the native weapons. Coronado also provided a detailed description of the native manner of dress.

Juan Gallego was charged with personally delivering the specimens of native handiwork and Coronado's message to Viceroy Mendoza at Mexico City. Juan was accompanied part of the way by Melchior Díaz and all the way by the discredited Fray Marcos de Niza. The captain-general was so bothered by the numerous false tales uttered by this delusional priest that he could no longer bear to have him in his sight. Given the disenchanted and disgusted mood of the troops, Coronado had little choice but to send him back for his own protection. Upon his return to Mexico City, the disgraced Fray Marcos retired to a monastery at Xochimilco. His self-imposed exile became permanent with the onset of a paralysis that crippled him for the remainder of life, which came to an end on March 25, 1558.

Though disappointed by all that he had seen so far, Coronado felt compelled to continue the search for native cities that might live up to the great expectations that he and his men had envisioned finding at the Seven Cities of Cibola. Too much money and manpower had been invested in this venture, which had been motivated by the fantastic tales of Fray Marcos, to simply give up now. There was still, he thought, the chance that the other native realms the friar claimed to have seen or heard about during his return from Cibola might prove more fortunate. There was also the possibility that the stories heard by Cabeza de Vaca and his comrades of rich kingdoms to the north might be somewhere near their present location. With these thoughts in mind, Coronado sent out three expeditions in various directions to see if there were promising regions or towns worth claiming for Spain. Meanwhile, Coronado and roughly eighty soldiers, mostly the advance guard who had marched by his side, remained behind at the Zuni pueblos where they had an opportunity to experience the way of life of the people who dwelled in this region.

The Zunis and the neighboring Hopi tribes were a settled people who farmed and hunted with a refined skill acquired from having lived off the land for many generations. Even in this dry region with few rivers and uncertain rainfall, they proved adept at cultivating fields of beans, corn, squash, cotton, and tobacco. They were able to make their land more fertile by digging irrigation ditches that connected to the nearest stream, which was sometimes several miles away. The residents of the pueblos also grew sunflowers, a plant that produces a voluminous number of seeds that are high in protein. The oil from these seeds was used for cooking and, when roasted, the seeds served as a nutritious and tasty supplement to their diet. The natives of the pueblo region also enjoyed eating the pine nuts produced by the small pinon tree, the same savory nut prized by many of the wandering tribes that Cabeza de Vaca and his comrades followed during their epic journey. When the cones fell and spilled their small nuts on the ground — which usually occurs in late September, the natives would gather the pine nuts, which they ate either raw or toasted — until the snows came. The fruit of the prickly pear was another delicacy enjoyed by both the wandering and settled tribes of the southwest region.

The Pueblo Indians hunted gophers, ground squirrels, and rabbits, the latter animal being their main source of meat. The occasional deer, fox, badger, antelope, and grey wolf were greatly prized additions to their cuisine. There were also periodic expeditions that went in search of buffalo. Some meats were preserved by being sliced into thin strips and dried in the sun so that it could be enjoyed during leaner times. The only domesticated animals were dogs and turkeys. Dogs were used to help with hunting, while turkeys were kept for their precious feathers. Eagles and other birds were captured and placed in cages, where they were well cared for in order to ensure there was a plentiful supply of feathers that they could pluck to fletch their arrows and to adorn their headdress.

The daily grind of the Pueblo Indians yielded more than enough food to meet their everyday needs but certainly not enough to sustain an additional group as large as the one led by Coronado. In the case of the Zunis, they generally stored enough corn to last one or two years—long enough to see them through extended periods of drought or famine. Food was often a source of friction between the Spaniards and the natives of the New World. The conquistadors often found their search for wealth in the New World sidetracked by a dire need to replenish their exhausted supply of food, a necessity used to justify the burdensome demands they placed upon tribes encountered along the path of their quest. Such taxing dictates often forced the natives to try to drive off the conquistadors before their own entire store of food was exhausted. Many natives died simply trying to protect what little they had on hand to feed their own people.

The tribes that chose to settle in such an arid region built unique styled homes designed to protect them from the extreme heat of summer and the bitter cold of winter. Such settlements consisted of a cluster of buildings made of adobe, which is simply a mixture of clay and sand that dries without cracking. Adobe apartments were built next to and on top of one another. The ground floor of these multistoried structures were generally used for storage and had no doors. Ladders were used for entering and exiting the different apartment levels. Many of these villages had an underground temple known as a kiva, a native term for "world below," where religious ceremonies were conducted by an audience made up entirely of men. As a rule, women were permitted to enter a sacred kiva only for the purpose of bringing food. Despite this restriction, pueblo women had more influence in their society than women belonging to many other tribes. Climbing a ladder that led out of the kiva was symbolically viewed as mankind's emergence from the womb of the Earth Mother. It was the Spaniards who took to calling the adobe dwellings of this region pueblos, the Spanish word for village or town.

Pueblo men were generally small in stature, barely surpassing five feet, and the women were even smaller. The men wore a breechclout and moccasins and the women wore cotton garments that covered much of their bodies. Buffalo and rabbit skins were used to make cloaks that shielded their bodies during the cold winter. Though generally a peaceful people, the Zunis were, as they had shown themselves against the Spaniards, certainly not averse to taking up arms to defend their homes. Before the arrival of the Spaniards, warfare was mostly confined to skirmishes with roving bands of Navajo and Apache who would periodically raid the Zuni pueblos for food. Like so many other Native American tribes, the Zunis were sun worshippers. They also believed in the legend of the Plumed Serpent, a sacred deity known as Quetzalcoatl to the Aztecs of Mexico, Kukulkan to the Mayans of the Yucatan, and Gucumatz to the Mayans of the highlands.

What Coronado and his men failed to realize was that the real wealth of the Seven Cities of Cibola stemmed from the fact that they were major centers of trade for pueblos and tribes both near and far. Turquoise, shells, buffalo hides, bird feathers, freshwater pearls, copper, and mica were just some of the precious items that found their way to these pueblos, many of which was traded for Zuni textiles.

Exploring All Possibilities

Melchior's Mission

Captain Melchior Díaz traveled with Juan Gallego and Fray Marcos de Niza as far as the Sonora Valley. There he met up with Tristán de Arellano, the captain who had been ordered to remain behind with a company of soldiers until his services were required. Díaz carried orders from Coronado instructing Arellano and the majority of his troops to join up with the army that was camped at Hawikuh. Captain Díaz, however, had been directed to stay behind with a squad of soldiers to establish a temporary outpost that was to serve as a vital supply line for the troops at Cibola. Once he had founded the settlement that was christened San Geronimo, Melchior was ready to follow through with the captain-general's additional order, which was to head westward in an effort to link up with Hernando de Alarcón, the naval commander who was transporting essential provisions for Coronado and his men. Diego de Alcaraz, the officer who had schemed to kill Cabeza de Vaca and his comrades in order to enslave the Indians who followed them, assumed command of the post established by Melchior Díaz, the officer who had rescued Cabeza de Vaca and his companions from such a terrible fate.

Melchior Díaz left San Gerónimo with twenty-five horsemen and several Ópata Indians. After a march of approximately one hundred fifty leagues, Díaz and his troops reached a section of the Colorado River, where they hap-

pened upon the Yuma Indians. By most accounts, the Yuma men were exceptionally well built, with many appearing to be much taller and stronger than
most of the Spaniards. Melchior was delighted to hear that the Yuma had met
with Captain Alarcón further downriver but disappointed to learn that a
great deal of time had passed since that encounter. The Spaniards trekked
downstream for three days, at which point they came upon a tree carved with
a message: "Alarcón came this far. There are letters at the foot of the tree."
The notes that were dug up informed them that the captain had waited for
news concerning the Coronado expedition but felt compelled to move on
when it appeared that his wait was in vain. Hernando de Alarcón, who led
the nautical expedition that was supposed to link up with Coronado's main
force, had departed nearly two months before Díaz arrived. Alarcón's ships
continued to search upriver for evidence of rich native civilizations or other
Spaniards in the area, only to return to Mexico without meeting any of their
objectives.

Though disappointed to learn that he had missed his chance to connect
with the supply ships dispatched from Mexico, Díaz decided to venture northward to see if there might be anything of interest that could help soothe the
distressing news he had to report to Coronado. The Spaniards and their Indian
companions marched for five or six days along the banks of the river before
deciding the time had come to cross to the other side. The Spaniards asked
for and received the help of a nearby Yuma tribe. Fortunately for Díaz and
his men, they learned in the nick of time that the Yuma were merely feigning friendship as part of a plot to kill them. This knowledge, coupled with
the aid of their superior weapons and their trusty Ópata allies, enabled the
Spaniards to prevail against their Yuma attackers.

In order to avoid another confrontation, the Spaniards and their native
allies quickly crossed the river, whereupon they resumed their search to find
something that would reward their time and effort. Unfortunately, their expedition came to an abrupt halt when the captain accidentally suffered a self-
inflicted injury that threatened his very life. When Díaz had spotted one of
the greyhounds harassing the sheep that accompanied them, the mounted
officer had charged and flung his lance at the dog in an attempt to scare the
canine away. His lance, however, took an odd turn and ended up planted in
the ground with the blade upright. While trying to retrieve his weapon, Melchior had found it impossible to steer his horse away in time to avoid the
exposed blade, which sliced through his groin and pierced his bladder. All
who saw what happened assumed that the captain was dead. Because of the
sensitive location of his wound, the soldiers were hesitant to render aid. Díaz
therefore had to tend as best he could to the severe laceration that caused him
excruciating pain.

The soldiers put their incapacitated captain on a hastily prepared litter and promptly began the long march back to San Gerónimo, where, it was hoped, he could receive proper medical attention. Their progress was greatly hindered by repeated struggles with unforgiving natives who had not forgotten their recent encounters with the Spaniards. The critically wounded Díaz braved the journey as best he could, but after twenty grueling days he lost the battle to save his own life. He was buried upon a hill close to where he died. The headstone was a plain cross erected by his grief-stricken comrades. All others who set out on this expedition eventually made it back to San Gerónimo. Messengers were sent to Cibola to inform Coronado of the death of Melchior Díaz and that they had missed the opportunity to link up with the supply ships under the command of Hernando de Alarcón

Tovar's Reconnaissance

Shortly before his messengers were dispatched to Viceroy Mendoza at Mexico City, Coronado had sent Pedro de Tovar and approximately twenty soldiers toward the northwest to investigate the province that Fray Marcos called Tusayán, a region where there were said to be another seven cities, The conquered Zunis told Coronado that these Hopi villages were built in a manner similar to their own except that they were made of mud instead of stone. Tovar was to determine if the Seven Cities of Tusayán were home to the vast wealth that the Spaniards had expected to find at the seven Zuni towns known as Cibola.

Shown the way by Zuni guides, Tovar and his men journeyed over the high-plateau country of north-central Arizona, where they saw, among other sights, the Petrified Forest and the Painted Desert — unusual terrain that was familiar to the Hopi and Navajo people. The Spaniards were awed by the sight of fossilized wood strewn across a remote patch of the Arizona Desert. But this sight paled before the discovery of the Painted Desert, a badlands region comprised of hills, flat-topped mesas and buttes accentuated by a varied mineral content consisting of slate, marl, and sandstone that produce an assortment of violet, blue, yellow, white, and red hues vibrantly reflected by the rays of the sun. (Both the Hopi and Navajo Indians use these brightly colored sands for their celebrated ritual paintings.)

Tovar and his troops reached Antelope Mesa during the night, whereupon they proceeded to make camp. From here, the Spaniards could see the Hopi village of Awatovi, a pueblo made of sun-dried mud bricks bound and covered with plaster. Just like the Zuni, the Hopi were a settled tribe who survived off the fruits of their labor. The men cultivated corn, melons, beans, and squash on plots of land that were owned by the women. Hopi men were also adept at making moccasins and weaving garments and blankets. The women handled most of the domestic chores, which included fetching water, making pottery, and helping with the gardening. Besides the fact that mesas were a suitable means of defense, the Hopi chose to live near mesas because many were home to a reliable source of spring water. The Hopi, a name that means "Peaceful Ones," were expected "to keep a good heart" and avoid confrontations. Their peaceful way of life, however, was suddenly shattered by the arrival of Pedro de Tovar and his soldiers.

The following morning, a number of armed Hopi warriors adorned with headbands and earrings came out to confront the Spaniards. The Hopi already knew about the conquest of the Zuni pueblos by these men clad in silver armor and mounted on strange and mighty beasts, and they therefore took up arms in a determined effort to make sure the same did not happen to their cherished town. Tovar had his native interpreters tell the warriors to lay down their weapons and peacefully submit to the will of the king of Spain and the God of the Christians. Annoyed by these demands, the Hopi told the Spaniards to leave their lands at once and, just like the Zuni at Hawikuh, they drew a line on the ground with sacred cornmeal, which Tovar and his soldiers were warned not to cross. A skirmish ensued the moment an overly zealous warrior struck one of the horses with his club. The Spaniards answered this insult by charging directly at the natives. Frightened by the speed and might of the horses, the Hopi retreated toward their village, but many were chased down and killed before finding sanctuary behind the walls of Awatovi.

Though fewer in number, Tovar and his cavaliers had so convincingly established their superiority on the battlefield that the Hopi elders quickly sued for peace with offerings of cloth, animal skins, maize, turquoise, and other items they deemed of value. News of the rout at Awatovi quickly spread to the neighboring villages and by the end of the day a number of emissaries from the other Hopi pueblos came to pledge their fealty to the Spaniards. Tovar was also invited to enjoy the hospitality of the other pueblos. The captain soon returned to Hawikuh to inform Coronado that he had succeeded in subjugating the Hopi pueblos that had a great deal in common with those of Cibola, including an absence of gold and silver. Tovar's most precious discoveries were some turquoise stones and news of a "great river" to the west of Tusayán that warranted an inspection.

Cárdenas Expedition

Eager to learn more about this mysterious "great river," Coronado instructed Garcia Lopes de Cárdenas to take twenty-five horsemen along the same path blazed by Pedro de Tovar. Once the stream had been discovered, the expeditionary force was expected to probe the course of the river in hopes of finding native cities situated along its path. Captain Cárdenas was given eighty days to complete this mission and report back to Coronado.

Cárdenas and his men were well received at Tusayán and fortunate to obtain the services of Hopi guides who were to lead them along an old path that led to the river they were anxious to see for themselves. A vigorous twenty day hike brought the Spaniards to the southern rim of the Grand Canyon, where they had an opportunity to gaze upon one of the seven natural wonders of the world. Far below they could see the Colorado River, which from this extreme height appeared to be just a small stream. The Hopi guides said that the river was a half-league wide, an assertion that the Spaniards found hard to believe. To verify this claim, a skeptical Cárdenas ordered three of his most agile soldiers to climb down a steep gorge of the Grand Canyon. A full day of cautiously descending the treacherous escarpment brought the three only a third of the way down the canyon, a point that proved close enough to ascertain that this truly was a river of immense proportions.

The Cárdenas expedition continued westward along the rim of the Grand Canyon once the three soldiers had climbed up to report on what they had seen. After traveling inland for nearly one hundred leagues, Cárdenas decided the time had come to return to Hawikuh. The decision to abandon this quest was prompted by the fact that there were no great native cities to be found and the Hopi warnings that there was little freshwater ahead to quench their thirst. Once reunited with Coronado, Captain Cárdenas reported that they had succeeded in finding the "great river," which had proved to be inaccessible, but failed to discover any towns other than those inhabited by the Hopi. One scout described the region beyond Tusayán as a "useless piece of country."[6]

A Sudden Revelation

While Captain Cárdenas was off in search of the Colorado River, a small assembly of Indians from a pueblo to the distant east came to Hawikuh to learn about the "strange people, bold men" they had recently heard about. This group, which had walked a great distance over barren land, was led by two chiefs who served as ambassadors for peace between the people of their village and the Spaniards. One of the leaders was a war chief that Coronado remembered as being a "young man, well built and robust in appearance"[7] and who, because of a pronounced sprout of whiskers on his face, he nicknamed Bigotes. The other was a much older chief who, for lack of a better name, the soldiers called Cacique, a title that the island tribes of the Caribbean bestowed on their rulers but which the Spaniards freely applied to the chiefs of all tribes in the Americas. Both chiefs had come to Hawikuh to invite Coronado and his soldiers to their homeland, which was more than two hundred miles east of where the Spaniards were presently camped.

The two visiting chiefs presented Coronado with an offering of animal hides, headdresses and shields. The captain-general reciprocated with gifts of little bells, colored glass beads, and some pearl beads. Sign language and interpreters helped Bigotes and Cacique communicate to the Spaniards that they were from a village called either Cicuique or Cicuye and later referred to as Pecos. Cicuique was located in a region that bore the same name and was situated along a path where massive herds of buffalo roamed. One of the natives who accompanied the two chiefs had a tattoo on his chest of a creature that, to the Spaniards, resembled a hairy cow. This was the first time that Coronado and his men had heard about this animal during their travels and it marked the first time that any Spaniard had seen the likeness of an American bison.

When Coronado inquired about the existence of precious metals or gems at Cicuique, the commander was disappointed to hear the chiefs say that they only had a large quantity of turquoise, a stone of great value to the natives but of little interest to the Spaniards. The captain-general decided to have Hernando de Alvarado and twenty cavaliers return with Bigotes and Cacique to their village to determine if it was worth bothering to claim for Spain. Alvarado, who left Hawikuh on August 29, 1540, was given eighty days to complete his reconnaissance mission, at which time he was to return to Hawikuh to report on his findings.

Serving as the guide for Alvarado and his troops, Bigotes led the Spaniards along an established path that brought them to Acoma, a large pueblo built atop a towering three hundred fifty-seven foot high sandstone mesa. Often referred to as Sky City, Acoma is derived from the native word Akome, which means "people of the white rock." Alvarado described the town as "one of the strongest ever seen, because the city is built on a very high rock. The ascent was so difficult that we repented climbing to the top. The houses are three and four stories high. The people are of the same type as those in the province of Cibola, and they have abundant supplies of maize, beans, and turkeys like those of New Spain."[8]

Bigotes met with the anxious warriors and elders of Acoma and it was his reassuring words that made it possible for Captain Alvarado and his soldiers to be welcomed with open arms. Alvarado and several of his men were invited to meet with the leaders of the village. The residents of Acoma came out in full force to greet the Spaniards and to present them with gifts of cotton, cloth, turquoise, buffalo hides, and a sampling of their daily cuisine.

The Spaniards and their guides pressed on along a northward road that led to a lake, and from there Bigotes steered the adventurers eastward to the banks of the Río Grande, which, because of their arrival on the eve of the Feast of Our Lady, Alvarado and his men christened the Río de Nuestra Senora. Armed with a Christian crossbow, Bigotes ventured upstream alone to meet with the Tigua chiefs of the nearby villages. The Indians of this region knew Bigotes and therefore were willing to trust him when he said that the Spaniards had come in peace. Alvarado's reliable guide returned with an assembly of chieftains and their entourage, who represented the twelve adobe pueblos of the Tigua province. They greeted the Spaniards with gifts of food, turquoise jewelry, blankets, and animal skins. Alvarado reciprocated by giving his gracious hosts an offering of trinkets he had brought for just such occasions. Pleased with this exchange, the embassy returned to their pueblos.

With the permission of the Tigua chiefs and the guidance of Bigotes, Alvarado proceeded to visit as many of the pueblos as he could. He was surprised to learn that there were nearly eighty pueblos stretched out over fifty leagues along the Río Grande. The Spaniards were greatly impressed by the abundant quantities of corn, melons, and beans that these natives were able to cultivate in this rather arid landscape. Alvarado made a thorough inspection of the pueblos called Santo Domingo, San Felipe, and Cochiti before venturing beyond White Rock Canyon, whereupon he entered the Española Valley. The conquistadors eventually came upon the pueblos that were home to the Taos Indians. Bigotes once again used his diplomatic skills to soothe a tense situation. The Taos chiefs invited the Spaniards to enjoy the comforts of their towns. Sensing their was nothing to be gained by such a visit, Captain Alvarado thanked them for their generosity but graciously declined their offer.

Hernando de Alvarado then returned to the lands of the Tigua, which the Spaniards preferred to call the province of Tiguex. Once there, Alvarado sent a message back to Hawikuh to inform Coronado that Tiguex was a much better place for the army to spend the upcoming winter. Besides including a map that would show his commander the route to these more accommodating pueblos, the dutiful officer sent "the head of a cow and several loads of clothing and tanned skins."[9]

Bigotes led the Spaniards to his hometown of Cicuique, a large pueblo with many four-and-five storied apartment buildings. The estimated fifty large houses, all of which were made with sun-dried bricks, were home to as many as two thousand residents, five hundred of whom were warriors. All came out to welcome the return of their beloved chiefs and to greet the Spaniards. Nestled within surrounding mountains and mesas, Cicuique was near the plains where the bison migrated; it also served as a gateway for trade between the settled pueblos of the west and the wandering tribes of the plains to the north and the east, the latter of which included the Apaches, Kiowas, and Comanches.

After resting for several days, Alvarado was eager to continue on to the Great Plains to see the buffalo—the creature he had seen a great many skins of and its likeness etched upon the chest of an Indian. Both Bigotes and Cacique asked to be excused from this expedition and offered in their place the services of two captive Indians from the prairies to the northeast who were slaves of Bigotes. The youngest of these offered guides was a native of Quivira named Sopete (aka Ysopete) who, because of the circles tattooed around his eyes, had the look of a raccoon. The older Indian hailed from Arahey (aka Arahe or Harahey), a place just beyond Quivira, and who, because his head wrapping resembled a turban, the Spaniards were quick to name El Turco (the Turk).

The Spaniards ventured forth with their new guides, who promised to lead them to the region where large herds of migrating buffalo were presently grazing. The expedition followed the Pecos River for a lengthy stretch before steering eastward along the course of the Canadian River. Just as promised, they soon came upon a vast herd comprised of thousands of buffalo grazing, a sight that was every bit as awesome as had been described. "There is such a quantity of them," a Spanish eyewitness wrote, "that I do not know what to compare them with, except with the fish of the sea."[10]

The field was so thick with buffalo that the Spaniards could not see where the herd began and where it ended. Alvarado decided they would venture to the other side by riding directly through the herd. The bold cavaliers strode into the horde and tried to clear a path by spearing the buffalo that refused to move. There was an unforeseen consequence to such an ill-advised action: several horses were gored to death and their Spanish masters barely escaped the same fate.

As the expedition ventured along the path of the Canadian River, the Turk, "by signs and in the Mexican tongue of which he knew a little," confessed to Alvarado that he did not know much about the lands to the east but claimed that he was quite familiar with the northeast region of Quivira, a place where the Spaniards could find an abundance of the gold, silver and precious gems that they so eagerly sought. Sopete, who was from Quivira, told the Spaniards that the Turk was exaggerating.

Though intrigued by the claims of the Turk, Alvarado wanted better proof than simply the word of an Indian guide before informing Coronado of this tale that sounded vaguely familiar to the one told by Fray Marcos. The Turk claimed that proof of the great wealth of this region could be found among the possessions of Bigotes, who had taken from him a gold bracelet and some jewelry made by the people of Quivira after the war chief had captured and enslaved him. What the Turk really wanted was an opportunity to return to Arahey and he believed this story was his ticket home. But instead of galloping off in search of the riches of Quivira, Alvarado decided they would all return to Cicuique to verify this rich claim. When he realized that his scheme to get the Spaniards to head to Quivira had failed, the Turk told Alvarado that it would not be wise to question Bigotes or Cacique about the gold bracelet or they might kill him and his men in order to protect this precious item as well as the secret of Quivira's wealth. The Turk failed to realize that there was no reasoning with men blinded by visions of gold: Quivira was destined to be added to the long list of legendary realms that the Spaniards were willing to risk believing in.

With a renewed sense of purpose, the Spaniards rushed back to Cicuique to confront Bigotes and Cacique about the gold bracelet and the rich kingdom of Quivira. Upon his return, Alvarado was given a warm reception and provided with additional supplies. The Spanish commander chose to disregard the Turk's advice and immediately questioned the two chiefs as to the precise whereabouts of the confiscated gold bracelet and the golden kingdoms of Quivira. Both denied that any such item or place existed and countered that the devious guide was simply trying to deceive them. Alvarado asked that the chiefs return with him to Hawikuh in order that Coronado could have an opportunity to determine which party was telling the truth. Bigotes and Cacique declined this request and all subsequent pleas of the Spanish captain. Choosing to ignore all that Bigotes and Cacique had already done for the Spaniards, a frustrated Alvarado lured the chiefs to his tent, ostensibly to discuss the matter in question, at which point he had both men clapped in irons as part of an effort to loosen their tongues regarding the golden item the Turk had told him about. The Turk was also detained inside the tent.

Once they learned what had happened to their esteemed chiefs, a large number of Cicuique warriors took up arms and rushed toward Alvarado's tent, a show of force they hoped would be sufficient to compel the Spaniards to release both Bigotes and Cacique. But Alvarado, who held the upper hand when it came to firepower, refused to back down and the warriors, who feared for the safety of their rulers, decided to withdraw. Worried that his tall tale was on the verge of being exposed, the Turk fled the village after cleverly finding a ready means of escape. Alvarado was convinced that the two chiefs had a role in the disappearance of the guide and pledged that he would keep them both in chains until he was found. An accord was reached whereby Cacique would, in return for his and Bigotes' freedom, take several warriors and track down the Turk. The fugitive was found and returned to Alvarado, who chose to reward Cacique by reneging on his promise. The chief once again found himself chained alongside Bigotes and the Turk.

Alvarado managed to restore a sense of calm by agreeing to join the warriors of Cicuique in a campaign against a rival tribe. The Spaniards accompanied an unchained Bigotes, Cacique and three hundred heavily armed warriors to the Nanapagua province. Sopete and the Turk, who also was released from his chains, were brought along on the raid. Two days into the march, the two native guides found an opportunity to slip away. Once their absence was detected, Alvarado again threatened to place both chiefs in chains unless the Turk and Sopete were returned at once. The runaway slaves were promptly found and brought back to Alvarado, who then decided to forgo this present course of action. The warriors were sent back to Cicuique while the Spaniards continued to Tiguex with the chained Bigotes, Cacique, Sopete, and the Turk in tow.

9

Native Unrest

Winter Camp

After receiving the message from Hernando de Alvarado that Tiguex would be a better location for the army to wait out the winter, Francisco Coronado sent García López de Cárdenas, who had just returned from his expedition, on ahead with as many as fourteen horsemen and several native allies to arrange accommodations for the entire army. Captain Cárdenas and his men proceeded to Alcanfor, the southernmost of the twelve settlements, where he ordered the residents to vacate their own pueblo in order to provide quarters for the coming of the Spaniards and their large entourage.

While still camped at Hawikuh, Coronado was reinforced by the arrival of Tristán de Arellano and his soldiers. The reunited troops remained at Hawikuh for another twenty days. Since the sheer size of his army was causing a severe drain on the natives' food reserves, the captain-general decided the time had come to march his army northward to the pueblos along the Río Grande. The conquistadors followed the course charted by Hernando de Alvarado. Unfortunately, Coronado did not have the services of either Bigotes or Cacique to act as mediators in their relations with the tribes they were to encounter.

Alvarado and his troops returned to the Tiguex province shortly after Cárdenas and his men had arrived. A vigilant watch was kept over the imprisoned Turk, Sopete, Bigotes, and Cacique while all awaited the arrival of Coronado and the remainder of the army. Once the captain-general reached Tiguex, he immediately met with Alvarado, who reported on all that he had seen on his expeditions to Cicuique and the Great Plains. It was, of course, what Alvarado had heard but not seen that was of the greatest interest to Coronado.

Intrigued by this new report of another rich native realm to the north, the captain-general was eager to learn more about Quivira from the enslaved Indian who was from that region. The Turk did not disappoint him. Knowing that the Spaniards were utterly obsessed by the thought of finding gold, the Turk told Coronado that Quivira was so rich with precious metals that they almost grew on trees. In addition to the story of the gold bracelet he claimed had been taken from him by Bigotes, the Turk spun a tale about a rich king named Tatarrax who slept under a tree filled with golden bells that tingled the most pleasing melodies as they gently swayed in the breeze. He told Coronado that his homeland rested near a great river that spawned fish as large as Spanish horses. The Turk claimed Quivira possessed so much silver and gold, the two metals dearest to the heart of every conquistador, that even the common folk had utensils, dishes, and cups made from these precious substances. Even canoes, he boasted, were fitted with eagle figureheads made of pure gold.

Thanks to the testimony of the Turk, the captain-general believed he was on the verge of a discovery that would make all the frustrations and disappointments of this expedition finally worthwhile. However, Coronado still wanted tangible proof that could support the claims of this Indian slave. He decided to question Bigotes and Cacique concerning the whereabouts of the missing bracelet. After all, it was the war chief Bigotes who supposedly had taken this piece of jewelry from the Turk when he captured him during a raid upon Quivira. Both chiefs told the Spanish commander that there was absolutely no truth to either the bracelet story or the fantastic tale of Quivira's riches.

Unwilling to accept the word of the two chiefs who had welcomed the Spaniards with open arms, Coronado decided that he would try to scare them into confessing the truth. It was Fray Juan de Padilla who recommended that Bigotes was deserving of a more intense interrogation. One or more dogs that were specially trained for inciting fear and inflicting pain were set upon the chief. Bigotes was bitten on one leg and one arm, but neither wound was severe. The hounds were called off and the chief's wounds were attended to when the only confession they obtained was his repeated claim that the Turk was a liar. Bigotes, Cacique, Sopete and the Turk remained in custody while Coronado decided upon his next course of action.

Frustrated by the series of letdowns up to this point, Coronado became noticeably less cordial in his relations with the natives after he reached the pueblos along the Río Grande. With the onset of winter the commander began making excessive demands upon the residents that, according to Casteneda, were "without any consideration or respect, and without inquiring about the importance of the person despoiled."[1] Spanish demands for clothing and blankets to shield them from the cold and food to feed them throughout the long winter had heavily taxed the patience of their hosts. While Coronado made sure that he complied with Viceroy Mendoza's order to compensate the natives for their goods and services, the Tiguex people felt slighted after having been

SPANIARDS HUNTING INDIANS.

Spaniards hunting Indians with the aid of horses and dogs.

forced to trade items that they needed for Spanish articles that were of little use to them. The numerous ultimatums and transgressions of the Spaniards were the source of a conflict remembered as the Tiguex War.

The insults and deprivations suffered by the Indians of these pueblos were compounded by reports of soldiers sexually assaulting the women. One such unseemly incident occurred at the pueblo of Arenal. Juan de Villegas, a soldier assigned to the company that was under the command of Cárdenas, had his way with a married woman of that village. Several natives, including the husband, went before the Spanish commander to complain of this soldier's sexual misconduct. The husband of the violated woman was able to identify the horse that belonged to Juan de Villegas but failed to recognize him as the wrongdoer. The language barrier also made it difficult for the natives to see that justice was done. Cárdenas would claim that Villegas was not disciplined simply because the offended husband was unable to identify him out of a lineup of similarly dressed soldiers. The more likely reason that Juan de Villegas was spared punishment is related to his brother's station in society: Pedro de Villegas was a high ranking official at Mexico City and a friendly acquaintance of Francisco Velázquez de Coronado.

The failure to bring to justice the soldier who had molested one of their women and the harsh treatment of Bigotes, Cacique, Sopete, and the Turk all contributed to a growing native hatred toward the Spaniards. The inhabitants of the Tiguex pueblos were also irritated that the horses were constantly grazing in their planted fields. The Tiguex natives were well aware of what had occurred at the Zuni and Hopi pueblos and they feared that the same was about to happen to them. The succession of Spanish abuses stirred up native discontent to a point where it was primed to erupt in violence.

The tense situation came to a head when a Mexican Indian charged with keeping watch over the horses unexpectedly returned to Alcanfor with blood streaming from several open wounds. He had rushed back to tell the Spaniards that a band of Tiguex warriors had killed his partner and stolen the horses they were guarding. Nearly seventy horses were taken from the fields where they were grazing as retribution for the rape of a Tiguex woman by a Spanish soldier cleared of all charges by his own officers. According to testimony later provided by Coronado, there were two Mexican guards and approximately thirty-five horses felled by a slew of arrows during this raid.

Coronado sent Cárdenas and eight cavaliers to track down the missing horses and to punish the impudent natives before their hostile actions turned into a full scale rebellion. The path they followed led directly to the pueblo of Almeda, which they were surprised to find deserted. Just outside the village the Spaniards were startled by the sight of two or three dead horses, their carcasses riddled with arrows. The tracks of the stolen horses led Cárdenas and his men in the direction of Arenal, the pueblo where the Indian woman had been molested. Along the way, they happened upon twenty-five more dead mounts— some of which were horses, while the others were mules.

Cárdenas and his cavaliers eventually reached Arenal, which they found to be well fortified. As they approached the pueblo the Spaniards were shocked by the sight of their stolen horses being chased around the plaza by warriors who repeatedly poked the frightened animals with their spears. They also saw a great many natives standing upon rooftops, several of whom were shouting and screaming while wagging the chopped off tails of horses they had already killed. Though greatly disturbed by what he had just seen, Cárdenas kept his composure and tried to negotiate a settlement with the natives. He promised that all would be forgiven if they laid down their arms and once again submitted to the will of the Spaniards. The riled natives refused all overtures made by Cárdenas. With so few men under his command, the captain was hardly in a position to force the issue. He returned to Coronado to report that the natives were in revolt. The captain-general sent Cárdenas back to Arenal to once again try to reach a peaceful accord but this effort fared no better than the first failed meeting.

The Tiguex War

Infuriated by the continual refusals of the warriors at Arenal to lay down their arms, Coronado decided the time had come for more persuasive action. Cárdenas was ordered to return to Arenal with an imposing squadron of soldiers and Mexican allies to make yet another offer for a peaceful settlement to their differences. If the rebellious natives refused to agree to these new terms then Captain Cárdenas and his troops were expected to take the pueblo by force. Coronado and the rest of the army was to remain at Alcanfor but were to be kept informed of all developments by means of messengers.

It was late December and snow had already begun to fall by the time the Spanish force reached Arenal. Cárdenas extended another offer for the natives to end their rebellion without fear of reprisal, but once again his efforts were for naught. After being spurned, the captain ordered his men to surround the pueblo in order to make sure no one could escape and that no one could come to their aid. Cárdenas issued the call to battle when the defiant warriors began to taunt his troops with all sorts of threatening gestures. Wading through a steady barrage of projectiles, the armored Spaniards managed to breach the pueblo but quickly found themselves pinned down by warriors who continued to assail them from their barricaded upper apartments. The captain ordered his troops to batter down the walls of the lower stories and to ignite brush fires, the smoke of which soon filled the occupied apartments. A great many natives were either killed or taken prisoner the moment they ran out to catch a breath of fresh air. The remainder of the Arenal warriors sued for peace by crossing their spears once they realized there was no hope of victory. Nearly two hundred warriors surrendered along with their families. The battle for Arenal was waged for several hours, a Spanish victory that resulted in the deaths of several Mexican allies and saw more than a dozen Spaniards suffer serious wounds.

The captured Indians were assembled into a covered area that was heavily guarded by soldiers. Meanwhile, other Spaniards were put to work driving stakes into the ground and then surrounding them with loose brush they had gathered. Once this task had been completed, a portion of the prisoners were escorted from their impromptu prison and tied to the planted stakes. These natives looked on in horror as their captors began to set fire to the brush that rested beneath their feet. This grisly act was approved by Cárdenas, who believed that such harsh punishment was justice served for their having killed so many innocent horses. Depending on which source is cited, between thirty and fifty natives were burned at the stake. To remind them of the dire consequences that one faced for offending the Spaniards, both the Turk and Sopete were compelled to watch this brutal execution of the Arenal warriors.

Pedro de Casteñeda wrote of it: "When the enemies saw that the Spaniards were binding them and beginning to roast them, about a hundred men who were in the tent began to struggle and defend themselves with what there was there and with the stakes they could seize. Our men who were on foot attacked the tent on all sides, so that there was great confusion around it, and then the horsemen chased those who escaped. As the country was level, not a man of them remained alive, unless it was some who remained hidden in the village, and escaped that night to spread throughout the country the news that the strangers did not respect the peace they had made, which afterward proved a great misfortune."[2]

The overpowering stench of charred and rotting flesh lingered long after the battle had been won. The women and children were spared from execution but were sentenced to a life of slavery, which by royal decree the Spaniards were permitted to do whenever the natives chose to challenge their authority. There were many instances during the conquest of the Americas in which unscrupulous conquistadors were guilty of purposely provoking the natives so they would have legal recourse to make them their slaves. The incident at Arenal was certainly not one of the finer moments of this mission. The rash order of Garcia Lopez Cárdenas would later bring ruin to his good name and tarnish the reputation of Francisco Vásquez de Coronado.

The inhabitants of the other pueblos learned of the terrible tragedy at Arenal and many began to assemble as one united group at Moho, the largest pueblo of the Tiguex province. Moho was built into a cliff that overlooked the Río Grande and fortified with a huge wall made from tree trunks pounded into the ground and plastered over with adobe — the same material used in the building of their homes. Coronado learned of their actions and sent Rodrigo Maldonado and a small squad of soldiers to Moho to try to talk them into peacefully submitting to Spanish authority. The actions of the Spaniards at Arenal had strengthened the resolve of the Tiguex people. Surrender no longer seemed to be an option, for to do so meant condemning themselves to a most horrible manner of death. It was, therefore, better to die fighting. Maldonado returned to Alcanfor with the news that the natives barricaded at Moho refused to comply with the request he had submitted on behalf of his commander.

Coronado responded by sending Captain Cárdenas and thirty horsemen to Moho to enforce his wish to bring closure to this protracted uprising. Just as he had done at Arenal, Cárdenas approached the fortified pueblo and communicated by way of signs and words that he greatly desired a peaceful resolution to their differences. Unfortunately for Cárdenas, the barbaric burning of their neighbors at Arenal was still fresh in the minds of all who took a stand at Moho. No one thought there was any truth to the captain's claim that they had come in peace and none believed the Spaniards would ever honor any promise they had made. The natives decided instead to turn the table on the conquistadors.

A chief, who bore an uncanny resemblance to someone the Spaniards knew at Mexico City and they therefore took to calling Juan Alemán, responded to the captain's peace overtures. Chief Alemán signified that he too desired a truce and indicated that the two should face one another so they could embrace as friends. As a sign of respect for their new friendship, Alemán asked that the soldiers withdraw and that Cárdenas meet with him on foot and without weapons. Agreeing to these conditions, the captain dismounted his horse and handed both his sword and lance to another soldier before proceeding on foot toward the pueblo.

As promised, Chief Alemán came out to meet with Captain Cárdenas. Once they were face to face, the chief greeted the officer with a smile and a warm embrace. Cárdenas soon realized that Alemán had his arms pinned so tightly with his hug that he was unable to move either of them. It was at that moment that several warriors appeared and rushed at him with clubs, which they used to knock the immobilized captain senseless. The stunned Cárdenas was then picked up and carried toward the pueblo. Once they realized they had been deceived, the soldiers rushed to the aid of their captured commander. A groggy Cárdenas came to his senses just in time to grab hold of a wall in a desperate effort to keep from being dragged inside the compound. By this time the soldiers had arrived and they managed to shield themselves from the torrent of rocks and arrows hurled at them just long enough to rescue their captain from certain death. In addition to the blows to his head, Cárdenas suffered an arrow wound to his leg.

A partially recovered Captain Cárdenas and several soldiers proceeded to another inhabited pueblo where the natives responded to his overture of peace with a slew of taunts and arrows. The frustrated captain rejoined the soldiers he had left behind to keep watch over the Moho pueblo only to soon find himself under attack from Alemán's warriors. With too few men to force his will on the natives, Cárdenas realized the time had come to return to Alcanfor.

After meeting with Cárdenas, the captain-general decided to assemble the might of his entire force to compel the rebellious Tiguex tribes to submit to Spanish authority. Coronado soon saw for himself that Moho was far better fortified than Arenal. Try as they might, the soldiers could not batter down these reinforced walls and when they attempted to scale them with ladders they were pummeled with a hailstorm of rocks and arrows. To their shock and horror, the Spaniards soon discovered that poisoned arrows were part of the arsenal of the opposition. The tips of these arrows were dipped in a mixture of putrefied deer liver and the deadly venom extracted from rattlesnakes. A strike from even one of these arrows was often fatal — a death sentence that lingered on for hours as the victim was left writhing in helpless torment. Even if a sufferer were lucky enough to survive the initial effects of such a ghastly wound he still faced the likelihood of developing either blood poisoning or tetanus, or having to endure watching his flesh rot like a cursed leper. Scores of Spaniards were wounded during this engagement and several later died from the effects of their festering wounds. At least five or six soldiers died during the assault on Moho.

Unable to take the pueblo by force, Coronado decided to have his troops form a blockade around Moho. Food was not a problem for the barricaded Indians but fresh water certainly was an issue. The Spaniards had cut off their access to the Río Grande, and in order to quench their thirst the Tiguex Indians had to rely on the falling snow as a source of fresh water. Coronado's troops laid siege to Moho from December 1540 through the following March. Some of the surrounding pueblos, according to later testimony, were destroyed in order to provide firewood for the Spaniards during this long siege.

An all-out attack occurred toward the end of February 1541. A popular and respected captain by the name of Francisco de Ovando was captured during this failed offensive and summarily put to death. Subsequent unsuccessful assaults began to frustrate the Spaniards. However, the arrival of spring and the inevitable melting of the snow saw the return of the ravishing thirst that plagued those hidden behind the walls of Moho. In a concerned effort to spare the women and children any further suffering, the Tiguex men asked if their families could leave without fear of harm. The captain-general promised to pardon all the warriors if they followed suit and crossed over to his camp. But because of their knowledge of how brutally the surrendering defenders at Arenal had been treated, the warriors at Moho were disinclined to believe such an offer. After Coronado agreed to their request, roughly one hundred women and children entered the Spanish camp as refugees. The warriors hoped that with less mouths for them to feed and more for the Spaniards to feed they could continue to hold on to their homes.

A sense of desperation set in among the Moho fighters once the water was gone. The warriors attempted to slip out of their pueblo as quietly as possible but, unfortunately, their movements were spotted by two Spanish sentries who immediately sounded the alarm. The fleeing Tiguex Indians silenced their calls by killing one of the lookouts and taking the other hostage. But it was already too late. The alerted Spaniards gave chase and the horsemen were able to quickly catch up with the escaping natives. The weakened warriors defended themselves as best they could, but one by one they were either brought down by the swords and lances of the Spaniards or taken prisoner. One soldier and one horse were killed during this confrontation and the conquistadors killed a great many natives as retribution for these losses. Many natives made it across the icy waters of the Río Grande while others drowned after losing the battle to the river's swift currents. Most of those who did make it to the other side of the river were soon captured and forced into servitude.

After a siege that lasted for nearly eighty days, Coronado and his men were finally able to lay claim to the town of Moho. Several Tiguex warriors who were too weak and frightened to attempt an escape with the others were found inside and taken prisoner. The Spaniards also discovered some food and a number of dead bodies, some of whom were found at a well that had caved in on them while they were desperately trying to dig for water. Several fallen comrades, including Captain Francisco de Ovando, were also found behind the walls of Moho and given a proper burial.

The victorious Spaniards proceeded to the other pueblo that had previously resisted and taunted Captain Cárdenas. The Tiguex Indians who resided there fled once they saw the approach of Coronado's troops. The soldiers searched for the inhabitants but they were nowhere to be found. The other pueblos of this province were also abandoned after the fall of Moho, which marked the end of the conflict known as the Tiguex War. The conquistadors suffered the loss of approximately twenty comrades during this military campaign, while roughly five hundred Tiguex Indians lost their lives trying to defend their way of life. A great many other natives were enslaved by the Spaniards.

Bigotes, Cacique, Sopete, and the Turk had been dragged to Moho where they were forced to witness the destruction of yet another pueblo. The Turk continued to curry the favor of Coronado by embellishing his already tantalizing tale of Quivira. The captain-general had already made up his mind to lead an expedition to Quivira to investigate the Turk's claims once the Tiguex revolt had been crushed. After the battle for Moho had been won, Coronado sought to make peace with the natives that Hernando de Alvarado had offended at the pueblo of Cicuique by returning Cacique and promising to free Bigotes once the army was on its way to Quivira. The natives were not entirely pleased but agreed to put aside their disdain for the deceitful Spaniards so that their beloved Bigotes would be returned to them.

Shortly after the siege of Moho, Coronado received the sorrowful news that Melchior Díaz had died during his quest to locate the much needed supplies that were slated to arrive by ship under the command of Hernando de

Alarcón. This report was carried from San Gerónimo by soldiers who had served with Díaz until the very end. They also informed the captain-general of the message left by Alarcón at a tree near the Colorado River that made it clear they had missed their opportunity to link up with the supply ships from Mexico.

Afterwards, Coronado sent Pedro de Tovar to the San Gerónimo post to restore order, which had fallen apart under the inept leadership of Diego de Alcaraz and to send more soldiers to join in the upcoming expedition to Quivira. Also accompanying Tovar were couriers who were to continue on to Mexico City to deliver a message to Viceroy Mendoza that would inform him of the battles at Tiguex and the tales of Quivira, a promising region that he was determined to investigate. A similar letter was drafted for the benefit of Emperor Charles V.

10

THE SEARCH FOR QUIVIRA

Where the Buffalo Roam

On April 23, 1541, Coronado led his army out of Tiguex to begin the search for the golden realm of Quivira. They marched to Cicuique where, as promised, the captain-general granted Cacique and, eventually, Bigotes their freedom. The people celebrated the return of their beloved chiefs and showed their appreciation to Coronado by willingly providing him with supplies for his upcoming expedition. Besides being permitted to retain the services of the Turk and Sopete as their guides, the Spanish commander was given another captive Indian who was also from the Quivira region. This lad, who was known by the name of Xabe, or Zabe, confirmed that there was indeed gold and silver to be found at his homeland but not nearly as much as the Turk claimed. The Turk, however, stuck to his story that Quivira was a land rich with precious gold and silver. The covetous Spaniards saw no reason to doubt his claims.

As the Spaniards prepared to leave Cicuique, the Turk told Coronado that because they would eventually pass through Ayas, a town of significant size that could provide enough food to feed them until the journey's end, there was no need to burden the horses with a heavy load of provisions. To put it in terms that the captain-general could appreciate, the guide said that the horses should not be overburdened or they would be too weak to carry back all the wealth they were certain to find at Quivira. Unbeknownst to the Spaniards, the Turk met privately with the chiefs of Cicuique shortly before the expedition got underway.

With rekindled dreams of discovering vast stores of gold, silver, and jewels, the Spaniards broke camp at Cicuique and set off for the riches that awaited at Quivira. In anticipation of the abundant amount of treasure they would have to haul back, nearly a thousand horses traveled in the company of the conquistadors. The multitude of mounts were accompanied by five hundred head of cattle and five thousand sheep brought along to make sure the soldiers did not have to march on empty stomachs. The pace of the expedition was significantly slowed by so many beasts on the move, many of which tended to stray from the herd. To gauge their daily progress, Coronado assigned one of his foot soldiers to keep an accurate count of the steps taken by one of the horses.

After a four day march the expedition reached the banks of the Pecos River. The river had swelled from the melting snows and a bridge had to be built in order for the men and animals to get across, a task that took four days to complete. Once all had crossed the Pecos the troops continued on an easterly course toward Quivira. The pace was further slowed by the need for the herds of cattle and sheep to have an opportunity to graze. The path they followed led them to the plains of Texas, where after several days of marching the Spaniards came upon a large herd of grazing bison. The herd was so immense that Coronado would remark, "there was not a single day until my return that I lost sight of them."[1] This vast tableland of grass, which extended in every direction as far as one could see, was an ideal grazing ground for the horde of American buffalo that blanketed the horizon. These buffalo roamed the plains by the millions in their search for grass and water.

During their crossing of the plains, Coronado and his troops came upon a trail marked with parallel lines etched into the earth. The curious Spaniards followed the tracks, which looked as if they were made by lances being dragged along the ground. The strange markings led them to a village that was the temporary home of a nomadic tribe that followed the migration of the buffalo. This band of approximately fifty Indians that they encountered were a group of plains Apaches known as the Querecho.

The Querecho way of life was almost entirely dependent upon the buffalo. The flesh of this animal was their principle source of food. The hide of the creature was used to make tepees, clothes, blankets, and moccasins. The sinews were stretched to make bowstrings and thread for stitching. A typical tepee (also spelled as teepee or tipi), the native word for dwelling, was made from as many as twelve buffalo hides sewn together to make a tent covering. The entrance usually faced the east so that the dweller could be greeted by the warmth of the morning sun. Bison organs were ground into a paste that was applied to aid in tanning hides. Hide scraps and bison dung were utilized as fuel for their fires. Bison bladders were used as containers for storing water and stomachs were made into a pouch that was ideal for cooking. Besides being woven into rope, buffalo hair was useful as stuffing for pillows, gloves, and moccasins. The bones were shaped into knife blades and various other tools. Buffalo hooves were boiled to produce glue and the horns were turned into drinking vessels. Buffalo hides and dried meat also served as a form of currency for the nomadic tribes of the Great Plains—items that were used to barter for blankets, pottery, corn and other food items harvested by the Pueblo tribes.

The Spaniards saw that the Querechos moved their belongings with the aid of domesticated dogs that served as their beasts of burden. What items the natives were unable to carry on their backs were hauled by dogs dragging two poles, which produced the markings that had attracted the attention of Coronado and his men. These poles were attached at the shoulder of the dog and the tail end supported a platform loaded with the owner's material belongings. These dogs could drag between thirty and fifty pounds in this manner. When French explorers later saw a similar mode of transport employed by natives up north they called it a travois. Many years later, the horse, which was known as either Spirit Dog or Holy Dog by many wandering tribes, would replace the dog as their beast of burden. When on the move, scouts went ahead to make sure the path was safe while armed warriors protected the rear. Women, children, and the elders walked alongside the dogs that lugged most of their belongings. The roving tribes of this region reminded the Spaniards of the tales of Arab nomads, the wandering tribes that knew the secret routes to the riches of Africa.

Misguided

Like many other tribes of the plains, the Querechos were adept at sign language — the almost universal dialogue between native people who did not share a common spoken language. The Querecho felt comfortable communicating with the Turk after he had eased their concerns over the rather intimidating appearance of the horses and soldiers. Coronado instructed his guide to ask the Querecho in which direction Quivira could be found. They responded by pointing due east, a direction that did not correspond with the northeast route that the Turk had originally told Hernando de Alvarado was the location of this magnificent realm. When questioned by Coronado over this obvious discrepancy, the guide simply shrugged it off as a miscalculation on his part and said they should now head eastward. The sly Turk had spoken with the Querechos before playing the role of Coronado's interpreter and informed them of the plan for revenge that had been concocted by Bigotes and Cacique. He wanted to know the most desolate course to take, one where the Spaniards would perish from hunger and thirst. That direction, the Querecho told him, was due east.

The Spaniards parted ways with this wandering tribe, and their subsequent two day march brought them to yet another Querecho camp. After conferring with the Turk, these Querecho also said that the kingdom of Quivira was further east, which seemed to confirm what the previous tribe had told them. Sopete, who had been forced to march at the rear of the procession because of his intense dislike for the Turk, stepped forward to tell Coronado they were being misled. Sopete, who was from Quivira, told the Spaniards that the cunning Turk had lied to them and that he had coerced the Querecho into his sinister scheme to lead the expedition astray. Quivira, he said, was a place steeped in poverty. Most of the soldiers thought Sopete was simply jealous that the Turk had the ear and favor of their commander. Coronado, however, was starting to become suspicious of the Turk's claims.

The Turk was as charismatic as he was crafty and together these traits enabled him to exert undue influence over others, especially the covetous Spaniards. The captain-general sent Diego López and several cavaliers on ahead to locate Ayas (aka Haxa), a native settlement that the Turk and the Querecho claimed was a wondrous sight to behold. While the main army remained camped at the second Querecho village, several soldiers decided to pass the time hunting buffalo. One of the soldiers suddenly found himself separated from the others while standing in the midst of a vast sea of grass. In a frantic effort to locate the friends he had lost sight of, the confused soldier darted off in the wrong direction. His concerned comrades built fires and sounded trumpets to help guide the lost soldier back but he was never seen again.

Meanwhile, Diego López and his men had their own unusual encounter with the buffalo. After happening upon a large herd that was calmly grazing, several soldiers decided, just for sport, to ride into the gathering of bison. Their loud noises and swift movements frightened the gentle beasts into a frenzied stampede, which the Spaniards found themselves caught up in. The galloping herd headed directly toward a deep gorge, whereupon they proceeded to tumble to their death. Ten horsemen were swept over a cliff and fell into a ravine that rapidly filled with the bodies of buffalo. After much effort, the riders were able to extricate themselves from the pile. But three horses were not so lucky, as they were crushed under the weight of the many creatures that rained down on them.

Because of their mishap with the buffalo, Diego López and his soldiers had not returned to the Coronado camp when expected. A search party was sent out and they soon located the badly bruised scouting expedition. Lopez returned to report that they had traveled for twenty leagues and saw no signs of either Quivira or Ayas. He punctuated this doleful news by stating "they saw nothing but cattle and sky." Despite this unpromising report, Coronado decided to continue trusting to the advice of the Turk and ordered the company to proceed along the same route. Sopete once again spoke up to say that the Turk and the Querechos were leading them in a direction away from Quivira. Once again, the Spaniards chose to ignore the warning of Sopete. The native of Quivira became so frustrated that no one would listen to what he had to say that he "threw himself on the ground and indicated by signs that he would rather have his head cut off than go that way because it was not the correct route to Quivira."[2]

Coronado and his men, including the reluctant Sopete, continued their march across the plains, a grassland region where in some spots the blades of grass grew so high that the rear guard had a difficult time keeping sight of the advance group. The soldiers had to maintain a disciplined file, for if one fell behind he could very easily suffer the same fate of the soldier who became lost while hunting buffalo. (This seemingly endless sea of grasslands extends from the Río Grande on up into Canada.) There were no hills, trees, or rock formations to provide a bearing or to break the monotony of the view. The sighting of a series of distant mesas that seemed to resemble the ramparts of a giant stone fortress helped make the journey a bit more bearable. Known as the Llano Estacado (Palisaded Plain), this flat plateau stretches over a vast region of southeastern New Mexico and northwestern Texas. Coronado and his men were now in the northern area of the Llano Estacado, which is located in the Texas Panhandle.

In a letter to Emperor Charles V, Coronado wrote, "I traveled as the guides wished to lead me until I reached some plains, with no more land-marks than as if we had been swallowed up by the sea, where they strayed about, because there was not a stone nor a bit of rising ground, nor a tree, nor a shrub, nor anything to go by."[3]

As they traveled these plains, the Spaniards at the front stacked sun bleached buffalo bones and dried dung to serve as guideposts for those bring-ing up the rear. The oft told tale of Spaniards hammering stakes in the ground to prevent getting lost seems to have little basis in fact. The soldiers had to keep a constant watch for packs of wolves that had caught a scent of the cat-tle and sheep. The soldiers were pleased to see that the Turk's claim that there was food to be found along the way had proved correct. Antelope were plen-tiful but their swift feet made them a difficult animal to catch. Prairie dogs were great in number and jackrabbits proved an easy prey to supplement their food supply.

The most plentiful animal of these lands was, of course, the migrating bison. Rodrigo Maldonado and a group of soldiers were off hunting buffalo when they happened upon some Indians performing the very same task. They were Teyas, a tribe that was an enemy of the Querechos. The Teyas met by Maldonado and his men should not be confused with the Tejas that were encountered by members of the Hernando de Soto expedition. The Teyas were nomads and the Tejas lived in permanent dwellings.

The Teyas hunters brought Maldonado and his comrades back to their village, which was currently located along the Tule Canyon. After being accorded a warm welcome by the members of the tribe, Maldonado sent a message back to Coronado to tell him they had found a village where there were a great many buffalo skins. When he arrived with the rest of the army, Coronado assumed that the great pile of skins laid before him was an offering from the Teyas and began distributing them to the soldiers until none were left. It was then that the Spaniards noticed nearly all the people of the village were weeping. The skins had been brought to Coronado to be blessed — just like the benediction that Cabeza de Vaca and his comrades had invoked during their wanderings between tribes.

The tales of the Christian healers were well known to the natives of this region. Cabeza de Vaca had passed through these lands as late as 1535 — just six years before Coronado— and therefore the memory of this legendary shaman was still fresh in their minds. Further evidence that Cabeza de Vaca and his companions had passed this way was accorded by Juan de Jaramillo, who wrote, "There was an old Indian, blind and bearded, who gave us to understand by signs that, many days before, he had met four others of our people near there but closer to New Spain."[4] It was assumed the "four others" were Cabeza de Vaca, Dorantes, Castillo, and Esteban.

The Teyas told Coronado that Quivira was a real place but in order to get there they would have to travel northeast instead of the due east course they were presently following. They then wanted to know why the Spaniards wished to go there, for the Quivirans, they said, lived a simple life that was entirely dependent upon the maize they grew and the buffalo they hunted. The Teyas added that the Quivirans did not possess any of the precious metals or gems that the Turk had bragged about. This seemed to confirm what Sopete had been trying to tell the Spaniards all along. Coronado then questioned his three guides: the Turk, Sopete, and Xabe. The Turk finally confessed that he was leading them astray but would not admit as to why he was deliberately misleading the expedition.

A Disappointing End

A frustrated Coronado sent scouts northward in the direction where Sopete and the Teyas said Quivira dwelled. It was at a nearby canyon that the Spanish scouts met up with an Apache tribe that warmly welcomed them to their village. A river ran through this canyon and fostered the growth of many edible fruits and nuts, which were a delectable delight to those who had been deprived for a long time of such savory items. As with most tribes of this region, there was more than enough buffalo meat to share among family and welcome guests. The Spaniards also had an opportunity to observe Apache expertise with the bow and arrow, a skill that favorably impressed their guests.

Meanwhile, Coronado and the army were escorted by Teyas guides to

Cona, a region inhabited by kindred tribes. They reached Cona after a march of four days, during which time they were reunited with the scouts who had been entertained by an Apache tribe. The Spaniards were surprised to find their tranquil surroundings suddenly interrupted. The sky began to turn black as night and a sudden gust of wind grew increasingly stronger. As the soldiers tried to calm the horses, all of whom were desperately trying to break free, they found themselves being pelted by a heavy downpour of hailstones. A tornado then appeared before them, a sight that the conquistadors had yet to experience during their many adventures in the New World. All were terrified by this Texas twister that swept past them with roaring force. They were relieved that the storm passed quickly. The horses and soldiers were battered and bruised but, thankfully, alive. Most of the damage was to the tents and the armor, the latter of which suffered from many noticeable dents. All of the clay pots and gourds the soldiers brought were smashed to pieces by the force of the hail.

Many of the soldiers, especially those given to superstitious beliefs, were convinced that this terrifying event was a portent of doom. Realizing that the morale of his men had been badly shaken by this tempest that had suddenly erupted, Coronado, who was not about to give up on this quest, called a meeting of his officers. Conceding that perhaps it was no longer wise to risk all of the army in search of a region that had lost much of its original appeal, the captain-general proposed that he would continue on to Quivira with just a small company of soldiers while the rest of the army returned to Tiguex. Coronado also understood that he could travel much faster to his intended destination without the constant burdens associated with the herds. The concern over the growing shortage of food and water also played a factor in his change of plans. The captain-general was also mindful of the Hernando de Soto expedition that was underway in Florida and hoped to find and claim any legendary cities of gold before his rival succeeded in his quest to do the same.

The army separated after reaching the Palo Duro Canyon on May 29, 1541. Coronado took thirty cavaliers, six foot soldiers, and several native guides, as well as Sopete, who was now in Coronado's good graces, and the Turk, who had fallen from grace, northward to find Quivira. Meanwhile, Tristán de Arellano led the bulk of the army back to Tiguex where they were to prepare camp while patiently awaiting the return of their commander. During their march back to Tiguex, Arellano and his troops encountered an unusual sight. Near a lake where no village was found they saw bones unexplainably piled "nearly twice as high as a man and three or more fathoms wide" and measuring nearly one hundred fifty yards in length. They had wandered into a vast graveyard of bison bones.

Sopete, who was asked by Coronado to lead the way for his expeditionary force, agreed to be their guide on the condition that after reaching Quivira he would be permitted to remain with his tribe. He also asked that the Turk, whom he loathed, not be included in the group that he was about to guide. Coronado agreed to the first request but not the second. Finding himself dragged along with bound hands while forced to wear a shackle around his neck, which was attached to a rope pulled by a cavalier, the treacherous Turk struggled as best he could to keep pace.

The Teyas guides who traveled with Coronado abandoned Coronado on the first day out and Captain Cárdenas had to return to the villages to obtain the services of other natives who could lead them through lands that were unfamiliar to Sopete. It was during the early days of this journey that a tattooed native woman, who had been a slave at Tiguex and now was a prized possession of Juan de Zaldívar, a conquistador who accompanied this expedition, recognized the lands around Cona and escaped to try to find her way home.

Coronado had a primitive compass to help him determine their direction but still had to rely on his guides to make sure he did not stray from the path to Quivira. Despite having significantly lightened his load, the captain-general found his progress slowed by the many twists and turns of the terrain. They spent four weeks trudging across the rugged northern plains of Texas and the open panhandle of Oklahoma. Coronado and his troops marched across the plains of Kansas until they reached the Arkansas River, where Sopete told them they were finally near Quivira. They continued on to Pawnee Rock and Great Bend, where the native trail they followed veered eastward toward the tribes situated along the banks of the Arkansas River and its tributaries.

On July 2, 1541, Coronado and company encountered a small band of Quiviran Indians who were hunting buffalo. The natives were frightened by the sight of strangely suited men sitting upon even stranger beasts and immediately took flight. Sopete chased after them and managed to calm their fears by conversing in their native tongue. After sharing camp with these hunters, the Spaniards proceeded to the Quivira settlements, which were located in the central highlands of Kansas. Coronado and his troops strode into the first village on the sixth of July. Though thankful for the warm reception they received, the conquistadors were disappointed to see that this village consisted of just a few round grass thatched homes, none of which housed any gold, silver, or precious stones. They could see that the Quivirans, who were most likely the Wichitas, were a settled people who lived comfortably off the buffalo they hunted and crops, such as melons, maize, and beans, that they grew. Everything that Sopete had said about Quivira proved to be true, while everything the Turk had claimed about this region was shown to be false.

Coronado spent several weeks exploring the Quivira province, during which time he either visited or learned something about the twenty-five neighboring native settlements, none of which had any form of wealth that would be of interest to Spain. There were no magnificent cities that rivaled the likes of Tenochtitlan or Cuzco. Instead, there were only small villages inhabited by people who were content to enjoy the fruits of their own labor. Coronado found Quivira to be a verdant land that could easily support a Spanish settlement, but without the promise of any precious metals or gems there was little that could be gained from such an endeavor.

The captain-general was determined to meet Tatarrax, the rich and powerful Quiviran chief that the Turk claimed slept under a tree filled with melodious golden bells. Though quite elderly, Coronado found the chief to be friendly and rather large in stature, as were most of the people of this land. The chief wore a copper ornament but it was still quite obvious to all that Tatarrax was no Montezuma or Atahualpa. This piece of copper was the only metal that Coronado ever discovered at Quivira. Only later did the Spaniards learn that tatarrax was the Quiviran name for their principal chief and not the name of an individual chief.

Realizing that Coronado's meeting with the chief he had greatly exaggerated about would expose yet another of his lies, and fearing there might be further repercussions because of this finding, the Turk desperately tried to encourage the Quivirans to turn on the Spaniards. Sopete learned of his devious efforts and immediately informed Coronado. Worried that the Turk had already implemented a plot against them, several soldiers urged their commander to execute their former guide. Coronado responded to this request by asking, "What honor would be gained by killing the Indian?"[5] The captain-general would soon have cause to change his mind.

Coronado was surprised to learn upon his arrival at the village of Tabas that the natives were unwilling to provide corn or any other food for his men and horses. When questioned as to why, the Quivirans told the captain-general that the Turk had instructed them to deprive the Spaniards and their animals of food and drink so they would become too weak to defend themselves. The scheme called for putting the natives on equal footing by killing all the horses before turning their wrath on the soldiers. Diego López was urged by Coronado to interrogate the Turk, who under intense pressure confessed not only to all of his misdeeds but also implicated the chiefs of Cicuique. He admitted that the bracelet story was a lie and that he purposely led the Spaniards astray so that he could escape and return to his homeland. According to the Turk, it was Bigotes and Cacique who had told him to lead the Spaniards out into the distant plains before abandoning them. It was hoped that they would all weaken and die from lack of food and water while trying to find a way out on their own. This was intended to be a fitting revenge for the harsh way the Spaniards had betrayed their friendship and trust.

Once he realized that the Turk had lied to him from the very beginning, Coronado instructed Diego López and Juan de Zaldívar to carry out the execution of the deceitful Indian slave, a task they were to perform secretly during the night in order to avoid the possibility of any Quivirans coming to his defense. Even Fray Juan de Padilla gave his blessing to the killing of the heathen Turk. The night after his confession the former guide was abruptly aroused from his sleep. The soldiers made the chained prisoner understand that he must die for the many lies he had told. The frightened Turk tried to talk his way out of his ordained fate by claiming "that the town having gold and other riches was farther on, and that he had led the Spaniards by way of Quivira merely to get his wife, who was there, in order to take her along."[6] The Turk understood that his words no longer carried any weight once he saw that he was about to be garroted by the very men who stood over him. Two Spaniards held down the body of the prisoner while a third soldier slowly tightened a rope wrapped around the Turk's neck, which was twisted from behind with a stick. The Turk's lifeless body was buried in a shallow grave that had already been dug near the tent.

11

THE ROAD TO RUIN

Return to Tiguex

After nearly a month at Quivira, and immediately following the execution of the Turk, Coronado decided the time had come to return to Tiguex. There were too few men and no compelling reasons to venture any further than the village of Tabas. He had learned all he cared to know about this land and simply wished to rejoin the rest of the army before winter began to announce its arrival. There were, however, two concerns that plagued the captain-general's thoughts. Coronado was worried that the Quivirans, who greatly outnumbered his troops, might attempt to exact revenge for the killing of the Turk. He was also concerned by the Turk's confession that Bigotes, Cacique and the other chiefs at Cicuique had plotted against him and therefore feared that they would attack them during their return to Cicuique.

Coronado had his men erect a wooden cross at Cow Creek while preparations were underway for the journey back to Tiguex. Chiseled into the rocks at the base was a message: "Francisco Vásquez de Coronado, general of the expedition, reached here."[1] Coronado kept his promise and granted the loyal Sopete his freedom. He was replaced with six Quivira Indians who were to guide them back to Cicuique, which was on the way to Tiguex. The Spaniards followed the same route they had taken to Quivira until they crossed the Arkansas River. It was then that Coronado and his entourage headed southwest, skirting the Kansas and Oklahoma border before returning to the Texas Panhandle.

In the meantime, Tristán de Arellano and a band of soldiers left Tiguex and headed to Cicuique, where the captain hoped to meet up with Coronado. After having parted company with his commander, Arellano and the main army reached Tiguex around the middle of July and, as instructed, they busied themselves making camp for the upcoming winter. A concerned Arellano took forty men and marched to Cicuique as the agreed upon time for Coronado's return drew near. They were also accompanied by Xabe, who served as their guide and interpreter. Once there, the Spaniards were surprised to see that the warriors of the town were prepared to oppose their return. The battle that ensued lasted for four days. The fierce determination displayed by the Cicuique warriors seems to support the Turk's claim that Bigotes and Cacique wanted to take revenge against the Spaniards.

Fearing that Coronado and his accompanying soldiers might walk into an ambush, Arellano decided to wait for his commander at Cicuique while his troops kept the angered natives at bay. Fortunately, the wait proved to be short. Coronado soon arrived and all were disheartened to hear that there was no gold or silver to be found at Quivira. The reunited conquistadors returned to Tiguex, where all prepared for a long winter of discontent.

Once back at Tiguex, Coronado dispatched a letter to Viceroy Mendoza to inform him of the many disappointments experienced at Quivira and the expedition in general. He included the copper medallion he had managed to obtain from Tatarrax, the elderly chief at Quivira, which he indicated amounted to the sum total of metal found on this expedition that was even remotely precious. Coronado also informed the viceroy that he had sent out scouting parties to follow up on every native hint of lands said to contain wealth, but all had been for naught.

Pedro de Tovar, the captain that Coronado had sent to San Gerónimo to restore order, returned to Tiguex with news that merely added to the expedition's mounting list of disappointments. Tovar had reached the Spanish settlement during the beginning of a native uprising that was a direct response to Diego de Alcarez's harsh treatment toward them. Diego was responsible for the brutal torture of several Ópata Indians. He is known to have ordered his men to hack off the nose of several Indians and to cut out the tongue of others. He also had a penchant for taking any native woman he pleased as his concubine.

After learning that a Spaniard had been killed by a poisoned arrow, Tovar sent Alcarez, at the head of a company of soldiers and a contingent of native allies, to crush the rebellion. The rebel leaders were apprehended but set free on the condition that they would furnish food and clothing for the Spaniards. Once released, the chiefs rallied the people to oppose the conquistadors with all their might. Infuriated by their thankless response, Alcarez ordered his men to attack but was forced to sound the call for retreat after being pelted by poisoned arrows. Seventeen of his men were to suffer extremely painful deaths. The surviving soldiers retreated to a garrison but were soon forced to abandon this for a new shelter.

In the meantime, Pedro de Tovar took half of the soldiers at San Gerónimo and headed back to Tiguex, where they were reunited with Coronado and their comrades. Diego de Alcarez suddenly found himself having to restore order with even fewer soldiers. Unfortunately for those who remained at San Gerónimo, the Ópata were in no mood to settle their differences peace-fully. Weary of Alcarez's cruel and covetous nature, the Ópata decided they would bring an end once and for all to the Spanish occupation of their home-land. Fearing for their lives, several soldiers deserted Diego de Alcarez and tried to find their way to Culiácan. Some of these Spaniards were killed by natives who had anticipated such a move. The Ópata managed to infiltrate the Spanish compound and there they killed three soldiers and several horses. At the time of the attack, Alcarez was in bed satisfying his lascivious desires with two native women. Aroused by the commotion, Diego tried to escape but was felled by a poisoned arrow that caused him to suffer terribly until relief came in the form of death.

Captain Cárdenas and a dozen other soldiers were en route from Tiguex to Mexico City while the native insurrection was taking place at San Gerón-imo. Cárdenas, who had suffered a badly broken arm during this campaign, had just received a dispatch from Mexico City informing him that his wealthy brother had passed away in Spain and that he needed to return home to han-dle the estate. While his comrades bemoaned the loss of their hopes of finding wealth at either Cibola or Quivira, Cárdenas could find solace in the vast for-tune he was about to inherit. San Gerónimo was on the way back and they arrived to see that the settlement had been abandoned and several Spaniards, including Alcarez, had been killed. Cárdenas learned the shocking details of the assault from some survivors and then returned to Tiguex to warn Coro-nado of the situation.

Coronado made Alcanfor his winter quarters for a second time. Since the expected supplies from Mexico had failed to arrive as planned, the Spaniards were forced to live off the land as best they could. Buffalo jerky became the main staple once their food was exhausted. Without the prospect of finding gold, a desire that had warmed their thoughts while waiting out the first winter, many of the soldiers began to voice their complaints. To con-sole his dispirited troops, the captain-general announced that, once warmer weather returned, he would lead them on an expedition just past Quivira, a region where Xabe claimed gold could be found. In the meantime, the bitter drop in temperature compelled Coronado to dispatch soldiers to procure garments from the nearby tribes. The Tiguex Indians, who needed the clothes and blankets for their own protection, had to watch as the Spaniards once again helped themselves to their belongings.

On December 27, 1541, Coronado decided to break the monotony of camp by engaging in a friendly horse race against Captain Rodrigo Maldon-ado. Prior to the start of the race, a new saddle girth was supplied for the cap-tain-general's benefit. Coronado had just taken the lead when one of the straps, which apparently had rotted, suddenly snapped, thereby causing the captain-general to tumble off his horse. Landing on his side, the fallen commander found himself directly in the path of his opponent's horse and, before either competitor could react, Coronado was struck in the head by the hoof of Maldonado's mount and knocked unconscious. Many who rushed to his aid feared that Coronado was near death. Even after he awoke, the commander's mind was in such a confused state that few believed he would survive much longer. Even Coronado thought the end was near.

Captain Cárdenas returned to Alcanfor while Coronado was confined to what many believed was his death bed. So as not to cause him any further distress, news of the tragic events that had taken place at San Gerónimo was deliberately kept from the incapacitated commander. However, after he made a sudden and surprising recovery, Coronado was immediately apprised of the native uprising that had resulted in the loss of many Spanish lives. The captain-general responded by launching into a tirade about how he would hang any soldier who mistreated the Indians, and then he suffered a debilitating relapse.

Once his head had cleared, an ailing Coronado felt a sudden longing to once again see his wife. The commander also was resigned to the fact that he had been duped into chasing one chimera too many and therefore announced that he no longer intended to venture back to Quivira, but instead would return to New Spain. Several officers attested to this new directive, which effectively ended the expedition, by affixing their signatures to the hastily written order. The officers agreed to delay their return to Mexico City until Coronado was strong enough to travel.

Return To Mexico

Fray Juan de Padilla requested and was granted permission to remain behind to carry on with the conversion of the many heathens of this land to the one true faith of the Christians. The hopes and dreams of all who had joined this expedition were dashed by Coronado's decision to return to New Spain. With nothing to go home to after having invested all that they owned in the success of this mission, sixty soldiers petitioned the captain-general to remain behind with Father Padilla. Coronado refused their request to help the padre settle the land. The captain-general had authority over the soldiers but not the priests, all of whom answered to a much higher authority. He then decreed that the army would begin the march back to Mexico City, in the early part of April 1542.

Fray Luís de Escalano (aka Luís de Ubeda) and Fray Juan de la Cruz, both of whom were lay brothers, were permitted to stay with the ordained Fray Juan de Padilla. Two Indian "donados," lay brothers who were christened

Lucás and Sebastián, also chose to remain behind. A few black servants were also allowed to stay as was Andrés do Campo, a devout soldier of Portuguese descent. After being escorted to Cicique by twenty armed soldiers, Padilla and his comrades ventured on their own to Quivira, where they preached to a receptive native audience. Besides their efforts to enlighten the Quivirans, the friars secretly hoped to find the Seven Cities of Antillia, the legendary realm founded by seven devout Portuguese monks and their faithful followers.

Andrés de Campo would return to New Spain several years later to report that Juan de Padilla was dead. This ominous news was soon confirmed by the return of the two "donados," Lucás and Sebastián. Father Padilla, they said, was killed by a neighboring tribe he had hoped to convert, even though they were known to be bitter enemies of the Quivira. Luís de Escalano and Juan de la Cruz are believed to have suffered a similar fate.

In early April 1542, and shortly after Fray Juan de Padilla and his followers set off for Quivira, Coronado and his troops departed Tiguex and headed in the direction of New Spain. The silence of the march was broken only by the steady pounding of hooves and feet upon the sun baked earth and the clanging of Spanish armor. The somber journey home was marred by a mysterious ailment that afflicted the horses, a sickness that caused the death of more than thirty of their trusty steeds during the ten day march back to Cibola. The soldiers finally had a reason to rejoice once they came near the San Pedro River. It was here that they met up with Juan Gallego, an officer who was leading a company of reinforcements and hauling much needed supplies from Mexico.

Gallego was elated to see Coronado but disappointed to learn that the expedition had failed to realize the objectives and expectations that had been so great at the outset. Convinced that the additional supplies and men would rejuvenate the captain-general's spirits as well as his sense of adventure, Gallego appealed to Coronado to resume the search for the legendary cities of gold. Much to the chagrin of Juan Gallego and his hopeful troops, Coronado made it quite clear that he no longer wished to waste any more time or risk any more lives on such a fanciful quest and that his only desire at this point was to return to Mexico City. Juan Gallego and his men could see from the sorrowful look on the faces of those who accompanied Coronado that most of the soldiers felt the same way.

Coronado was still weak from the blow to his head and for much of the way home he had to be transported on a cowhide litter latched between two mules that advanced in single file. Coronado's army continued to march southward while accompanied by Juan Gallego and his troops. The soldiers came under attack during their return to Sonora, the region where many natives had suffered at the hands of the malevolent Diego de Alvarez. Guerilla attacks with poisoned arrows felled a number of horses, one of which was the horse ridden by Tristán de Arellano. The captain was in danger of falling victim to this assault but was rescued by the timely intervention of several comrades. One of the Indians who had killed Arellano's horse was captured and the officer exacted his revenge by cutting off the nose and hands of this guilty archer. The mutilated native was sent back as a warning to the others.

The Spaniards soon learned that Arellano's stern warning had failed to deter the warlike ways of their enemy. As the army entered a nearby pass, a soldier by the name of Mesa was suddenly struck by a poisoned arrow. His comrades did all that they could to try to save him. Quince juice had seemed to help in some similar instances but in Mesa's case it only prolonged his agony. For two hours he suffered the horror of watching the flesh around his wound decay and peel off. The rot started at his wrist and climbed to his shoulder before he finally succumbed to the inevitable.

Finding most of the natives of this region up in arms and fearful of another deadly encounter with warriors armed with poisoned arrows, Coronado decided it was best to alter their course. The army headed eastward to Batuco, which is in the vicinity of Corazones. Few felt safe until they finally reached Culiácan, where the expedition unofficially disbanded. Many of the soldiers had families at Culiácan and therefore preferred to remain there while Coronado and the remainder of the army continued on to Mexico City. Coronado began the last leg of his long journey home following a brief stopover for much needed rest.

Still feeble from his injury, Coronado was transported by litter to Compostela accompanied by what remained of his army. The flooded rivers of the region presented several new sets of danger for the returning Spaniards. A great many alligators lurked along the banks and one unsuspecting soldier found himself seized by one of these mighty beasts and swiftly dragged away and devoured before anyone could come to his rescue. On another occasion, one of the horses drowned while attempting to cross a badly flooded area.

Coronado surely relished the warm reception he was accorded at Compostela. Francisco de Goday, the provincial treasurer, presented him with a horse that had a gentle gait that would provide the captain-general a more comfortable and dignified entrance to Mexico City. Coronado agreed to take Goday's horse on the condition that it was received as a loan, which he pledged to bring back once he returned to fulfill his duties as governor.

The captain-general returned to Mexico City with less than one hundred soldiers. What remained of the expeditionary force was officially disbanded by Viceroy Antonio de Mendoza. Many accounts claim that Coronado was not well received by Mendoza but, given the close nature of their relationship beforehand, it is more likely that the viceroy's displeasure was reserved mostly for Fray Marcos de Niza. It was, after all, his glowing reports of the riches that awaited at the Seven Cities of Cibola that led to this expedition, a failed quest that resulted in the loss of numerous lives and the fortunes of many investors.

Coronado's expeditionary force had spent nearly two years trekking across the lands of Mexico, Arizona, New Mexico, Texas, Oklahoma, and Kansas only to discover that the golden realms of Cibola and Quivira were but an illusion. His return to Mexico City with the disappointing news that there was no gold, silver, precious stones, or magnificent cities to the north curtailed Spanish plans to conquer and colonize these lands. To settle these regions would have cost the Crown more than they could ever expect to receive in return. Coronado's official report to Emperor Charles V helped put to rest the rumors of finding another Tenochtitlan or Cuzco to the north of New Spain. The emperor, however, was still hopeful that Hernando de Soto would fare better in his quest.

Despite not having fully recovered from the severe trauma to his head, Coronado still felt strong enough to resume his duties as governor of New Galicia. Two years later, Coronado's judgment and honor were called into question when he was required to stand before a judge who had been sent from Spain to investigate the many failures associated with the Cibola expedition. He unexpectedly found himself the target of a changed political climate toward the treatment of the New World natives. Most of the charges brought against him centered around the complaints of those who were still bitter about not finding the fame and fortune they so desperately sought on this failed campaign. Thanks to the supportive testimony of Viceroy Mendoza and the loyal officers who served alongside him, Coronado was able to overcome the numerous accusations of criminal wrongdoing brought against him. García López de Cárdenas, however, was not as fortunate as his commanding officer. He was condemned for the brutal execution of the Tiguex warriors he had captured at Arenal, a conviction that deprived him of the opportunity to enjoy the benefits of his newly inherited wealth.

Francisco Vásquez de Coronado had, for the most part, proved himself to be a compassionate commander who was sincerely concerned for the welfare of his men and the natives who supported his efforts. He was never hesitant to praise his officers and never reluctant to give credit to those who were deserving. Unfortunately, Coronado never fully recovered from the damage done to his body, his finances, and his reputation. He passed away in 1554 at the age of forty-four.

De Soto Claims His Prize

Leaving Havana

Hernando de Soto spent a year at Havana, where most of his governing efforts were concentrated on preparing for his upcoming expedition to the mysterious lands of Florida. Not all who made the journey from Spain with Hernando would choose to continue the adventure across the waters that separated Cuba from the mainland of North America. Some deserted due to illness and others went into hiding after hearing the frightening tales of the previous ill-fated expeditions to the Florida region. Those who decided to remain at the island were replaced by Cuban colonists eager for a chance at finding gold and glory.

There were a large number of horses, dogs, mules, and pigs rounded up to accompany Hernando de Soto and his crew of conquistadors. The governor had a total of two hundred twenty-three horses stowed below the decks of his ships. Hernando was convinced that the horses, which were few in number on the previous expeditions, would mean all the difference between success and failure for his upcoming Florida campaign. After all, the horse had served him well during the conquests of Panama, Nicaragua, and Peru. De Soto introduced the pig to North America when he unloaded three hundred swine along the shores of Florida. The herd multiplied rapidly and numbered as many as seven hundred at one point.

The adelantado of Florida fully expected the tribes encountered along the way to provide sustenance for his large army and therefore brought just enough food to sustain them until a firm foothold had been established. De Soto also made sure to bring along plenty of iron collars and chains, a clear indication that from the very outset he planned to enslave Indians to serve the needs of his expedition. It was only a matter of time before those iron collars were clamped around the necks of subjugated natives and then attached to chains that bound several slaves together.

Shortly before setting sail, Hernando de Soto was reunited with his good friend Hernán Ponce de León, a fellow conquistador who served alongside him during many rewarding experiences in Nicaragua and Peru. These two soldiers of fortune were like brothers and this bond had led to the forging of a pact whereby each agreed that the earnings from their conquests were to be shared equally. Hernán was in the process of returning to Spain to enjoy the ample riches he had acquired in the New World when the sudden onset of foul weather forced his ship to drop anchor at Cuba. Ponce feared that his former partner would lay claim to his vast treasure to help finance his expedition to Florida and tried, but without success, to conceal the wealth he carried with him. De Soto assured Hernán that he had no intention of claiming his money and only wished for his friend to have an opportunity to invest and share in the riches that awaited at Florida. Hernán Ponce de León was supposed to sail to Florida with additional supplies and reinforcements after the governor departed. Instead, Hernando's former partner weighed anchor and sailed to Spain to enjoy a life of luxury. This was perhaps the most fortuitous choice that Ponce ever made.

While most accounts agree that Hernando de Soto left Havana on May 18, 1539, few sources seem to agree on the number of ships and troops that accompanied the governor. One report states there were five ships and two caravels that transported five hundred seventy conquistadors and colonists. Another account claims that de Soto sailed for Florida with nine boats: five ships, two caravels, and two brigantines. Garcilaso de la Vega claims that, according to his source, an anonymous conquistador who participated in this campaign, there were nine hundred fifty Spaniards and eleven ships that departed Cuba. Rodrigo Rangel and Gonzalo Fernández de Oviedo both assert there were seven hundred men who sailed with Hernando de Soto. It seems that the governor made sure to bring as many as ten longboats with him.

Shortly before leaving, Hernando de Soto named his wife, Dona Isabel de Bobadilla, who was the daughter of Pedro Arias de Avila, his former commander, as governess of Cuba during his absence. Fray Marcos and Esteban were already two months into their search for the Seven Cities of Cibola by the time Hernando began his voyage to Florida. While it is true that de Soto suffered from a lack of accurate maps and firsthand knowledge of those who had been to this region, the governor did, however, have in his possession the most up to date maps and the benefit of information supplied by Cabeza de Vaca. They certainly knew where they planned to sail. Juan de Añasco had already probed the Florida shoreline to find a suitable harbor for the ships to drop anchor. He even returned with several natives that the governor hoped could be trained to serve as interpreters. However, little was known about the interior of Florida, for most who ventured beyond the coast had failed to return.

Hernando's ships dropped anchor somewhere in the vicinity of Tampa

Bay during the late afternoon of May 31. The voyage from Cuba to Florida had been particularly difficult for the horses confined below the decks: as many as twenty horses are believed to have perished during this short trek. A squad of soldiers were sent ashore the following morning to see if there were any nearby Indians. The search party soon found what they were looking for. They encountered a small band of natives—probably Timucuan Indians—who were also on a scouting mission. Startled by the sight of these encroaching strangers, the Indians attacked the Spaniards with such swiftness and ferocity that the soldiers were forced to fall back to the water's edge. An alarm was sounded and a number of alerted soldiers rushed to the aid of their besieged comrades. The horse of officer Vasco Porcallo de Figueroa was felled by an arrow dipped in poison. Two warriors were killed before the rest retreated into the woods. Besides escaping with their lives, the Spanish scouting party returned with grass to feed the horses and some berries they had found in the woods.

The following day, which was the second of July, Hernando de Soto ordered his men to disembark. Everyone was ashore by the third day of July, at which time the governor officially laid claim to La Florida for Spain, the emperor, and himself. Since these lands had already been claimed for Spain and its ruler by both Juan Ponce de León and Pánfilo de Narváez, de Soto's claim to Florida was primarily for his own benefit. Shortly thereafter, the governor decided to lead one hundred of his soldiers in search of a better site to dock the boats and to establish a camp. Approximately eight miles north of where the ships were then docked, Hernando and his soldiers came upon the village of Ocita. A daring dawn raid resulted in the capture of the small village that was ruled by Hirrihigua, the disfigured chief who endured the many atrocities committed more than a decade earlier by Narváez. De Soto attempted to lure Hirrihigua out of hiding with gifts and promises but the chief was not about to be fooled again.

The nearby and more suitable harbor convinced Hernando that Ocita would make an ideal base to begin the conquest and settlement of the vast region that had been granted to him. The governor then sent orders for the rest of the troops to make their way to Ocita. While the passage by water went without difficulty, the journey by land was hindered by treacherous swamps and the thick growth of trees and shrubs. Once reunited, de Soto had his men unload the ships and store their numerous supplies at the village. After this task was completed, the governor decided to send his largest ships back to Havana to obtain additional provisions and recruits to aid in the conquest. As many as four ships were to remain at Florida.

The Timucuan Indians of Ocita and the surrounding lands shared many of the customs and practices that were common to the Mississippi cultures.

They were sun and moon worshippers who built earthen mounds to elevate their palaces and temples. The villagers lived in circular homes that were thatched with palmetto leaves. A mighty chief such as Hirrihigua often lorded over several villages. Their towns, however, were smaller than those of the Mississippian societies later encountered by the Spaniards. The Timucuans tattooed their bodies with etchings of creatures such as birds and snakes, which they considered sacred. The men, as well as the women, were quite tall. The lean and muscular males covered themselves with only a breechclout.

A Fortuitous Find

Hernando de Soto soon discovered that he was in need of interpreters and guides. Three of the Timucuans captured by Juan de Añasco during his reconnaissance mission had managed to escape shortly after the armada dropped anchor. This left Hernando with only one native to act as both interpreter and guide. The adelantado seized several natives to replace those who had abandoned him, but they purposely led the conquistadors astray in an effort to elude their captors. While camped at Ocita, the governor learned that a stranded Spaniard was living as a member of another tribe along the Florida coast.

Baltasar de Gallegos was instructed to take one hundred twenty soldiers, forty of whom were cavaliers, and scour the region for natives that could be pressed into service as porters, guides, and interpreters for the inland search for empires equal in magnificence and wealth to those forged by the Aztecs of Mexico or the Incas of Peru. It was also hoped that Gallegos would learn if there was any truth to the rumors about a Spaniard living among the natives. Led by their native guide, the soldiers soon happened upon a band of twenty or more Indians with faces painted bright red, a color commonly associated with war and death, the Indians were armed with bows and arrows. A chief by the name of Mucozo had learned of the arrival of the Spaniards and immediately sent out a scouting party to investigate.

The natives ran for cover once they had been spotted by the much larger Spanish scouting party. The horsemen gave chase and easily overtook four of the warriors as they attempted to flee across an open field. The cavaliers knocked three to the ground with their lances and as Alvaro Nieto was preparing to bring the fourth down in the same manner he was surprised to hear his intended victim cry out in Spanish, "Sirs, for the love of God and St. Mary do not kill me: I am a Christian, like you, and I am a native of Seville, and my name is Juan Ortiz."[1] The Spaniard, who was dressed, painted, and tattooed in the manner of the local natives, also begged the soldiers not to harm the others, for they were his friends. Alvaro Nieto put Ortiz on his horse and quickly brought him to Captain Gallegos who, in turn, made sure he quickly found his way to Hernando de Soto.

Even though Juan Ortiz was delighted to once again be in the company of fellow Spaniards, his return to Ocita surely forced him to relive many of the painful memories he had tried so hard to suppress. After having gone so long without speaking his native tongue, Ortiz found it somewhat difficult to carry on even a simple conversation with his rescuers. Cabeza de Vaca, who had been stranded with the natives of the New World almost as long as Ortiz, at least had other Spaniards he could converse with in Castilian. Hernando's troops made sure Juan was given plenty of opportunity to sharpen his speaking skills.

The soldiers were shocked to hear Juan's woeful tale of suffering imposed by a vengeful chief. He spoke of how he came to be a prisoner of Hirrihigua, the native ruler who was brutally tortured by Pánfilo de Narváez after being forced to watch his own mother savaged to death by a pack of ravenous Spanish dogs. Ortiz described the horrific way that his captured comrades had been executed by Hirrihigua and how he owed thanks to the chief's wife for being saved from the same dreadful fate. Her compassion, however, could not entirely save him from Hirrihigua's wrath. The ghastly scars that covered one whole side of his body, which he received when the chief had him roasted over an oven pit, was visible evidence of Juan's physical and emotional torment. He surely would have succumbed to this horrendous ordeal had it not been for the timely intervention of Uleleh, the chief's daughter, who helped him escape to the safety of a village lorded over by Mucozo, a chief she was pledged to marry. All who heard this tragic tale could not help but feel pity for Juan Ortiz.

Hernando de Soto was perhaps the most delighted of all to see Juan Ortiz reunited with his countrymen and embraced him as if he were a long lost son. After all, he now had an interpreter who was fluent in both Spanish and the tongue of the local natives. The commander could not help but view this as a promising sign. His experiences in Panama, Nicaragua, and especially Peru had taught him the value of a good and reliable interpreter. Only later did he learn, much to his dismay, that because each tribe spoke a varying dialect, communication with the natives would prove far more difficult than he had anticipated. An appreciative de Soto sent a message, which was delivered by two natives, to Chief Mucozo that expressed his deepest thanks to the ruler for his kindness toward a son of Spain and that he greatly desired to meet with him. Mucozo did come to meet with the Spanish commander, who warmly received him with much thanks and many gifts. Mucozo remained in the company of Hernando de Soto for a week, during which time he satisfied his curiosity about Spanish customs and learned more about the peculiar items they brought on their voyage across the water, especially their weapons.

Juan Ortiz told Hernando de Soto that he was familiar only with the surrounding regions and therefore knew nothing about cities or kingdoms where gold could be found. He had, however, heard mention of a tribe further inland that was ruled by a chief named Urriparacoxi who was so powerful that even Hirrihigua and Mucozo had to pay tribute to him. News of Urriparacoxi's empire and the fact that they now had a reliable interpreter were viewed as fortuitous signs by many of the Spaniards, especially Hernando.

Chief Hirrihigua, who remained hidden in the woods with his warriors, continued to refuse all Spanish overtures of peace. The probability that the fearful chief would reveal himself lessened once he learned that de Soto had met with Juan Ortiz and Chief Mucozo. Lieutenant General Vasco Porcallo de Figueroa was dispatched with a company of soldiers to apprehend the reluctant chief. Their native guide led them into the neck of the woods where there was a village in which Hirrihigua was most likely located. As they neared the settlement, Vasco Porcallo attempted to rally his men by leading the charge. Unfortunately, the commander was not mindful of his surroundings and quickly found himself and his horse slowly sinking into the muck of a large swamp. Other soldiers found themselves in a similar predicament but their dilemma was not as precarious as that of their commander, who had plunged into the quagmire first. Fearing they would suffer the same fate if they attempted to rescue their leader, the soldiers helplessly looked on as Vasco struggled to extricate both himself and his horse from the swamp's firm grip, which he finally succeeded in doing. The muddied Porcallo was disappointed to discover that the village where he expected to find Hirrihigua had been abandoned. The officer vented his frustration by ordering the village razed and putting to death their guide, who was torn to pieces by the powerful jaws of a greyhound.

Vasco Porcallo and Hernando de Soto exchanged words after the embarrassing incident in which the lieutenant general almost drowned in a swamp while pinned under his fallen horse. Hernando was perturbed by Vasco's inability to locate Chief Hirrihigua and Vasco was irritated by Hernando's inability to find gold or any other items of value. The elderly Porcallo decided that he had had enough of this dubious enterprise and asked for and received permission to return to Cuba. After resigning his command, Porcallo sailed home with the soldiers, slaves, and servants he had brought to Florida. He did, however, agree to leave behind the horses, armaments, and Gomez Suárez de Figueroa, his son by a Cuban woman.

Hernando de Soto now focused his attention on locating the realm of Urriparacoxi, and on the 20th of June he dispatched Baltasar de Gallegos at the head of one hundred eighty soldiers to pursue this new objective. Chief Urriparacoxi learned of their approach and immediately sent thirty emissaries to meet the Spaniards at a small village located along their route. These ambassadors came bearing gifts of maize and animal furs, which they presented to Gallegos while informing him that the treasure the conquistadors sought was not to be found in their lands but instead at a place to the north called Ocale. Baltasar was skeptical of this claim but decided to send four messengers back to camp to inform his superior of this new information. Believing that Urriparacoxi's envoys had freely provided them with promising news about Ocale, the governor sent Gonzalo Silvestre along with twenty cavaliers to inform Gallegos that the main army would soon join him.

The Spaniards had been camped at Ocita for roughly six weeks before Hernando decided to join up with the troops under the command of Baltasar de Gallegos. Before leaving Ocita, de Soto placed Captain Pedro Calderón in charge of a company of eighty soldiers, the remaining sailors, and forty horses to protect the supplies left at the village and the ships docked in the harbor. Calderón was also instructed to keep an eye peeled for supply ships from Cuba and to maintain the peace with the natives. Shortly after Hernando departed, a young man named Juan Muñoz, who was assigned to Calderón's command, was captured by Indians. Muñoz would spend the next ten years as a tribal slave until he was finally rescued by another Spanish expedition.

De Soto ventured first to the village ruled by Mucozo, which was roughly two leagues from the harbor, to say goodbye to the kind chief he looked upon as a friend and to ask him to keep a watchful eye on the soldiers he had left behind at Ocita. The adelantado also wished to thank Mucozo once again for shielding Juan Ortiz from the harm that Chief Hirrihigua intended to do him. Hernando gave Mucozo some Spanish armor as a show of his appreciation and the chief reciprocated by supplying the commander with natives who would serve as porters. Once all that had to be said was said, de Soto and his soldiers set off to join forces with Baltasar de Gallegos.

Native Resistance

Despite staying on the beaten path wherever possible, the Spaniards found the way to the realm of Ocale a more daunting undertaking than they had envisaged. The native trails were designed for travel by foot and because of this there were sections of the route that were extremely difficult for the horses to follow. Size also proved to be a factor: the narrow paths were created for only one or two persons to walk abreast. The expedition had to cross swamplands that were difficult for both man and beast to trudge through. The slow pace of the constantly foraging herd of pigs that accompanied the

Spaniards also hindered their progress. Even though pigs are generally good swimmers, they had to be ferried across the deeper and wider rivers and streams in order to avoid being swept away by the swift current. There was no food to be found along the way and what little the expedition had brought was rapidly diminishing. The insufferable heat of the region also weighed heavily on the armored Spaniards.

The Río de Mocoso was the first major obstacle the Spaniards had to overcome on this leg of the journey. Here they had little choice but to build a bridge in order to get to the other side of the river. De Soto had planned for such a contingency by making sure to bring along plenty of tools, nails, and an engineer by the name of Maestro Francisco. This may very well have been a lesson learned from Cabeza de Vaca when he spoke to him of the difficulties encountered by the Narváez expedition. Once across the river, Hernando and his army of conquistadors continued north toward the realm of Urriparacoxi.

The main army rendezvoused with Baltasar de Gallegos at the village of Luca. De Soto was disappointed to learn that Urriparacoxi had gone into hiding and all the conquistadors were disheartened to see that the village of this chief was smaller and less prosperous than they had been led to believe. The commander sent messages to Urriparacoxi expressing his desire for peaceful relations but the chief could not be coaxed out of hiding. The ruler had led his warriors deep into the woods where they were shielded by swamps that were, especially for horses, extremely difficult to cross. The chief was clever enough to realize that the surest way to rid himself of this invading army was to feed them stories of faraway lands rich with precious stones and metals. The blighted hope of the Spaniards was rekindled with the native tales of a wealthy province called Ocale. After a week of disappointment at the region ruled by Urriparacoxi, who was a brother-in-law of Mucozo, Hernando decided it was time to seek the riches that awaited at the province of Ocale.

Convinced that the Ocale province was near, Hernando took eleven mounted soldiers and pressed on ahead of the army. On the third day of their march to Ocale, the Spanish vanguard faced the formidable task of having to cross a treacherous swamp, a vast and muddy morass where one misstep could cause either man or beast to sink to their inescapable death. They had reached the swamp that they called Cale but which was most likely the Withlacoochee Swamp, the same quagmire that the Narváez expedition had previously found itself bogged down in. De Soto's predicament was compounded by a sudden attack from warriors who shot arrows at them from behind trees. Diego de Mendoza would succumb to a wound he received from this furious onslaught. A message was sent back to tell the main force to quicken their pace. Forty-five solders soon arrived to bolster Hernando's advance force while the rest of the army pushed ahead as fast as possible under such difficult circumstances.

The Spaniards managed to capture a few natives, all of whom were compelled to serve as guides. Just like the Indians pressed into service at Ocita, these guides purposely misled the conquistadors. This deception became painfully obvious when the natives led Hernando and his advance troops to yet another bog. A frustrated de Soto responded by feeding four of the captives to the dogs. One guide was forced to watch the others die so that he would know the terrible fate in store for him if he dared to lead them astray again. They soon reached the village of Uqueten where the famished Spaniards were able to fill their bellies on the maize that was grown in the surrounding fields. A significant amount of corn was collected and sent back to the troops who were still trudging through the swamps.

Once reunited, the army made its way to the central Florida province that was ruled by a proud and powerful chief named Acuera. As they approached the village that bore the same name as its ruler, Hernando sent a message to the chief requesting that he peacefully submit to his will. The mandatory Requerimiento was read aloud, which stipulated that the natives must become vassals of Emperor Charles V and accept the Lord Jesus Christ as their savior. The message closed with a promise to use force if these demands were not met.

Unfortunately for Hernando and his troops, the Indians of this region could still recall the numerous transgressions of the Spaniards who served under Pánfilo de Narváez. Seeking to avoid another unpleasant incident, Chief Acuera sent a reply to Hernando that emphatically warned him to stay off his lands. He also made it clear that he had no intention of ever submitting to Spanish demands, proclaiming, "I am king in my land, and it is unnecessary for me to become the subject of a person who has no more vassals than I. I regard those men as vile and contemptible who subject themselves to the yoke of someone else when they can live as free men. Accordingly, I and all of my people have vowed to die a hundred deaths to maintain the freedom of our land. This is our answer, both for the present and forevermore."[2]

Chief Acuera promised to wage war against de Soto and his men if his demands were not heeded. He punctuated this threat by stating that he had commanded his warriors to bring him the severed heads of two Christians every day for as long as the Spaniards dared to remain on his land. This ultimatum sounded to the governor as if the native ruler had something of great value that he wished to conceal from Spanish eyes, perhaps something as precious as gold. Hernando responded with a more conciliatory message that he hoped would persuade the chief to change his mind, but Acuera remained resolute in his defiance.

The warriors acted on the orders of Acuera to bring him the heads of the Christians once they saw that the Spaniards were not making any effort to leave their land. Two unaware soldiers were ambushed and their severed heads were laid before the feet of Chief Acuera. The horrified Spaniards buried the headless bodies of their fallen comrades, but that night the warriors returned. They dug up the buried bodies and proceeded to chop the corpses into many pieces, which they hung from the trees as a warning to de Soto and his troops. Two more soldiers soon suffered the same fate; they were decapitated and their grave sites defiled. After fourteen such gruesome deaths, Hernando de Soto decided the time had come to leave this wretched place. They marched away to the ominous threat of the natives, who cried out, "Advance, thieves and traitors, for here in Acuera and further on in Apalachee you will be treated as you deserve, since all of you, after being quartered and cut into pieces, will be hung on the largest trees along the road."[3]

With their pace quickened by a pervasive nudge of fear, the conquistadors soon reached the province of Ocale. They passed many small villages along the way before finally reaching the town that was their intended destination. The Spaniards discovered that the natives had abandoned their homes and gone into hiding once they learned of their approach. De Soto and his soldiers were disappointed to learn that there was no gold or silver to be found at Ocale. The only item of value was maize, which they found in quantities great enough to feed the entire army. The soldiers helped themselves to the food that had been left behind and enjoyed a much needed rest by taking comfort in the deserted huts.

Just as he had done with Chief Urriparacoxi, de Soto attempted to lure the ruler of Ocale out of hiding with the promise that he had come to their land with only good intent. The skeptical ruler responded that he was already familiar with the lies of the Spaniards and was well aware of the fact that their true purpose was to conquer and plunder. After six days and numerous messages the chief finally agreed to meet with the Spaniards. The ruler was permitted to return to his tribe once their cordial encounter had concluded, but only after he pledged to send some of his people back to aid the Spaniards in whatever capacity they required. It was a promise that the chief never intended to keep.

Perhaps the most rewarding sight beheld by the Spaniards during their brief stay at the province of Ocale was the opportunity to gaze upon the crystal clear waters of Silver Springs, one of the largest limestone springs on earth. The Indian name for Silver Springs is Sua-ille-oka, which means "sun-glinting water." Since Ocale appeared to be a region of little material promise, Hernando decided to lead the expedition to Apalachee, the hostile region he had learned about from the survivors of the Narváez expedition. De Soto hoped that Apalachee would yield enough food to replenish their rapidly dwindling supply and provide him with an opportunity to take revenge against the tribe that had chased off Narváez's troops. More likely than not, Hernando had convinced himself that the reason the Apalachee were so aggressive was that they possessed something worth risking their lives to protect.

As he had done so many times before, Hernando de Soto decided he would personally scout out the region ahead. He set off in search of Apalachee with fifty cavaliers while Luís de Moscoso was left in charge of the army at Ocale, which was busy preparing to follow the lead of their commander. De Soto was guided simply by the knowledge that Apalachee lay to the north, a direction that coincided with the path of the Indian trail they were following. The main army was instructed to remain several days to the rear of Hernando's scouting party.

Four days after setting out from Ocale, a patrol led by Juan de Añasco happened upon a group of natives who were busy tending to their cornfield. Añasco and his cavaliers swooped in and captured many, all of whom were immediately brought back to Hernando. Shortly thereafter an Indian of regal appearance strode into the Spanish camp. The man told de Soto that he was the chief of the tribe that inhabited these lands and he had come before the Spaniards to offer himself in exchange for the release of his many subjects. To sweeten the offer, the ruler promised to provide the conquistadors with food and drink to fill their bellies and guides to lead them wherever they wished to go. Preferring the advantage of having a chief as his hostage, Hernando agreed to this offer and released the captured natives.

The following day the Spaniards were shocked to see a large number of armed warriors gathering near the village. The usually intuitive Hernando failed to realize he had been duped by an impostor. The real chief had been busy gathering his forces while the man who pretended to be him was cleverly negotiating the release of his loyal subjects. The trickster kept up his act by volunteering to go and speak to his people. Convinced that the tense situation could be diffused with a few reassuring words from their chief, the governor permitted his lone hostage to leave with several Spanish guards by his side. Once he was near the assembled warriors the charlatan suddenly turned on his escorts and, after stunning the soldiers with his violent actions, he ran toward his people. De Soto saw what happened and released a hound that alone was responsible for bringing down the runaway native, an act performed so swiftly and frighteningly that it caused the warriors to disperse out of fear. As for the captured impersonator, one can only assume that he suffered greatly for having dared to deceive the Spaniards.

With nothing further to gain from the village that Hernando called Mala Paz, or "Bad Peace," the conquistadors continued on to the river now known as the Santa Fe. The recent heavy rains had caused the river to swell to a width and depth that could be crossed only with the building of a bridge. A dispute between the commander and some of his officers regarding their present course seems to be the reason that this overflowing river came to be called El Río de las Discordias, "The River of Discords." By adhering to the plans of Maestro Francisco and utilizing the abundance of wood that was there for the taking, the Spaniards were able to build in just three days a bridge strong enough for the men and horses to cross.

One day after crossing the river, Baltasar de Gallegos, who had been sent to scout the land ahead, succeeded in capturing seventeen Indians, one of whom happened to be a princess. Soon thereafter, Chief Aguacaleyquen met with Hernando to beg for the freedom of his beloved daughter. He promised to provide the Spaniards with whatever they might require and even offered to take her place. When the chief failed to provide, as promised, guides who knew the way to Apalachee and interpreters who could aid Juan Ortiz, de Soto decided he would keep both the father and the daughter. Aguacaleyquen's warriors began massing in large numbers when they realized that the Spaniards were not going to release either the chief or the princess. Finding himself greatly outnumbered, the governor sent a message back to Luís de Moscoso urging him to come to their aid as quickly as possible. Fortunately for Hernando de Soto and his small band of soldiers, the natives merely meant to intimidate the Spaniards into surrendering their ruler and his daughter.

The entire army left Aguacaleyquen's province shortly after de Soto and Moscoso were reunited. Their date of departure was the ninth of September. The chief and his daughter traveled with the Spaniards, both of them compelled to serve as guides and human shields for the conquistadors. This heartless act seemed to set a precedent for the remainder of the expedition. Upon entering a new village, Hernando would attempt to seize the chief and other nobles for the purpose of extorting food and items of value. The soldiers would continue to the next village with their hostages, most of whom were granted their release once they had taken sufficient hostages from their new location. Native guides, who were treated no better than the other captives, were used to locate the next village that could furnish the army with additional food, valuables, and slaves. In the instance of this captive chief and his daughter, the warriors of Aguacaleyquen continued to follow the Spaniards in the hope of finding a way to liberate them. De Soto eventually granted the chief and his daughter their freedom but not until he was within reach of another village that could adequately provide for him and his men.

The conquistadors reached the village of Ochile (aka Uzachile), which was ruled by a chief of the same name and who, according to Garcilaso de la Vega, shared power over the region with two brothers. The Spaniards announced their arrival at this frontier outpost, which protected the border of the province from its neighboring enemies, with the blaring of trumpets and fifes and the banging of drums. The natives who came out to investigate the strange clamor were seized and held hostage as the Spaniards laid siege to the fortified village. The Gentleman of Elvas wrote that many of the native villages they encountered before Apalachee were protected by a palisade: "The enclosure, like that in the other towns there afterward, was of thick logs set solidly close together in the ground, and many long poles as thick as an arm placed crosswise. The height of the enclosure was that of a good lance, and it was plastered within and without and had loopholes."[4]

De Soto sent messages to the barricaded chief that promised no harm would come to him or any of his people if he surrendered his village. However, should the chief dare to deny him this request, then, the governor pledged, the full fury of the conquistadors would be unleashed against him. This, he vowed, would commence with setting fire to the town. Realizing that the chief was not intimidated by his bombastic threats, and not wanting to destroy a village that surely had food and possibly even items of value, Hernando decided he would send several hostages to testify they had been treated kindly by the Spaniards. This tactic achieved the desired result and de Soto's troops were permitted to enter the village the next day, which they did with much fanfare and ceremony.

True to his word, Hernando treated Chief Ochile and his subjects with much kindness and respect. His benevolence was most likely prompted by the realization that this village was part of a much larger province subject to the rule of Vitachuco (aka Uriutina), a mighty chief who was also the older brother of Ochile. Thanks to the help of Ochile, de Soto was able to persuade yet another brother who ruled another tribe, and whose name has long been forgotten, to submit to his will. Messages of peace, however, were not as well received by Vitachuco, the oldest and most powerful of the three brothers. The chief made it clear that he had no desire to befriend the Spaniards and emphasized that he would welcome the opportunity to punish those who had dared to trespass on his lands.

Chief Vitachuco was also the spiritual leader of his tribe and it was in this capacity that he promised to protect his people from harm by summoning sacred spirits who were to unleash a host of natural catastrophes that would prevent the Spaniards from ever setting foot in his village. Vitachuco vowed to cause the earth to open wide enough to swallow his enemies whole and to impel the hills to clash until all were buried beneath the ground. If these calamities were somehow overcome, the chief promised to command the wind to uproot trees and fling them at the Spaniards like spears and pledged that the birds above would rain down a toxic venom that would poison the waters and the ground, which would cause the intruders to suffer a slow and agonizing death.

Hernando de Soto learned of these brash threats uttered by Chief Vitachuco and decided to call his bluff. When the natural disasters that were supposed to halt the advance of the Spaniards failed to appear, Vitachuco sent a message that declared if de Soto and his men persisted along their present course he would seize every one of them and promised they all would die screaming while being slowly baked or boiled over a fiery pit built just for them. The conquistadors continued their advance, fully expecting that at any moment they would have to defend themselves against an attack. Hernando decided to send to Vitachuco the two chiefs who had welcomed the Spaniards as friends in the hope that they could persuade their elder brother to be more receptive to his peaceful overtures.

All of the conquistadors were taken aback when Chief Vitachuco suddenly altered his belligerent tone and announced that he now desired to have a cordial meeting with the chief of the Spaniards. The ruler set off in the company of his two brothers and five hundred well-armed and finely attired warriors to meet with Hernando de Soto. Vitachuco and his large entourage met the governor and his army along the path that led to his village. The chief offered up apologies for the many threats he had made and invited the Spaniards to enjoy the hospitality of his tribe.

Vitachuco, however, was simply feigning friendship in order to lure the Spaniards into a trap. The scheming chief confided to four native attendants who served Hernando de Soto that it was his plan to gain the full confidence of the Spaniards and once their guard was down he would order his warriors to fall on them. It was Vitachuco's wish that most were to be taken alive so he could savor the extreme suffering they would endure as punishment for having the audacity to ignore his commands. As previously promised, many captured Spaniards were to be boiled or roasted alive. Several were to be buried up to their necks, leaving their heads exposed to the wrath of nature. Some soldiers were slated to die by poisoning and others were to be hung by their feet from the tallest tree to serve as fodder for the birds. For their help in achieving this end, the chief promised to reward the four natives with freedom, wives, or whatever else they might desire. After the natives agreed to help his cause, Vitachuco then informed his nobles of the plot that was set to unfold. The four newly recruited conspirators, however, broke their promise to the chief and told the details of the sinister scheme to the interpreter Juan Ortiz, who in turn informed the governor. De Soto then assembled his captains to advise them of his measures to counteract this threat. The conflict that the Spaniards had hoped to avoid was now inevitable.

It was Vitachuco's plan to create a state of confusion among the Spaniards by seizing their commander during his upcoming inspection of the troops. Hernando now planned to use the same tactic against the cunning chief. The conquistadors surprised the warriors by attacking first. Twelve soldiers immediately seized the chief and shielded him from the battle that raged all about them. The warriors put up a valiant fight but, as was often the case in such confrontations, native weapons were simply no match for the steel and firepower wielded by the Spaniards. Add to this advantage the might and maneuverability of the horse and it becomes easier to understand why the larger force of warriors, which one source estimated to have swelled to ten thousand strong, was forced to make a hasty retreat. A multitude of natives were slaughtered while trying to escape the fury of the Spaniards. Many fleeing warriors sought shelter in a nearby lake but soon surrendered when they realized that their enemy was prepared to wait until they dared to make a move. After fourteen hours of treading water, nearly nine hundred cold and exhausted natives chose to surrender and were held as prisoners of war, which meant the Spaniards were legally entitled to use them as servants and porters. The imprisoned Vitachuco managed to get a message passed to the other captives commanding that on a designated day, hour, and signal they were to attack the Spaniards with whatever means were at hand.

As a veteran of many campaigns in the New World, Hernando de Soto could not help but admire the bravado of the proud Chief Vitachuco. Given that the other brothers had shown their willingness to befriend the Spaniards, the governor decided to try to win the eldest chief over with an overt show of friendship and respect. Most likely Vitachuco reminded the Spanish commander of Atahualpa, the Inca ruler he had come to know and admire after his capture and imprisonment by Francisco Pizarro.

Vitachuco pretended to accept Hernando as his friend until an opportune moment presented itself to enact his plan for revenge. That moment arrived when the chief was invited to share food and drink with Hernando de Soto and several officers. Once the meal was finished and all were preparing to relax, Vitachuco suddenly stood up and began stretching and contorting his body with such force that his bones could be heard to snap and pop. The officers believed he was putting himself into a deep trance in order to perform some sort of ritualistic dance. The entertained Spaniards watched as the chief began to sway back and forth. Vitachuco clenched his fists and flapped his elbows as if he were summoning an animal spirit that would transform him into a mighty bird. The gait of the chief slowly straightened and once fully erect he suddenly lunged at Hernando. The chief firmly grabbed the collar of the startled governor with his left hand while he repeatedly pummeled the face of his sworn enemy with the fist of his right hand. The seated officers looked on in disbelief as the enraged chief continued to bloody the face of their helpless commander. De Soto fell to the ground unconscious as Vitachuco continued to beat him while letting out an ominous bellow, which was the signal for the other captives to follow his lead. It was then that the startled officers finally came to their senses and rushed to the aid of their fallen leader. It took a dozen sword thrusts to permanently extinguish the rage of Vitachuco.

Recognizing the cry of Vitachuco as their signal to attack, the captive natives grabbed sticks, pans, the chains that bound them, and whatever else was available to attack their captors. They were able to severely beat many of the Spaniards before the uprising was crushed. All who participated in the revolt were put to death by the victorious conquistadors. Hernando remained unconscious during most of the fight. Blood streamed profusely from his battered eyes, ears, and mouth. Those who feared the worst were greatly relieved to see their commander regain consciousness after a half-hour. Besides the wounds to his face and pride, de Soto suffered the loss of two teeth.

13

Pearls before Swine

On to Apalachee

Five days after the failed attempt to assassinate Hernando de Soto, the Spaniards left the village of the fallen Vitachuco and headed off in search of the neighboring province of Osachile. By this time the commander had partially healed, though his face was still badly bruised and swollen. A march of four leagues brought the conquistadors to the banks of a river that served as a natural boundary between the two native provinces. Hernando had his troops make camp along the banks, where they set about to build another bridge to get them across yet another river. Their attempt to cross was nearly foiled by a sudden barrage of arrows shot by a slew of warriors concealed in the fields on the other side. The Spaniards succeeded in driving off their attackers and once this nuisance was removed they were free to resume their march to the main village of Osachile.

The conquistadors marched for nearly two leagues over an open field before reaching a cornfield, which to the hopeful Spaniards was viewed as a sign that they had reached the domain of a more civilized people. This increased, at least in their minds, the likelihood of finding the precious metals that were dearest to their hearts. Their sense of elation was soon shattered by the realization that they were not alone. Osachile, the chief who bore the same name as his province and village, had learned of their approach and had the women and children seek refuge in the surrounding woods while his warriors took cover in the cornfields where they would attempt to halt the advance of the intruders. The Spaniards suddenly had to shield themselves from a torrent of arrows that seemed to come at them from every direction. Several soldiers were severely wounded as they desperately fought their way through a dense field that made it extremely difficult to see their enemy. Strength and courage enabled the beleaguered conquistadors to overcome yet another obstacle. De Soto and his men entered the abandoned town of Osachile, one of many native villages they would encounter on their journey that built mounds to elevate their sacred temples and the homes of their elite nobles.

Hernando sent messages to Chief Osachile that pledged all was forgiven; he added that he merely wished, in the true spirit of friendship, to meet with the chief. The answer was understood to be *no* when the messengers failed to return when expected. Frustrated by this rebuff, de Soto ordered his soldiers to capture as many natives as possible. A number of Osachile's subjects were rounded up and placed "in chains with collars around their necks" and thereafter forced to serve as porters for the conquistadors. The threat of death was constantly employed to motivate these bearers, who were referred to as tamemes. When a chained native grew too weary to carry his own weight, a Spanish soldier simply lopped off his head, a deadly blow that permitted the torso to slip from the collar without having to stop and unlock the chains that kept him in his place. The severed head and body were left where they happened to fall. The train of porters was halted just long enough to distribute the items of the deceased tameme among the other shackled Indians. Hernando would exert much time and effort in finding natives to replace the porters who were executed in such a horrific manner, or those who had run away in an effort to avoid suffering a similar fate.

The fierce response of the Florida natives from the time they had set off in search of Apalachee seemed to provide Hernando de Soto with the excuse he needed to inflict the harsh treatment he now believed was necessary to ensure the success of his mission. The fact that the hostility they encountered from the Indians of this region was mostly a response to the transgressions of the previous Spanish expedition was given little consideration. The brutal beating that Hernando suffered at the hands of Vitachuco also contributed to his growing sense of disdain for those he had come to view as little more than savages. This lack of compassion, combined with the frustration over failing to find anything of value, gave rise to the committing of additional Spanish atrocities, which included the killing of Indians simply for sport. Native women who were pleasing to the eyes of the Spaniards were baptized so the men could satisfy their salacious desires with righteous Christians and not with godless heathens.

The Spaniards spent only two days at the village of Osachile before setting off for Apalachee, a region the natives had told them was not very far away. Four days of marching brought the expedition to the edge of a large swamp that rested beneath the shade of a dense forest. Thanks to information provided by the survivors of the Narváez expedition, this was but one of many obstacles de Soto anticipated encountering during this stage of his expedition. He knew that this large and treacherous swamp had to be crossed in order to reach Apalachee. He was also aware of the fact that the hostile Apalachens had found ways to use the swamp to their advantage when they forced Narváez and his troops to make a hasty retreat to the coast. With these thoughts in mind, the governor sent one hundred foot soldiers on ahead to probe for a passable route, especially for the horses, and to make sure they were not about to walk into an ambush.

The natives of Apalachee were well aware of Hernando de Soto's approach and had taken steps to make sure that he did not have the same opportunity to harass their people as Pánfilo de Narváez had during his campaign. The Apalachee were somewhat familiar with Spanish weapons, tactics, and the capabilities of the horse following their violent encounter with the previous Spanish expedition. They knew to keep their distance while striking fast and hard with their longbows. The warriors were quick to realize it was the horse that gave their enemy superiority on an open field of battle and they therefore used the forest and the swamps to help neutralize this advantage.

The Spanish reconnaissance party followed a narrow trail that led them directly into the line of fire of warriors who had taken cover behind the surrounding trees. The soldiers could not help but notice that many of the arrows seemed to target the horses. De Soto and the rest of the troops rushed to the aid of their besieged comrades and a fierce, full-scale battle ensued. Losses steadily mounted on both sides as the fight was carried into the water. The Apalachee warriors eventually withdrew from the battle, leaving the battered and weary conquistadors to contemplate their next move as they made camp.

The next day a narrow path beneath the water was discovered and Hernando sent a company of foot soldiers on ahead to blaze a trail for the rest of the troops and horses. Armed with crossbows and arquebuses for protection and hatchets and axes to clear the brush and branches that barred the way, the advance party of Spaniards slowly waded through waist deep water to get to the other side of the swamp. As the narrow path forced them to march in single file, the soldiers were thankful that the warriors did not contest their crossing. De Soto and the remainder of the army had little trouble following the trail cleared by the others and therefore were able to quickly catch up with their comrades. Their reunion coincided with the reappearance of Apalachee warriors determined to protect their homeland. Now that they stood on firmer ground, the Spaniards had an easier time defending themselves and, after much effort, were able to force their adversaries to withdraw. With renewed confidence, the conquistadors pursued the retreating warriors to a clearing where, thanks to the quickness of the horses, they were soon able to overtake their enemy. The Spaniards gave no quarter and when the battle was over the field was left littered with a great many slain warriors.

The victorious Spaniards made camp for the night but were prevented from getting much rest, thanks to the constant interruptions of the surrounding warriors who whooped, hollered, and shot arrows at them from a safe distance. The next morning de Soto and his troops resumed their march toward the main village of Apalachee. The terrifying thought of being way-laid at any moment was compounded by the dire warnings of the captured natives, all of whom claimed that the chief of Apalachee was expecting the Spaniards and planned to either kill or enslave every one of them. The path led the soldiers to a ravine where they were ambushed by warriors who had taken cover in the dense forest. A desperate fight ensued during which several conquistadors were killed and a great many were wounded before Hernando and his soldiers could claim victory.

The Spaniards would have to endure several more skirmishes during their trek to Anhaica, the prominent town of the Apalachee province. After so many hostile encounters, the conquistadors were relieved to find Anhaica deserted and still intact. The village, which stood where the city of Tallahassee now stands, had been ordered abandoned by Capafi, a chief who was large in both stature and girth. The conquistadors made themselves at home in the numerous round thatched houses of Anhaica and helped themselves to the stores of food that had been left behind. But the fulfillment of these basic needs were of little consolation for those who were disappointed to discover there was nothing that could satisfy their pecuniary desires. Hernando sent messages to Capafi, the ruler of the region, but the chief could not be persuaded to come out of hiding. His only response was the continual harassment of the Spaniards by his warriors.

Using this deserted village as his base, Hernando sent out three expeditions to see if there were any towns richer than Anhaica, which had certainly proved disappointing in the extreme. Captain Arias Tinoco and Captain André de Vasconcelos led their scouts along separate trails, both of which led northward, while Captain Juan de Añasco ventured south with ninety soldiers, forty of whom were cavaliers, to find the sea and to locate a suitable harbor for the ships still docked at Tampa Bay. Those who trekked northward returned after a week to report that they were unable to locate any large cities or learn the whereabouts of any precious metals. They did, however, happen upon some villages where the people grew crops, which the commander took as a sign that the civilizations he sought were still further inland.

As for Captain Añasco and his troops, their progress was slowed by the swamps and the thick undergrowth that made it increasingly difficult, especially for the horses, to proceed. They were guided by a native of Apalachee who had volunteered to show the Spaniards the quickest way to the coast, a route that was somewhat off the beaten path. However, Añasco and his soldiers became suspicious of their guide when it seemed that he was steadily leading them away from the faint sound of the distant surf. The Indian led them further into a dense forest where he secretly hoped the conquistadors would waste away from the lack of food and the rigors of such an arduous journey. Frustrated that these men were proving stronger than he believed, the guide turned on one of the soldiers and struck him in the face with a burning piece of wood used to fuel the campfire. Such an infraction would have normally meant a swift and brutal end for such an offender but Captain Añasco, who did not relish the thought of continuing on without a guide, decided to spare him from such a punitive measure.

Shortly thereafter, the Indian guide repaid Añasco's kindness by attacking another Spaniard in the exact same manner, an unprovoked assault that this time did not go unpunished. Even after receiving a severe beating delivered by the vindictive hands of several soldiers, the determined guide once again tried to harm yet another conquistador. This time the defiant guide was shackled in heavy chains while forced to continue leading the Spaniards toward the coast. Sensing the hopelessness of his predicament, the guide used the chains that bound him to try to strangle the man assigned to watch over him. It took the combined strength and swords of several soldiers to keep the spiteful Apalachen from satisfying his grudge against the Spaniards. This time, however, there would be no pardon from a benevolent commander. Captain Añasco, who was counted among those delivering a steady round of punishing blows, decided he had had enough of this native's treachery and unleashed one of the trained attack dogs, who viciously tore away at the bloodied torso of the guide until his screams were silenced forever.

Unsure of which route to follow, the lost Spaniards decided that their only hope of recovering their bearings was to try to retrace their steps. The path they followed soon led to the village of Aute, where Añasco and his weary men found a few Indians who were willing to lead them to the coast. True to their word, these natives promptly guided them to the seashore by following a path that was free of any major obstacles. As Añasco and his troops probed southward along the coast in the hope of finding a suitable harbor for de Soto's ships, they happened upon a chilling sight. They discovered an area where the ground was littered with the bleached skulls and bones of horses and other items that were evidence that this was once a Spanish camp that had met with a terrible disaster. They also found some rotting native canoes that had been stored along the shore. From what they saw with their own eyes and what they heard from their knowledgeable guides, the Spaniards were able to correctly ascertain that this was La Bahia de Caballos (the Bay of Horses), the very spot where the starving and wounded soldiers of the Pánfilo de Narváez expedition had built rafts in a desperate attempt to reach New Spain. Many of Añasco's men surely must have wondered if a similar fate was in store for them.

Juan de Añasco returned at once to Anhaica to report his findings to Hernando de Soto, who decided that La Bahia de Caballos would make an excellent harbor to serve as a link to the port at Havana. De Soto then sent Añasco and a company of soldiers back to Ocita to instruct Pedro Calderón and his men to make their way to Anhaica. Juan was expected to steer the ships to the bay he had just discovered while Hernando and the rest of the soldiers sat out the winter at Anhaica. The dutiful captain and his thirty cavaliers raced to Ocita, traveling as fast as they could over difficult terrain and resting as little as possible in order to avoid the steady sling of arrows directed at them. Their travels brought them back to the village of Vitachuco, the home of the defiant chief who administered a severe beating to the face of Hernando de Soto. The Spaniards were surprised to find the town burned and abandoned. A search of the area led to the discovery of a mass of dead bodies piled and left to rot. Añasco and his men soon resumed their journey to Ocita. They continued to suffer numerous hardships along the way, including a mysterious ailment that claimed the lives of two cavaliers while they were still seated upon their horses. They eventually found their way to Ocita, where the soldiers were glad to hear that de Soto and their comrades were still alive but disheartened to learn that the expedition had failed to locate any magnificent cities awash with items of wealth.

Shortly after he had dispatched Añasco and his cavaliers to Ocita, Hernando de Soto learned where Chief Capafi was hiding and decided to lead a company of men to try to apprehend him, a capture that the Spaniards hoped would bring an end to the incessant guerilla attacks they had been forced to endure ever since they had laid claim to this village. After much effort, the soldiers succeeded in capturing the chief and brought him back to Anhaica. Much to the consternation of the conquistadors, the Apalachens, who were greatly angered by the seizure of their revered ruler, increased their assaults against the Spaniards, attacking any and all who made the mistake of venturing too far from camp.

The governor sought the aid of the captured Capafi by beseeching him to use his influence to bring a halt to the escalating violence. The chief told his captor that he would have to deliver such a message in person, otherwise his people would not believe these were his true words. Convinced that Capafi realized there were benefits to both sides by calling for a truce, Hernando had a company of soldiers escort the chief to a place where he was to meet with several other nobles. A brief meeting took place between twelve Apalachens and Capafi, after which the ruler assured the Spaniards that those he met with would carry de Soto's message of peace to the others in hiding. The Spaniards relaxed their guard following such comforting news. That very night, the corpulent Chief Capafi managed to escape by crawling on his hands and knees until he was reunited with those he had schemed with at the meeting.

Soon after Juan de Añasco and his troops reached Ocita, a ship under the command of Gomez Arias was dispatched to Havana to inform the governess, Dona Isabel de Bobadilla, and the citizens of Cuba that the expedition was gradually making progress and of the governor's plan to establish an outpost at La Bahia de Caballos, which is also known as the Bay of Aute. Meanwhile, Pedro Calderón and his company of one hundred twenty soldiers prepared to comply with the instruction to join up with Hernando de Soto at Anhaica while Juan de Añasco readied the remaining vessels to seek the Bay of Aute, which they would successfully find by closely hugging the coast.

Captain Calderón and his soldiers experienced few difficulties in the march to rejoin their commander, that is until they entered the realm of Apalachee, where the conquistadors had to fend off frequent and vicious Indian attacks that were both physical and verbal. The warriors taunted the soldiers by shouting, "Since we have already slain your captain and all of his soldiers, where are you thieves going now?"[1] As no one from the governor's camp had come out to greet them, the Spaniards had good reason to fear that the claims of the Indians were true. A dozen of Calderón's men and seven horses succumbed to the wounds and the fatigue of such a difficult crossing before finally finding their way to Anhaica. De Soto and his troops were delighted to see them, for they had been led to believe by the taunts of the Apalachens that they had been ambushed and killed in the woods.

Shortly after reaching the Bay of Aute, Juan de Añasco set off to rejoin Hernando de Soto while the mariners stayed behind to keep watch over the docked boats. Once Añasco returned to Anhaica to report on the success of the mission, de Soto decided to send Captain Francisco Maldonado to the Bay of Aute to take command of the brigantines and venture another hundred leagues along the coast to locate other suitable harbors and to search for rivers that might be a gateway to the rich kingdoms they sought. Maldonado was given two months to complete this task.

During Maldonado's absence, Hernando and his officers continued to inquire as to where they might be able to find any gold or silver. Their luck finally appeared to change when they obtained the services of a captured and enslaved native lad by the name of Perico who spoke of a fabulous kingdom that was a fortnight's journey from Anhaica. Perico, who was thought to be around seventeen years old, said he was originally from a place called Cofitachequi, a distant realm that was ruled by a powerful empress who had grown rich off the tribute periodically paid to her by a great many other tribes. He claimed that besides an abundance of gold and silver, Cofitachequi had large storehouses filled with lustrous pearls. This story was confirmed by another captive native who claimed to know this region well. Hernando and the rest of the conquistadors were delighted to hear that there was finally a native kingdom worthy of their best efforts and gave thanks that they had a guide who was willing to lead them there. While all were eager to set off for Cofitachequi, de Soto decided to wait for Maldonado to return before undertaking a new quest. After all, this commander did not want to make the same fatal mistake that Pánfilo Narváez did when he rushed off in search of rich empires without knowing precisely where his boats were docked.

After sailing sixty leagues up from the Bay of Aute, Captain Maldonado found a harbor that appeared as if it might serve as an excellent port for Spanish vessels arriving from Cuba to support the launch of new expeditions to locate the rich inland kingdoms just waiting to be discovered. There are some accounts that speculate this site was Mobile Bay but, given the recorded distance from the Bay of Aute, Pensacola Bay seems the more likely spot reached by the two brigantines. Maldonado captured two Indians from the town of Achuse (also spelled Achusi, which was located near the harbor), who had come out to greet the Spaniards. Adhering to the directives of his commander, Maldonado returned to Anhaica to report that he had discovered an excellent harbor that could safely support many ships and to present the two natives who might serve the future needs of the expedition.

Hernando de Soto was pleased with Diego Maldonado's findings and entrusted the loyal officer with yet another task: He was to take the two brigantines back to Havana to inform the governess of their progress since the earlier report issued by Gomez Arias and to procure more men, horses, and provisions for the next stage of the conquest, which was to include the establishment of a permanent settlement. Unless he heard otherwise, Diego was expected to return to Florida after sixth months. Once at Havana, Captain Maldonado was warmly received by Dona Isabel de Bobadilla, who was delighted to hear that her husband was well and that the expedition was proceeding as planned. She made sure that he received all that was required to ensure the continued success of her husband's mission.

Meanwhile, de Soto and his troops would spend the next five months battling the cold as well as recurrent attacks by Apalachen warriors determined to drive the Spaniards off their homeland. Two soldiers who sought to relieve their boredom and satisfy their taste for something sweet made the fatal mistake of climbing a nearby tree to collect some of the succulent fruit it bore. Surprised by the sudden attack of a band of warriors, one soldier was shot through the back with an arrow as he desperately tried to escape. The other hapless soldier was riddled with arrows while still sitting in the tree and once he fell to the ground the Apalachens removed his scalp, a native practice that horrified the Spaniards.

It was during their stay at the province of Apalachee that the Spaniards abandoned the chain mail they typically donned to protect their bodies. This decision was made after having witnessed a demonstration provided by an

Apalachen archer who, at fifty paces, was able to put an arrow clear through a basket cloaked in their protective gear. These longbows, which were nearly as tall as a man, had bowstrings strung so taut that many of the soldiers found it nearly impossible to pull them back far enough to launch an arrow. A display of the might of this weapon was called for after Luís de Moscoso was wounded during a confrontation while strapped in his armor. After the powerful force of this weapon had been substantiated, the natives helped de Soto's men make quilted armor — similar in style to that used by the Aztecs and adopted by Hernán Cortés and his men during the conquest of Mexico — that was less cumbersome and offered better protection against the longbows that launched arrows capable of piercing armor.

Onward to Ocute

It was toward the end of March 1540 before Hernando de Soto was ready to lead his troops out of Anhaica to begin the much anticipated search for the magnificent stores of treasure that awaited at Cofitachequi. The Spaniards collected as much maize and other food items as they could possibly carry for the long journey ahead. Because so many of their native slaves had perished from the hardships of their forced labor and exposure to the cold temperatures, the conquistadors were now forced to haul the bulk of their supplies themselves. Fortunately for the Spaniards, the Apalachens made their departure easier by not launching any further attacks. De Soto and his men were also grateful to have the young Perico to guide them to the rich realm of Cofitachequi.

The conquistadors had to cross marshes that were natural breeding grounds for leeches, mosquitoes, ticks, alligators, and poisonous snakes such as coral, copperheads, and even rattlesnakes. After a difficult three day trek through treacherous marshlands and dense forests, Hernando and his troops came to the recently abandoned village of Capachequi. The famished soldiers helped themselves to the stores of food that had been left behind. The commander decided to make camp at this location for the next few days in order to give the men and the horses a brief but much needed rest. It was during this period that a band of seven soldiers were sent out on patrol and not far from camp suddenly found themselves under attack from a band of Capachequi warriors who were also out on patrol. Five Spaniards were killed during this confrontation, most being felled by the initial onslaught of arrows. Francisco de Aguilar was saved by soldiers from camp who, upon hearing the commotion, rushed to his aid while he was still desperately fighting for his life. The men were shocked to see that besides arrows still embedded in his thighs, Aguilar's hair and skin had been stripped from the top of his head to reveal a bald and bloody skull. The natives retreated and Aguilar was brought back to camp where his wounds were tended to. Andrés Moreno, the seventh soldier, who suffered numerous arrow wounds and had been left for dead by the warriors, was found alive but soon succumbed to his injuries.

Hernando de Soto and his army left this hostile region and soon entered the realm of the Mississippian chiefdoms, which were inhabited by natives far more civilized than any they had encountered up to this point. As a precautionary measure, the commander made it a point to send messengers ahead to inform the chiefs that he had come to their land in the spirit of friendship, which was his customary way of learning whether or not the natives were friendly. Juan Ortiz continued to serve as de Soto's trusted translator, but his effectiveness as an interpreter gradually waned the further the expedition ventured from the coast of Florida. Since each village seemed to have its own dialect, the string of interpreters grew larger as the expedition continued and consequently misunderstandings inevitably occurred.

The Spaniards crossed the southern region of Georgia, where they soon reached the town of Toa, the size and magnificence of which greatly impressed the wandering conquistadors and convinced them that they were finally on the verge of finding the great cities they so desperately sought. When the chief of Toa learned of the approach of the Spaniards, he ordered his people to seek refuge while several nobles remained behind to learn the true intentions of these intruders. Through Ortiz and a lengthy line of interpreters, Hernando was able to convince the native nobility that his army meant the citizens of Toa no harm and that they were merely passing through their lands in order to reach Cofitachequi. De Soto appreciated the warm reception he received from these natives but was anxious to resume his quest. However, the soldiers, especially those who traveled by foot, did not share their commander's eagerness. Weary from the long and difficult journey, they simply wished to remain there long enough to rest their bodies and fill their bellies before heading off on the next leg of the journey.

The restless Hernando de Soto took forty horsemen and continued northward to explore the region ahead while his troops rested at Toa. The scouting party soon reached the realm of Ichisi, a native kingdom also referred to by various participants and historians as Achese, Altapaha, or Chisi. The first village encountered had little to offer in the way of value to de Soto and his men except for some much needed food and a few apprehended natives who might suit their purpose. Hernando knew that the tribes of these lands were devout sun worshippers and decided to exploit their religious beliefs by drawing on his experience with the Incas of Peru, who truly believed they were children of the sun god Inti. After the mandatory Requerimiento was read aloud, the commander sought to win the respect and allegiance of the natives by declaring that he was a "son of the sun and came from where it dwelt."[2] Once he learned that the main village of Ichisi was still a good way off, de Soto sent a message back to Toa that ordered the army to join him at once.

The expedition proceeded to the town of Ichisi once the forces were reunited. The Spaniards were guided by several natives who were familiar with the way to the capital of this province. A hard rain slowed their progress considerably but their determination helped them prevail over the elements. The Spaniards were delighted by the warm reception they received from the inhabitants of the outlying villages, many of whom came out to greet them with offerings of food and drink. De Soto and his troops were escorted to the town of Ichisi, where they were warmly received by the chief, "who was one-eyed." While he had no precious metals or stones to satisfy the rapacious desires of the conquistadors, the chief was able to console them with a bountiful offering of food and guides who could lead them to Ocute, a chiefdom to the north that he claimed was far wealthier than his. Eager to see what awaited at Ocute, Hernando spent just one day at Ichisi, which was long enough for his men to erect a large wooden cross on one of the ceremonial mounds.

A three day march brought Hernando de Soto and his troops to the neighboring province of Altamaha. They were greeted along the way by emissaries of Chief Camumo, who in anticipation of their arrival had ordered a nearby village abandoned and stocked with a great quantity of food to satisfy the Spaniards. War canoes were provided to carry the soldiers across the Oconee River to meet with the chief. According to Rangel, the Spanish commander presented his gracious host with "a large feather colored with silver," a gift that the chief said he would cherish forever. Camumo told Hernando that he paid tribute to a powerful chief named Ocute and wondered whether he should now pay tribute to de Soto instead. Hernando replied that he considered Ocute a brother and that Camumo should continue paying tribute as before until he commanded otherwise.

The Spanish commander sent a message to Ocute that requested the chief's presence at Altamaha. Chief Ocute accepted this invitation and on the seventh of April he met with Hernando de Soto at the village lorded over by Camumo. De Soto presented the compliant Ocute with "a hat of yellow satin, and a shirt, and a feather"[3] and the grateful chief reciprocated by inviting the Spaniards to the town that bore the same name as his. The Christian soldiers erected a large wooden cross upon one of the Altamaha mounds before setting off for Ocute.

A two day march along the banks of the Oconee River brought Hernando and his army to the principal town of Ocute. Here the Spaniards were presented with a vast array of gifts, much of which was fish and game for the soldiers to feast upon. Though impressed by the size of the town and the magnificence of the reportedly six sacred mounds, the Spaniards were once again disappointed to learn that there was no precious gold, silver, or gems to be found. The chief, however, offered encouraging words regarding the wealth that awaited at Cofitachequi, which he said was not very far away. For the next five days, the chief made sure the Spaniards had adequate food and shelter, and Hernando de Soto expressed his appreciation by erecting another large Christian cross.

The Spaniards left Ocute on April 12 in the company of four hundred armed warriors who helped to lighten the load of the conquistadors by serving as their porters. The chief offered to guide the expedition part of the way to the province lorded over by Cofaqui, an elderly ruler who had strong blood ties to Chief Ocute. Before returning home, Ocute sent a message to Cofaqui, in which he informed the neighboring chief that the Spaniards had shown themselves to be very courteous. This news was accompanied by a request from Ocute that Cofaqui show the Spaniards every possible courtesy. Such an eloquent introduction paved the way for a friendly reception for de Soto and his soldiers. Cofaqui came out to greet Hernando with his nephew, whom the aged chief had relinquished much of his power to, and an entourage of nobles, all of whom were regally attired with large colorful feathers and elegant capes and animal skins.

Hernando told Chief Cofaqui that he was bound by the orders of his chief, the Emperor Charles V, to explore all the lands thought to be part of La Florida and that it was his wish to visit next the rich region of Cofitachequi. The chief confirmed the stories of the great wealth that was housed at the neighboring province but added that the natives of that realm were their sworn enemy. He also warned the Spanish commander that the warriors of Cofitachequi were extremely fierce fighters. Cofaqui proceeded to tell de Soto that their realms were separated by a vast wilderness that would take as many as seven days to cross.

In addition to giving his guests plenty of corn and dried fruits to replenish their nearly exhausted food supply, Chief Cofaqui provided the Spaniards with additional porters. The armed natives in Hernando's ranks swelled to somewhere between eight hundred and twelve hundred, a number deemed suitable enough to safely escort him and his men to the region said to be home to an abundance of gold, silver, and pearls. De Soto took note of the rivalry that existed between the neighboring tribes and hoped to use their discord to his advantage. Unfortunately, Hernando failed to realize that he was the one being used: Ocute and Cofaqui had supplied him with many warriors for the purpose of waging war against Cofitachequi, a victory they believed would be assured by the addition of this imposing Spanish force.

Into the Realm of Cofitachequi

A noble by the name of Patofa, who served as Cofaqui's war chief, volunteered to lead the way for the Spaniards. Hernando de Soto, who felt fortunate to have another guide in addition to Perico who knew the way to Cofitachequi, gladly accepted Patofa's offer. The Spanish commander was unaware of this chief's true agenda, which was to lead his warriors on a campaign to exact revenge for a past transgression they attributed to their neighbors at Cofitachequi.

The expedition hadn't ventured very far before a heated dispute erupted between Hernando's two guides. Patofa questioned Perico's choice of direction as well as his claim that it would take just three or four days to reach the boundary of Cofitachequi. De Soto continued to place his full faith in Perico, the enslaved lad who claimed he was from that region. Since the neighboring realms did not carry on commerce with one another, there were no direct paths for the Spaniards to follow. Perico led them along an old trail that passed through several villages that were both small and inconsequential, a disappointing sight that caused many a soldier to question the native stories that this was a region laden with gold, silver, and pearls. After nine days of seemingly aimless wandering, a visibly frustrated Hernando summoned Perico and threatened to have him thrown to the dogs unless he could tell him precisely where the rich kingdom he had spoken of was located. Perico confessed that he was lost. All that saved him from being ravaged by the bloodthirsty hounds was his worth as an interpreter who knew the Muskogean dialects, which he translated to the Timucuan tongue for the benefit of Juan Ortiz, who, in turn, interpreted into Spanish for Hernando. However, Perico's value to the mission could not save him from being bound in heavy chains.

Many of the warriors provided by Chief Cofaqui had grown weary of Perico's wandering ways and begged Patofa to allow them to return to their homes. After all, dying at the hands of their sworn enemy was considered honorable but to die of starvation in the wilderness was simply foolish. The equally disillusioned war chief presented the concerns of his warriors to the Spanish commander. As a sign of respect, de Soto did agree to consider Patofa's request. In addition to worrying about rationing his rapidly dwindling food supply, Hernando was concerned that such a large number of native auxiliaries might incite the ire of the people at Cofitachequi. After a moment's thought, the governor decided he was not yet willing to acquiesce to Patofa's request to return to Cofaqui. Convinced that Perico's confusion about the way to Cofitachequi stemmed from the fact that he had not been this way for a long time, de Soto decided to give the chained guide another chance to find his way home.

Four more days of roving through the woods failed to reveal the whereabouts of their intended destination. Their food supply was now precariously low and there was little to be found along the way to feed so many mouths. The expedition was hopelessly lost. Even Patofa was unsure of which way to proceed, for he rarely ventured so far from home. Many began to suspect that Perico was purposely leading them astray. Sensing that the patience of the conquistadors had been tested to the limit, the guide came up with a clever way to save himself: Perico claimed he was possessed by a demon. The guide put on a convincing show for all to see. He dropped himself to the ground and began rolling back and forth as if in great torment. One account says that the guide even began to foam at the mouth. The performance was persuasive enough for Hernando de Soto to summon a priest to perform a hasty field exorcism. The padre succeeded in casting out Perico's chimerical spirit, but this did not change the fact that the expedition was stranded along the banks of a river with little food and no idea of which direction to follow.

Having reached the point of desperation, de Soto and several horsemen went on ahead to scour the region, hoping to at least find a village that could provide the troops with much needed food. After venturing nearly twenty miles without encountering a single encouraging sign, the commander returned to camp to discuss with his close circle of officers their extremely precarious predicament. The primary concern was that the food supply was nearly exhausted. They all realized that to turn back now would entail following a route they knew had nothing to offer in the way of sustenance, which, of course, meant many would starve to death before ever escaping this inhospitable wilderness. The general consensus was it would be better to take a chance on continuing forward. In an effort conserve what little food he still had on hand, Hernando decided the time had come to permit Patofa and his large entourage to return home.

Unsure of which route to follow, the governor provided four of his trusted captains with eight horsemen apiece and then sent each group off in a different direction to search for Cofitachequi or a village that could provide them with food. Juan de Añasco searched downriver, Baltasar de Gallegos probed upriver, and Juan Lobillo and Alonso Romo ventured inland in opposite directions. A cleansed Perico was permitted to join one of these scouting missions. Hernando would remain at the river's edge, where he would tend to the morale of the rest of the troops while patiently awaiting the return of his captains. At this point, the Spaniards found it necessary to slaughter several of the pigs that traveled with them in order to satisfy their ravenous appetite.

Captain Añasco and his men returned after two days to report that they had found a small village that was roughly a dozen leagues away. As proof of his discovery, Añasco brought back some food from this village as well as a native woman and boy who dwelled there. Since their supply of food was precariously low, Hernando de Soto decided it was too risky to wait for the return of the three other expeditions and therefore gave the order to march to the village. De Soto made sure to leave a message that informed the others of the direction they were headed. The Spaniards marched as quickly as possible toward Himahi, a village also referred to as Aymay. Unfortunately, the lateness of their start and the weakness in their legs forced the Spaniards to make camp just a few miles short of their intended destination. Luckily for them, they happened to make up camp where there was a great store of maize and edible berries.

Captain Alonso Romo and his men managed to rejoin the expedition the following day. They were accompanied by four or five captured natives, all of whom were dragged before de Soto for interrogation. The Spanish commander questioned them as to the exact whereabouts of Cofitachequi and when they refused to talk he had them all tied to stakes and then set one on fire to demonstrate his resolve to learn the answer to this question. When the fiery death of their comrade failed to loosen the tongues of the others, a frustrated Hernando de Soto had them all burned at the stake. Captain Baltasar de Gallegos showed up the following day with a woman captive who claimed to know the way to Cofitachequi. Captain Juan Lobillo and his soldiers returned that same day to report having followed a northward road where he received word that the chieftainess of the realm they sought was aware of the Spaniards' presence and eagerly awaited their arrival. The governor was probably surprised to learn that many tribes of this region functioned as a matrilineal society — noble status being determined by the bloodline of the mother rather than of the father. Hernando immediately dispatched a message to the queen of Cofitachequi to inform her highness that his men would make haste to visit her fair city.

The Kindness of a Princess

Encouraged by the words of welcome from Cofitachequi's ruler and the fact that they now had a guide who knew the way to this promising province, the Spaniards pressed on with a renewed sense of spirit and purpose. On May 1, 1540, after two days of trekking across difficult terrain, the weary conquistadors reached a river — which is believed to be the Wateree River near the present site of Camden, South Carolina — that separated them from the town they had been seeking for more than a fortnight. Words of peace were conveyed to a gathering of natives on the opposite shore and they quickly carried this message back to their village. Shortly thereafter, a canoe carrying a

The Indian princess of Cofitachequi presenting a necklace of pearls to Hernando de Soto.

delegation of six emissaries paddled across the river to ascertain whether the Spaniards came to their land as friend or foe. Hernando de Soto made sure they understood that his army meant them no harm, a choice of words that obviously pleased the emissaries. He also stressed the fact that his soldiers were in dire need of food. This request did not elicit the response that the governor hoped to hear. They replied that because of a terrible pestilence that had ravaged their land the previous year, the people of Cofitachequi barely had enough food to satisfy their own needs.

Shortly after the delegation carried Hernando's message of peace and request for food back to the village, the Spaniards noticed a large canoe rowed by several men headed directly toward them and towing another large canoe. The second canoe carried a woman who appeared to be of such importance that many Spaniards believed they were about to be greeted by the queen of Cofitachequi herself. She sat regally upon an elegant litter, her face obscured by a thin veil of white cloth. Seated alongside this royal figure were eight women thought to be her ladies in waiting. Once ashore, the curtains of the litter were slowly pulled back to reveal a young woman of exceptionally fine appearance. She welcomed Hernando de Soto to her land by presenting him with a "large strand of pearls as thick as hazelnuts which encircled her neck three times and fell to her thighs."[4] The grateful commander returned the favor by plucking from his finger a gold ring set with a large ruby, which he offered to her as a pledge of his friendship.

Hernando soon learned that this young woman was not the queen, but instead a relative — most likely a niece — of the empress. The Spaniards either failed to learn or had a difficult time pronouncing her real name and thus respectfully addressed her as Senora. She was fondly remembered by the soldiers as the Lady of Cofitachequi. When de Soto made his habitual demand for food, the royal emissary apologized that she would be unable to fully honor his request, which she blamed on a mysterious malady that was the cause of much suffering and had claimed the lives of a great many of her people. Her woeful words seemed to confirm what the other emissaries had previously told him. The Lady of Cofitachequi promised that the soldiers would have access to a store of corn equivalent to six hundred bushels, but she could spare no more lest her own people might starve. She also extended an invitation for the Spaniards to visit her town, where temporary lodgings would be provided for all.

The Lady of Cofitachequi furnished a small fleet of canoes to transport Hernando de Soto and his army across the river. The current of the Wateree, however, proved too strong for several horses, seven of which — according to one eyewitness account — drowned while attempting to cross the river. Even though the town and the surrounding region had fallen on hard times, the Spaniards were impressed by the magnificence of Cofitachequi, and many felt that they were finally going to be rewarded for all their travails. The plague that had recently decimated the region might very well have owed its origin to diseases introduced by the ill-fated expedition of Lucás Vázquez de Ayllón, which had landed along the Carolina coast several years earlier.

The lingering question that needed answering for the Spaniards was where all the gold and silver was that the natives had said could be found at Cofitachequi. De Soto ordered the guide who had bragged about the abundance of precious metals that could be found in this region to ask the Lady of Cofitachequi if she could bring some for them to see. She complied with their request by commanding several of her subjects to round up some metallic items that resembled the gold and silver jewelry worn by the conquistadors. These natives eventually returned with a large quantity of copper that had a golden hue and slabs of mica that shone like silver.

Despite their disappointment over the misunderstanding regarding which metals were considered precious to them, the Spaniards took consolation in the knowledge that there were plenty of elegant freshwater pearls similar to those presented by their hostess to Hernando de Soto. The Lady of Cofitachequi pointed to a nearby temple and said, "That structure is the burial place of the nobility of this town. Within it you will find large and small pearls and in addition many seed pearls. Take what you want, and if you still desire more, they may be had in a place a league distant which is the residence and family seat of my own ancestors and the principal village of our province. In that town is a still larger temple which is the burial place of my kinsmen. Within it you will find so many seed pearls and pearls that you will never be able to remove them all even though you load each of your horses and as many of your own selves as may come. But take them, and if others are necessary, then we can obtain more and more each day in the pearl fishing that is done in my land."[5]

De Soto and approximately thirty of his officers and royal officials went to investigate the treasured belongings of the sacred temple. All took note of the rather imposing life size statues that stood guard over the temple's entrance, each of which brandished menacing weapons. Once inside, the Spaniards were surprised to see a large collection of items that were quite familiar to them. They saw rosaries with crosses, two axes similar to ones made by Europeans to chop wood, and glass beads like those commonly used by Spanish explorers to barter with the natives. The also noticed several chests of Old World design that now served as coffins for deceased Cofitachequi nobles. The natives admitted that many of these items were from an abandoned colony near the coast and not far from their town. It was generally assumed that these were salvaged remnants of the failed settlement of Lucás Vázquez de Ayllón. In spite of these distractions, the conquistadors were pleased to see that the Senora had not exaggerated her claim regarding the vast quantity of pearls housed at the temple. Hernando and his men estimated that this one temple held more than twenty-five thousand pounds of lustrous pearls.

After taking a few moments to revel in his first rewarding discovery, Hernando de Soto decided they should immediately set off to learn what treasures awaited at the other temple mentioned by the Lady of Cofitachequi. Many soldiers were disappointed to learn that their commander planned to relieve the temple of only a little more than three hundred fifty pounds of pearls, fifty of which was earmarked for shipment back to Havana to serve as proof that there truly were riches to be found in this land. Since at this point they were still in search of native cities that rivaled the wealth of Tenochtitlan or Cuzco, Hernando thought it prudent not to burden his troops with a heavy treasure that they could easily claim upon their return. After all, the temples were sacred sites and therefore would remain untouched. Unable to sway the governor's mind, the soldiers tried to take comfort in the thought that the inhabitants of Cofitachequi would continue to deposit more freshwater pearls at the charnel house during their absence.

A march of little more than a league brought Hernando and his companions to Talomeco, a large town that they found abandoned. The temple was easy to spot: the roughly one hundred foot long and forty foot wide structure had a cane and reed roof that was decorated with numerous shells and pearls. Once inside, the Spaniards saw that the ceiling was designed in a manner similar to the roof. There were, however, more statues at this temple, most of which were carved in the likeness of well-armed and gallant warriors. Of course, the most rewarding sight was the vast quantity of freshwater pearls that had been continually collected and deposited at the temple for almost as long as the tribe had lived in this land. This treasure trove of lustrous pearls greatly exceeded the find at the first temple. Once again, the soldiers were disappointed to learn that their commander intended to delay the plundering of the temple until their return from the quest that still had to be completed.

After realizing that there were few other rewards to be had at Cofitachequi, Hernando decided the time had come to resume his search for those elusive cities paved with gold. A number of soldiers felt it would be best to remain at Cofitachequi long enough to found a settlement that might serve as a base for future expeditions. But de Soto was quick to veto such a plan. They had been at this province for nearly two weeks, which was far longer than Hernando had originally intended to stay. The commander was determined to locate a chief he had been told ruled over a rich and mighty province called Chiaha. De Soto also hoped that at some point the expedition would happen upon the supply ships that were slated to be dispatched from Havana, a task he had entrusted to Francisco Maldonado. Baltasar de Gallegos and a portion of the army would remain at Cofitachequi for a few more days to collect additional provisions while Hernando and the majority of the army marched off in search of the gold they were told could be found at Chiaha.

From this point on, there are conflicting accounts regarding the relationship that existed between Hernando de Soto and the Lady of Cofitachequi. Given his undignified penchant for using native rulers as a human shield while making his way across their province, it is reasonable to assume that Hernando forcibly persuaded the Senora to serve in a similar capacity. Such a request was surely sweetened by an offer to grant the Lady of Cofitachequi her freedom once the expedition had safely passed the border of her land.

14

ACROSS THE WIDE MISSISSIPPI

The Bloody Battle of Mabila

On the morning of May 13, 1540, Hernando de Soto assembled his troops to begin the march to the promising realm of Chiaha. The addition of several natives to help lighten the heavy load and the Lady of Cofitachequi to shield them from anticipated Indian reprisals helped to ease the nagging doubts that were gnawing away at the spirit of the conquistadors. The abduction of the Senora would also help fulfill many basic needs of the Spaniards: Hernando instructed her to command the nobles at the towns they visited along the way to furnish his army with food, shelter, guides, and additional porters. The expedition continued northward before veering westward to explore the mountain regions. The guides led them down a path that would eventually deposit the expedition at the foothills of the Appalachian Mountains, which de Soto deemed to be a fortuitous sight. Here he expected to find rich and powerful cities similar to Cuzco and Quito, two large Inca cities that were perched upon the slopes of the Andes, or discover another Tenochtitlan, the magnificent Aztec city that was nestled in valley of a surrounding mountain range in Mexico.

It was at the French Broad River Valley, located at the far edge of the Cofitachequi domain, that the expedition suffered an incalculable loss. It was here that the shackled Lady of Cofitachequi asked for a moment of privacy in the woods without her chains so that she might properly relieve herself. The Spaniards granted the Lady her wish. Several soldiers were sent to retrieve the Senora after the patience of the conquistadors had been tested by her long absence, but all they discovered was that everyone had been duped by her charming demeanor. Unconvinced that the Spanish commander would keep his word and release her once they reached the border, the Senora, along with several loyal subjects, had planned her escape for quite some time. With her shackles removed, the lady of Cofitachequi had little trouble keeping up with those who safely guided her through the woods and back to their village. Some accounts claim that she made her escape on the 26th of May with a Spanish slave, and these tales are divided over whether he was a baptized Indian or African, whom she supposedly took as her lover.

Hernando's troops would spend fifteen days resting their horses and themselves at Xuala, a town that shared the name of a sparsely populated province that was a vassal state of Cofitachequi. During this time and shortly thereafter, as many as six soldiers took the escape of the Lady of Cofitachequi as their cue to also desert the expedition. Two of these deserters were captured but the records are silent regarding the severity of their discipline. More likely than not, the two were put to death as a means of discouraging any further breakdown in the chain of command. Baltasar de Gallegos and the rest of the troops rejoined Hernando de Soto at the town of Xuala.

The next leg of the journey deposited the Spaniards at the town of Guasuli (aka Guaxule), which they reached on the 30th of May. De Soto and his men were relieved to find themselves warmly welcomed with a bountiful offering of food, a simple but nutritious fare that included dog meat and a variety of corn dishes. A four day march from Guasuli brought the expedition to their intended destination of Chiaha, an island town that rested upon a river. Once again, Hernando and his men were well received by natives who willingly shared their food and offered them shelter. But once again, the conquistadors were disappointed to discover that tales of a faraway rich kingdom had failed to live up to their lofty expectations. There was no silver or gold to be found anywhere, only more stores of freshwater pearls. The chief of Chiaha was kind enough to provide the governor with a demonstration of how they removed the pearls from their shells, which was accomplished by placing the oysters over a fire until the heat caused the shell to expand. The one disadvantage to this ingenious method was that the high temperature often caused a noticeable discoloration in the pearl.

As was often the case, the conquistadors managed to overstay their welcome. The Spaniards remained at Chiaha for nearly a month, and during this time the Indians endured without complaint a seemingly ceaseless list of demands from their guests that grew more excessive and tiresome with each passing day. An exasperated chief drew the line at Hernando's demand that he provide him with thirty young and attractive women to satisfy the salacious desires of his troops, particularly those of the officers. Because their reputation as fierce warriors had preceded them, the chief was understandably wary of challenging the conquistadors to combat. Instead, the ruler commanded his people to abandon their town in the hope that the unruly Spaniards would also leave. Angered by their refusal to honor his request, de Soto ordered his soldiers to destroy the surrounding fields and then sent cavaliers to flush out and round up the natives. Unable to force the Indians out of hiding, the Spanish commander coaxed them to return to their homes by promising to forgive their actions and to forget his unseemly demands. Hernando also pledged to leave Chiaha at once, his only condition being that the chief supply him with a number of men to serve as porters.

De Soto adhered to his pledge to depart Chiaha once he had been provided a sufficient number of Indians to carry the brunt of the expedition's supplies and provisions. On June 28, 1540, the Spaniards renewed their hunt for rich kingdoms to claim. This time, the search was for a Mississippian empire called Coosa, after which Hernando hoped to rendezvous with the ships under the command of Francisco Maldonado. The path they followed passed through Coste (aka Acoste), a province that bordered Coosa. As the army set up camp a short distance from the main town of Coste, de Soto took eight soldiers with him to meet with the chief. While the commander was busy paying his respects and negotiating for food to feed his troops, a few soldiers slipped away and committed an egregious error in judgment by helping themselves to some corn stashed at the royal storehouse. Caught in the act, the thieves found themselves the recipients of a harsh beating delivered by several greatly angered warriors. The bloodied and frightened looters were dragged before the chief, who was still conversing with the Spanish commander. The offended ruler, who was backed by several thousand warriors sporting colorful headdresses and brandishing a deadly array of weapons, demanded from an embarrassed Hernando de Soto, who had but a handful of unarmed men at his side, an explanation for such insolent behavior. Realizing the situation was rapidly spiraling out of control, the governor remained calm and used his wits to come up with a way to quell the looming crisis. He chastised the guilty soldiers with a powerful acting performance, which surely drew upon his own frustration over the thoughtless action of these men, that satisfied the chief and thereby averted a confrontation between the tribe and his men.

Hernando and his men were permitted to return to their camp. However, according to one account, instead of being grateful for having barely escaped harm, the commander decided that, regardless of how terrible the behavior might have seemed, these natives deserved to be punished for having dared to lay their hands on a Spanish soldier. A surprise raid resulted in the capture of the chief and several warriors, all of whom were held against their will just long enough to instill fear and respect for the might of the Spaniards and to ransom whatever provisions, especially food, that they needed for the long journey ahead. Another popular chronicle of this episode paints a more harmonious picture, one in which the chief of Coste freely provided the Spaniards with much needed food after granting them permission to cross his land without fear of harm.

Though the Spaniards were thankful to have escaped Coste without the loss of any men, many were surely disappointed over their failure so far to find any of the magnificent cities they had hoped to find in the mountains. All, including Hernando de Soto, clung to the hope that Coosa, a vast chiefdom spread throughout the northern regions of Alabama and Georgia, would turn out to be the realm that fulfilled their great expectations. The actual location of the principal town of Coosa is a subject of much debate among historians. Some say it was located near present day Childersburg, Alabama, while others place the town at Carters, Georgia. It is generally agreed that the realm of Coosa had eight major towns, all of which were accentuated with a number of large earthen mounds.

A seven day march brought the Spaniards within a half mile of the capital of Coosa. It was here that they were unexpectedly greeted by the chief of Coosa, who was held aloft on an elegant litter while graced by the presence of many nobles. The chief had learned of the conquistadors' approach and had come out to welcome them to his land and offer the hospitality of any village they should happen to pass through in his province. Garcilaso de la Vega wrote that this was a cordial meeting between the two leaders, even claiming that the chief begged him to establish a settlement in his land. He goes on to say that the governor declined this generous offer, presumably after having concluded that Coosa had little to offer that would satisfy his avaricious desires. The Gentleman of Elvas and Rodrigo Rangel, however, remember this meeting quite differently. They report that, after being given food and shelter, their ungrateful commander repaid the generosity of his native host by taking him prisoner. Startled by this unexpected betrayal of trust, many natives sought shelter in the surrounding woods, but most were quickly rounded up by the Spaniards.

It was on the 20th of August that the restless Hernando de Soto resumed his search for the elusive kingdoms of gold that still awaited his discovery. Under the protection of the chief and his sister, and with the additional company of many native porters, the Spaniards were able to proceed through the province of Coosa with relative ease. Their biggest hindrance during this stage of the journey was having to wait several days for the swift current of the rain fed waters of the Coosa River to subside until it was safe for the soldiers and horses to cross. De Soto and his troops headed southwest, stopping to refresh themselves and replenish their supplies at several towns that were subject to the omnipotent chief who accompanied the expedition. At the town of Ulibahali the local chief was persuaded to provide the Spaniards with additional porters and to part with between twenty and thirty women to serve as concubines. The expedition suffered the loss of Francisco Rodríguez el Manzano, a common soldier, and Joan Vizcaíno, an African slave, during this stopover at Ulibahali. Both seized upon an opportunity to desert the expedition and take their chances living among the natives.

The Spaniards finally reached the boundary of Coosa on the 16th of September, at which point they entered the province of Talisi. A two day march brought de Soto and his troops to the principal town of Talisi, which they found deserted. They were soon greeted by a delegation of nobles sent by Tascalusa, a powerful lord of the region. One of the ambassadors was Tascalusa's son, an eighteen year old prince who towered a head above most of the Spaniards. The tall and dignified prince told the governor that he had come on behalf of his father to welcome the Spaniards to his land and to invite them to enjoy his hospitality at the town of Atahachi. When the commander agreed to meet with Tascalusa, the prince said to him, "My Lord, although it is no more than twelve or thirteen leagues to the place where he now is, there are two routes. I beg Your Lordship therefore to have two Spaniards go there by one route and return by the other in order that they may ascertain which is the better for your use. I myself will provide guides to direct these men and bring them back safely."[1] Hernando agreed that this was a wise course to follow and sent Juan de Villalobos and another soldier to observe which was, especially for the horses, the surest route to the town of Atahachi.

Once the two soldiers returned from their brief reconnaissance, Hernando de Soto permitted the chief of Coosa to return to his homeland but did not show the same courtesy to the chief's sister, who was retained as a human shield. After a stay of ten days at the town of Talisi, the expedition — under the guidance and protection of the young prince — headed toward the town of Atahachi. By following the recommended route of Juan de Villalobos, the expedition was able to reach its destination by the 10th of October.

Once the village was in sight, Hernando dispatched fifteen soldiers to officially announce their arrival to Tascalusa, a mighty chief who held sway over a great many tribes. The Gentleman of Elvas describes Tascalusa as "very tall of body, large limbed, lean and well built."[2] The chief was as tall, if not taller, than his son and therefore stood as a giant among the Spaniards. The chief seemed little impressed with either the soldiers who came to pay him homage or the horses that they rode upon. Sensing that his presence was required, de Soto soon arrived but was disappointed to see that the proud Tascalusa paid him little mind, which he demonstrated by not even bothering to rise and greet the Spanish commander. The chief chose to assert his authority by letting the Spaniards do all the bowing and talking. After all the salutations were completed, Hernando, who was used to dealing with native royalty, stepped forward and greeted the chief in a respectful manner that was met with approval from Tascalusa.

A grand feast accompanied by lavish dances and other assorted entertainment was held to celebrate the arrival of the Spaniards. At the conclusion of the banquet, Hernando put a damper on the festivities by demanding that the chief provide him with a number of men to serve as their porters and a number of women to nurse their manly needs. Tascalusa defiantly replied that he did not take orders from others but others took orders from him. The Spanish commander then decided the time had come to teach this proud chief who really was in charge here. That evening de Soto had the ruler of Atahachi imprisoned in the palace that had been provided for the comfort of the Spanish officers. It was an order that the governor would later regret having given.

To Hernando it seemed that a night of confinement had brought the arrogant chief to his senses. Come morning, Tascalusa agreed to provide four hundred men to help lighten the load of the conquistadors. As for women and food, the chief promised that all they required would be provided for them at the neighboring town of Mabila (aka Mauvila or Mavilla). While Hernando and his men were busy preparing for the next leg of their journey, Tascalusa sent messages to Mabila to make sure everything was prepared for the arrival of the Spaniards. De Soto led his army out of Atahachi the following day. The Spaniards had the added company of four hundred native porters and Chief Tascalusa, who, because of his great height, was seated upon the largest horse the Spaniards had in their possession.

A march of three days led the expedition past the town of Piachi and to a stretch of the Alabama River that had to be crossed by rafts that took the Spaniards two days to build. It was during this time that two soldiers went missing and it was soon discovered that they had been killed in an ambush by a roving band of warriors. One of the slain was Juan de Villalobos, the soldier who previously helped reconnoiter the more practical route to the town of Atahachi. Suspicious minds were quick to focus on Tascalusa as the mastermind behind this attack. Hernando certainly held the chief personally culpable. He threatened Tascalusa with torture by fire unless he promptly handed over all who were responsible for this unprovoked attack. The chief managed to assuage de Soto's anger with a pledge that the guilty parties would be turned over to him the moment they reached Mabila, where he immediately sent a message to make sure his subjects understood this was his command.

De Soto, however, still had his suspicions about the true intentions of Tascalusa and therefore sent two scouts on ahead to make sure the path was safe. This responsibility was assigned to Gonzalo Quadrado Xaramillo and Diego Vázquez. Both soldiers were accompanied by several porters from Atahachi who served as guides to Mabila, which was approximately a league and a half from the Spanish camp. One of the scouts soon returned to report that armed natives were massing in great numbers and were busy fortifying the village as if they were making preparations for war. Luís de Moscoso and several other officers expressed their concern about a possible trap and advised their commander to avoid venturing to Mabila. The governor was determined to proceed as planned. After all, to do otherwise might be construed as a sign of cowardice by the natives. Like Pánfilo de Narváez before him, Hernando de Soto was not one prone to heed the advice of a subordinate.

As he had done so many times before, Hernando de Soto went on ahead with a small company of officers and soldiers while the main army followed close behind. Included in this advance guard were Luís de Moscoso, the interpreter Juan Ortiz, and Tascalusa. The chief of Mabila came out to greet de Soto and his companions as they made their approach to the main entrance of the town. The ruler, who was accompanied by a large entourage of nobles, warriors, and musicians, welcomed the Spaniards to Mabila with gift of blankets and animal furs. The commander was delighted by the ceremony that surrounded his arrival and was now inclined to believe that his scouts had misconstrued what were merely native preparations for his grand entrance.

Several soldiers were instructed to keep watch over the horses while Hernando de Soto, his officers, and Tascalusa entered the town on foot. As they proceeded toward the plaza, the Spanish officers saw that Mabila was a fairly large town protected by a high wooden wall punctuated with several towers that could hold many warriors. A quick count seemed to indicate that there were roughly three or four hundred people on hand to greet them. The Spaniards, however, were unaware of the several thousand warriors who remained well hidden. They would later learn that Tascalusa had recruited warriors from the neighboring tribes for the purpose of exacting a fitting revenge against his captors. He bought their allegiance with offerings of gifts and promises of granting them a fair share of the captured Spaniards who could serve as their slaves.

Hernando de Soto and his officers were treated to a splendid banquet of food and fermented drink while being entertained by a bevy of beautiful maidens who danced before them. The suggestive gyrations of the young women managed to distract the Spaniards while the warriors hurriedly made preparations for battle. As the dancers were nearing the end of one of their evocative routines, Tascalusa excused himself from the group and went to a hut where the war council was presently convened. The chief then gave the order for the warriors in hiding to commence with the attack.

The absence of Tascalusa did not escape the notice of Hernando de Soto. One eyewitness account states that the commander immediately sent one of his captains to retrieve him, while another version says it was Juan Ortiz, the interpreter, who was sent to fetch the chief. Whoever actually went found that it was impossible to coax Tascalusa from the place where he met with the other chiefs. It was during this time that some of de Soto's men spotted some hidden bundles of bows and arrows. Upon further inspection, it was noticed that the huts they believed were empty were secretly housing a great many warriors. This information was relayed to the commander but by then it was too late to stop what had already been set in motion by the actions of one of the Spanish captains.

During the search for the missing chief, Captain Baltasar de Gallegos apprehended a native noble who had crossed his path and demanded that he make Tascalusa show himself at once. But when the noble accentuated his refusal to comply by breaking free of the officer's grasp, Gallegos drew his sword and hacked off the Indian's left arm. This violent act signaled the start of the bloody confrontation that was to follow. It was at that moment that several thousand warriors stormed out from their places of hiding and charged at Hernando and his men. This small group of Spaniards suddenly found themselves trapped within the walls of the town while the main army was still making its way to Mabila.

Five soldiers were quick to fall before the fury of the initial assault. Despite the protection of his helmet, Baltasar de Gallegos was struck in the

The Spaniards are forced to do battle with Tascalusa's warriors at Mabila.

head with such force by a warrior that blood flowed freely down his face. De Soto was pelted by several arrows, but luckily his armor shielded him from harm. The commander and his surviving comrades, including the wounded Gallegos, managed to escape — though just barely — by fighting their way past one of the town gates. The natives quickly closed the gates behind them and proceeded to taunt the fleeing Spaniards with a flurry of wild whoops of joy over their victory. The humiliated Hernando and his battered troops continued their retreat until they caught up with the army that was advancing on Mabila.

Infuriated by the hostile reception he had just been accorded, Hernando de Soto decided to repay his ungrateful hosts by unleashing all at once the full force of his army. The thunderous discharge of an arquebus announced the start of the attack, which came from all sides. These warriors gleaned from Atahachi, Mabila, and surrounding tribes fought the Spaniards with a tenacity and ferocity equal to that of the Apalachee. Even the women of Mabila took up arms against the conquistadors. It was a fierce contest waged both in the town and on the open field. The warriors were able to repulse the attack of Hernando's men several times, but each time the Spaniards regrouped and attacked with even greater determination. The battle raged for nearly nine hours without letup. By now it was clear that the warriors had no plans of surrendering and the soldiers had no intention of capitulating.

The stalemate ended when the Spaniards were able to penetrate the fortress walls after having hacked openings with the blades of their axes and swords. Once inside, they began setting fire to the town. The wood structures and thatched roofs were quick to erupt into a blazing inferno that trapped a great many natives. The terrifying screams of those being burned alive could be heard above the roar of the fire. Soldiers patiently waited outside the burning buildings to kill any native who tried to escape the flames. One warrior eluded capture by climbing a tree and hanging himself. The bloodstained ground was littered with hundreds, if not thousands, of dead or dying natives. The Spaniards were able to confirm the death of Tascalusa's son, but the fate of the father was less certain. Some believed that he escaped during the heat of battle and others were convinced that he perished in one of the fires that consumed the village. Having succeeded in killing all who opposed them, the victorious conquistadors laid claim to the charred remains of Mabila.

The conquistadors paid a dear price for their hollow victory. More than twenty soldiers died during this confrontation and few survived unscathed. Captain Diego de Soto, a nephew of the governor, was killed, as was Don Carlos Enríquez, Diego's brother-in-law, who was married to the niece of the expedition's commander. Hernando de Soto, who fought and bled alongside his men throughout the long battle, suffered the pain and indignity of an arrow that penetrated his left buttock. Most of the soldiers endured multiple wounds, some serious enough to require the immediate attention of the surgeon. The less serious flesh wounds were treated with whatever remedy was readily available. Once such treatment involved the dissection of dead warriors to obtain body fat, which was used as an unguent for their open wounds. De Soto ordered his men to give the dead soldiers a proper burial; the fallen natives were left as fodder for nature's scavengers.

In addition to the loss of so many lives, the Spaniards suffered a number of tangible losses that would radically alter the future course of the expedition. The soldiers had brought their supplies much too close to the front, a tactical error that resulted in their reserve clothing, most of their food provisions, and the few pearls that were in their possession to perish in the fires they had set at Mabila. They also lost their valuable supply of gunpowder, which rendered useless what were perhaps their most forceful weapons on this campaign. The expedition's priest suffered the loss of their sacramental wine and the wheat flour that was essential for making the wafers used during the ritual of Holy Communion. Forty-five horses and a great many pigs died during the battle of Mabila.

The victorious conquistadors would spend the next several days at Mabila tending to their wounds and taking stock of what was salvageable. Since most of the village had burned to the ground, the Spaniards were forced to find shelter as best they could. The clothing of their fallen comrades was torn into strips to make bandages. The flesh of the dead horses was flayed, cooked, and fed to the troops. Thirteen gravely wounded soldiers would succumb to their wounds during this brief period of recovery. With only one doctor to administer aid and little in the way of medicine to provide relief, several more soldiers would soon pass away from the serious effects of their injuries. It has been calculated that as many as forty-seven Spanish deaths can be attributed to the battle that occurred at Mabila. On the other side, the death of so many natives doomed the Atahachi chiefdom to a state of abject poverty and near extinction.

Mississippi Travels

While camped at Mabila, Hernando de Soto sent out several small scouting parties to search for food and to gauge their distance to the coast, where he hoped they would meet up with Captain Diego Maldonado and the much anticipated supply ships that were supposed to sail from Cuba. It was hoped that Maldonado would have returned by now with livestock, food, building materials, weapons, and additional recruits for the founding of a permanent settlement. It soon seemed as if their prayers had been answered. The interpreter Juan Ortiz learned from some natives that Spanish vessels had been spotted along the coast, a distance of approximately thirty leagues away. This information was made available only to de Soto and his inner circle of officers. As Hernando began formulating plans to meet up with the flotilla along the coast — which he was sure had to be the ships under the command of Maldonado — he suddenly had second thoughts.

The fierceness of the battle just fought was sufficient enough reason for many soldiers to question the soundness of a decision to establish a permanent settlement in such a hostile region. The bruised and battered army had grown weary of the expedition and many openly spoke of a desire to return to Cuba. After all, they had yet to find any evidence of the vast amounts of gold and silver that had been promised at the start of the expedition and the few precious pearls that represented the only evidence of wealth so far were lost to the fires at Mabila. Hernando feared that many of the disgruntled soldiers would desert the expedition and return to Havana once the ships were discovered. Concerned that such a loss would pose a threat to his plans, the commander ordered Ortiz to keep silent on the subject of the ships. Hernando de Soto simply could not afford to abandon his quest, for to do so would result in the ruin of both his good name and his once considerable fortune. Much to the chagrin of those who had knowledge of the boats, the governor decided to chart a course that would lead the expedition away from Maldonado's fleet.

After more than three weeks at Mabila, Hernando led his expedition inland in search of riches that he hoped would quell the mounting doubts and concerns of his troops. This time they chased the promise of golden dreams that were to be fulfilled at a province known as Chicasa (aka Chicaza or Chicasaw). It is possible that de Soto had previously learned of Fray Marcos de Niza's claim of having sighted one of the Seven Cities of Cibola and may have thought that Chicasa was a part of this golden realm. If so, this might help explain his rash decision to continue on even when there was no evidence of rich kingdoms in this region.

A proud Hernando de Soto led his tattered troops out of Mabila and headed northwest on a path that plunged them ever deeper into the unknown wilderness of Alabama. What little food they possessed had to be strictly rationed. A four day march brought the Spaniards to the town of Talicpacana where a host of fifteen hundred armed warriors came out to persuade them to leave. The famished soldiers made an immediate and desperate charge at the warriors. Fearing to engage these invaders on an open field, the natives wisely chose to retreat across the river. The victorious conquistadors then took possession of the town, which they found had been abandoned by all of its inhabitants. Luckily, in their haste to leave, the natives left behind some of their maize, but unfortunately it was not enough to fully satisfy the needs of the soldiers.

The luck of the Spaniards failed to improve at the next town. The inhabitants of Mozulixa quickly gathered all their belongings, including every morsel of food, and ferried themselves across the river, which was most likely the Black Warrior River, once they learned of the conquistadors' approach. Hernando and his army entered the abandoned town only to be rewarded with the sight of eight thousand warriors on the opposite bank who stood prepared to prevent their crossing the river. The natives taunted the starving Spaniards by laying out in plain view a bountiful spread of their food while warriors with longbows in hand dared them to try to cross. The Spaniards bided their time before accepting such a challenge.

Determined to make it across the river, Hernando instructed his men to build two large piroques, a vessel very similar in structure to a raft. The Spaniards gathered and ate whatever food they could find while secretly spending the next twelve days feverishly working to build the boats that would ferry a company of men across the river in an effort to capture a generous portion of the enemy's food supply. Once this task was completed, approximately sixty men and several horses attempted to cross over at a site downriver that was believed to be out of view of the warriors. As they reached the other side, the soldiers suddenly found themselves confronted by a gathering of several hundred warriors who had correctly guessed what they were up to. A heavy barrage of arrows was unleashed but the desperate conquistadors were determined to achieve their objective, regardless of the cost. The charge of the cavaliers, led by Diego García, Gonzalo Silvestre, and Hernando de Soto, was able to push the warriors back, but they soon returned in greater numbers. After six unsuccessful attempts to drive off the Spaniards, the natives abandoned the battle and retreated to the surrounding woods. Hernando and his troops succeeded in capturing enough food to satisfy the appetite of the entire army.

The victory and the accompanying spoils of war earned at Mozulixa helped revive the crestfallen spirits of the Spaniards as they pressed on in search of Chicasa. De Soto and his men helped themselves to the food found at the next two towns, one of which was the main village of the Apafalaya province. It was here that the paramount chief of this realm was captured and forced to serve as both a guide and a human shield for the expedition. A sense of urgency came over the soldiers as the falling temperatures and the first flakes of snow signaled the rapid approach of winter.

It was the early part of December 1540 before the expedition finally reached the province of Chicasa. The Spaniards came upon yet another river, which might very well have been the Tombigbee, where they once again found a throng of armed warriors positioned on the opposite bank who were determined to prevent their crossing. De Soto and his men used the nails saved from the dismantled boats at Mozulixa to build another boat. Once across the river, the conquistadors were able to quickly drive off the opposing natives. The Spaniards soon reached the capital of Chicasa, which they found abandoned. All hopes and dreams of finally finding riches were dashed the moment the soldiers saw that the main town of this province was little more than a collection of huts (accounts range from as few as twenty to as many as two hundred), none of which housed any precious metals or gems. All they had to be thankful for was that the village and the surrounding fields yielded enough food, especially corn, to sustain them for several weeks.

Once their commander decided they would wait out the winter at this location, the soldiers began gathering food and building additions to the existing huts so there would be enough sustenance and shelter for all. The displaced Chicasa continually harassed the efforts of the Spaniards with their guerilla-style attacks, which were designed more to instill fear than cause harm. Forced to fend for themselves in the woods during a winter that was exceptionally harsh, the Chicasa schemed to get rid of these intruders who had stolen their food and shelter. A temporary truce occurred when the chief and several nobles strode into the town that was once theirs bearing gifts of animal skins and one hundred fifty rabbits. The chief feigned friendship with Hernando de Soto by asking for his help in defeating an enemy tribe. The veteran commander suspected this was a ploy to divide his forces and wisely chose not to commit himself to such a cause.

The severity of the winter season caused both sides to take risks that threatened to undo the fragile peace that existed between the opposing camps. The first such incident occurred when three Indians were caught trying to steal several pigs to feed the starving men, women, and children of their tribe. De Soto ordered the execution of two and had the hands of the other chopped off. The mutilated native and the lifeless bodies of his comrades were returned to the tribe to make sure they understood that the Spaniards would not tolerate any such blatant acts of thievery. While the message had the desired impact on the Chicasa, it failed, however, to resonate with many of his own men. Shortly thereafter, several soldiers decided on their own to find relief from the bitter cold by riding into the native camp and stealing a significant number of their blankets and animal hides. Angered that by taking matters into their own hands they had unduly risked the lives of every soldier, Hernando made sure they were severely punished before ordering their execution. The commander would later rescind this harsh sentence but only after several soldiers and officers begged for a show of mercy on behalf of the guilty parties.

Hernando's decision to leave the Chicasa village toward the beginning of March was prompted by nature's hint that spring was just about ready to escape winter's grasp. The commander informed the Chicasa chief of his plans to leave and demanded that he provide him with porters to help lighten the load of his men. The ruler had previously scoffed at all such requests, but this time Hernando made an offer that was backed up by the threat of bodily harm, which was directed specifically at the chief. Even though he knew the Chicasa ruler had agreed to his demand out of a sense of fear, de Soto probably deluded himself into believing that the chief's change of heart was motivated by a desire to see the Spaniards leave his land. The truth of the matter would soon be revealed.

That very night the Chicasa chief decided the time was right to implement his long-awaited plan for revenge. Darkness provided enough cover for small bands of warriors to sneak past the posted sentries and enter their former village where the Spaniards now took comfort. The Spanish guards eventually took notice and quickly sounded the alarm. But by that time more than three hundred armed warriors had managed to gain entrance to the town. The Chicasa soon set fire to the buildings with torches and flaming arrows. The soldiers who had not heard the initial alarm were quickly awakened by the smoke and flames that rapidly engulfed their shelters. Many blindly ran out into the open for a breath of fresh air only to be met by a barrage of arrows as they desperately tried to locate their weapons. It was a battle somewhat reminiscent of the clash at Mabila, only this time it was the Spaniards who perished while trapped inside burning buildings.

Hernando de Soto, a true warrior who relished the challenge of battle, was among the first Spaniards to strike back at the enemy. Once he located his lance, the commander mounted his horse and charged directly at one of the Chicasa warriors. De Soto thrust his lance with such force that he threw himself from his horse as he succeeded in slaying his rival, who according to most accounts was the only warrior to die during this battle. Hernando continued to fight on foot as other soldiers quickly rallied to his side. The Chicasa were on the verge of a decisive victory until a strange twist of fate interceded on behalf of the Spaniards. The Chicasa warriors called off their attack after mistaking the pounding hoofs of frantic horses trying to escape the fury of the surrounding flames for the deadly charge of the cavalry.

The estimated number of Spaniards who died during this bloody battle range from eleven to as many as forty. We do know that one of the two Spanish women who accompanied the expedition was counted among the dead. Francisca de Hinestrosa made the fatal mistake of rushing back into a burning building to retrieve the few pearls she had managed to save from the fires at Mabila. Her husband was powerless to save her when the flaming walls came tumbling down. Ana Méndez, however, managed to survive the massacre at Chicasa. More than fifty horses were lost while barely one hundred pigs survived the battle. The fires also consumed what little remained of the spare clothing and laid claim to the saddles and a great many weapons. The loss of so much and so many, especially the horses, which the warriors seemed to target first, dealt a devastating blow to the expedition. Once again, the meat of the dead horses served as sustenance for the surviving Spaniards.

Fearing that the Chicasa would soon return to finish what they had started, Hernando had his men hurriedly gather all that was salvageable and then promptly led them away from the charred and smoldering remains of the village that had served as their home for the past several months. The movements of the retreating conquistadors were steadily tracked by Chicasa warriors who made sure their presence was known, but only from a safe distance. The battered and demoralized army took up residence at the winter camp of the natives, which had been abandoned following the Chicasa raid to reclaim their village. Knowing that their present whereabouts would be revealed by those who spied on them, the soldiers quickly tended to their wounds and chopped down trees to make replacement lances for those lost in the fires. They also improvised with whatever materials were readily available to make replacement saddles. The soldiers built bonfires to fend off the cold and maintained a vigilant watch for signs of the attack that was sure to come.

Luckily for Hernando and his fatigued troops, the Chicasa delayed their next assault for nearly a week. This time they waited until the early light of dawn before charging at the Spaniards in full force, which they did from three separate directions. However, the rested conquistadors were prepared for such an attack. The soldiers managed to drive the warriors into an open field where, thanks to their recovered horses, they were able to earn a swift and decisive victory that ended with the slaughter of a great many natives. The Chicasa survivors returned to their homes and chose never again to bother their enemy.

The battered, disheartened, and diminished company of conquistadors realized the time had come to leave this hostile region. Hernando de Soto led his men along a trail that the natives had told him would take them to a large Indian kingdom situated along a mighty river. Several days later, after having made camp for the night, the governor sent out scouts to see if there were any nearby villages and to determine if they might be friend or foe. They soon returned to say that the path ahead was blocked by a manmade barricade that was guarded by a great number of warriors. Hernando sent out fifty horsemen to make a more accurate assessment of the situation and they promptly returned to inform their commander that these natives appeared aggressive and advised it would be best to attack before they decided to do the same to them. De Soto agreed with their recommendation.

Not wanting to repeat the mistakes made at Mabila and Chicasa, Hernando left a third of the army behind to watch over their meager supplies while he led the rest of the troops to face the obstacle situated along the road. The advancing conquistadors soon encountered the barricade they had been warned about. Blocking their way was a recently constructed fortress made of earth and wood that shielded three hundred armed warriors determined to contest any attempt to cross their path. The Spaniards could see that many of these warriors wore brightly feathered headdresses and their faces and bodies were streaked with menacing looking bands of war paint.

The warriors made it clear that there was no room for negotiations by letting fly a great many arrows in the direction of the advancing Spaniards. Convinced that these defenders had something of great importance to protect, De Soto ordered his troops to storm the barricade. The Indians were able to stop several soldiers in their tracks by aiming their arrows at the unprotected legs of the enemy. This fierce struggle ended in favor of the conquistadors. A great many natives were killed in this conflict and those who survived were taken prisoner. It was then that Hernando and his troops discovered that these proud warriors had nothing to protect except their honor, which they sought to do with a display of valor on the field of battle. The Spaniards lost as many as fifteen men, and several soldiers sustained serious wounds in order to claim a barrier that simply barred the path ahead.

Hernando and his battle weary soldiers spent the next four days burying their fallen comrades and tending to their own wounds. Once these tasks were completed, the still determined Spaniards pressed on through a thick forest of towering pines that soon delved into treacherous swamplands shielded from the sun by the canopy of very tall timber. Food soon became scarce, which meant the troops had to spend a great deal of time scouring for edible roots and hunting for game. On May 8, 1541— nearly two years after first making landfall along the coast of Florida — the Spaniards came to a clearing that offered them a first glimpse of the Mississippi River, which they christened the Espíritu Santo.

The first sighting of this mighty river was not a particularly glorious moment for Hernando de Soto and his exhausted troops. The mile wide river was a grim reminder that they would once again have to build boats, only this time they would have to be bigger and stronger to ferry the men, horses, and supplies across such a great divide if they wished to continue their search for cities paved with the wealth of mighty rulers. What proved more comforting to the famished Spaniards was the belief that they were finally within reach of native towns that could provide them with sorely needed food.

The Spaniards were now deep in the heart of the Mississippi mound civilizations. The tribes of this region generally lived in large villages fortified by a surrounding palisade. The pointed stakes that enclosed the town were usually about twice the height of a man and, as these soldiers had already experienced during their previous encounter at Mabila, they had towers in place to defend against an assault. These sturdy walls guarded a society that graced itself with magnificent public buildings, ceremonial structures, earthen mounds, and even a ball field.

De Soto and his men were greatly impressed with the towns of the Mississippian tribes they happened upon and attempted to describe their unique building techniques, especially the earthen mounds: "Then on the top of these places they construct flat surfaces which are capable of holding the ten, twelve, fifteen or twenty dwellings of the lord and his family and the people of his service, who vary according to the power and grandeur of his state. In those areas at the front of the hill ... they construct a plaza, around which first the noblest and most important personages, and then the common people build their homes."[3]

The manmade mounds, which were sometimes referred to as earth islands, elevated the rulers, priests, and nobles to a point where they were closer to the spirits of the sky, sun, moon, and stars above. To reflect his higher status, the home of the chief was usually erected on the largest mound. The Indians of the Mississippi region were sun worshippers, and Hernando de Soto, who was familiar with the sun worshipping cult of the Incas, hoped to use his knowledge of such religious practices to exploit the natives of this region.

The Mississippian tribes thrived off the rich soil found along the banks of the great river and the neighboring valleys that provided the right conditions for corn, sunflowers, squash, and beans to take root and sprout in great abundance. A river flush with fish and forests teeming with game, berries, nuts, and herbs also helped ensure that the people of these lands never suffered from a lack of food. The Mississippian cultures developed and nurtured extensive trade routes that brought them many items not inherent to their region. The exchange of goods and ideas, such as in the manner practiced by the Mississippian tribes, is a cornerstone trait common to all great civilizations.

The first native town sighted along the banks of the Mississippi River was Chisca, which is sometimes referred to as Quizquiz. In dire need of food and thoroughly convinced that all the natives of this region were combative, De Soto and his starved soldiers stormed one end of the village. Luckily for the Spaniards, most of the able-bodied men were away at the time tending to their fields. The lightning raid resulted in the capture of more than three hundred natives, mostly women, and the confiscation of a great many hides

The discovery of the Mississippi by Hernando de Soto and his followers.

and blankets, but not nearly enough food to satisfy the basic needs of the soldiers. Hernando hoped to remedy this dilemma by bargaining his new batch of prisoners for much needed food.

While the Spaniards were busy sacking a section of the village, several warriors ascended the royal mound to inform their ruler of this sudden and unexpected intrusion. The elderly, bedridden chief, who was known by the same name as the village he lorded over, suddenly found the strength to pick himself up and reach for a trusty tomahawk, which he intended to use against these insolent intruders. The chief, who was once a mighty warrior, still possessed the memories of his great valor in battle but, unfortunately, he no longer had the physical strength to execute his will. After being constrained by his wives, concubines, and servants, the agitated chief was compelled to listen to the counsel of his warriors. They told him that these numerous and well-armed men were unlike any they had seen before. They advised the chief to feign friendship until they were in a stronger position to fight such an unfamiliar enemy.

De Soto and his troops ceased with their pillaging when the men who had been away tending to their crops suddenly reappeared and demanded the immediate return of all that belonged to them, especially their women. The

Spanish commander sought to make amends by sending a message to the chief in which he apologized for the actions of his men and expressed his fervent desire to reach a peaceful accord. When his apology for sacking and plundering the town was not received as well as expected, Hernando de Soto countered with another offer that he hoped would appease the aggrieved Indians. The governor pledged to return all the items pilfered and every native taken against their will in exchange for enough food to feed his army and a place to rest for a few days, after which, he promised, they would depart the domain of Chisca forever. Based on his past experiences in the New World, de Soto believed that the best way to earn the respect of the natives was to follow a show of military might with a seeming act of compassion. Though inclined to respond with his own show of force, the elderly chief reasoned that the best way to resolve this delicate situation was to agree to these terms. The Spaniards were permitted to enter the town unopposed once Hernando fulfilled his end of the deal. They were then allowed to help themselves to food and shelter so long as they remained respectful of their hosts. After a stay of six days, the well nourished and rested conquistadors met briefly with the elderly chief of Chisca before resuming their quest.

The expedition continued to be slowed by the vast number of sick and wounded soldiers who struggled to keep pace with their healthier comrades. The Spaniards traveled for four days along the banks of the Mississippi before finally finding a spot they believed was the least difficult to cross. Four natives unexpectedly strode into the Spanish camp while de Soto and his men were busy building boats sturdy enough to carry everyone and everything to the other side of the great river. They were emissaries of the chief of Aquixo who had been sent to extend a hearty welcome to the Spaniards and to offer their lord's pledge of friendship. Hernando met with the envoys and then sent them back to their chief with expressions of thanks and a pledge of his peaceful intentions toward the people of this land.

Shortly thereafter, an imposing armada of two hundred large canoes appeared on the river. The surprised Spaniards could see that this fleet carried a great many armed Aquixo warriors, all of whom appeared to have their faces painted with red ochre and many of whom sported brilliant plumes of feathers. If Hernando and his soldiers believed they were about to be greeted by the chief himself they soon found it was mistake to think this was the case. The soldiers had to run because the warriors began pelting them with a steady stream of arrows. Besides trying to save themselves, the Spaniards were primarily concerned with protecting the boats they had worked so hard to build. The soldiers were finally able to drive off their attackers with several well aimed bolts delivered by the few crossbows still in their possession.

The Aquixo warriors would continue to harass the Spaniards with periodic canoe raids, but their best efforts failed to deter the resolve of those who were determined to cross the river. Though impressed with their fleet of canoes, de Soto once again convinced himself that the hostile actions of the natives was an indication that they had something to protect that might be deemed of great value to him and his men. The soldiers slaved for twenty days building large boats sturdy and maneuverable enough to carry an entire company of men and beasts across this wide and raging river. Once the boats were completed, the Spaniards crossed the great river during the early morning hours of June 18th without being noticed or suffering loss of life. The warriors who had constantly troubled their efforts with taunts and a steady volley of projectiles had departed once they saw the Spaniards had finished building their boats and were prepared to cross the river.

Once on the other side, the Spaniards dismantled the boats they had labored so long to build, taking care to save the nails they would surely need for the next river to cross. Hernando de Soto was now in search of a golden realm called Pacaha (also known as Capaha), a province the natives told him was ruled by a powerful lord who received tribute from a great many tribes. Hernando and his troops were relieved that the warriors of Aquixo chose not to contest the crossing of their province. A near week long march upriver and across sparsely inhabited lands led the expedition to Casqui (Casquin), a large fortified town that, according to Garcilaso de la Vega, had four hundred houses.

As soon as he learned of their approach, Chief Casquin, who is sometimes referred to as Yeasqui, sent emissaries to greet and invite the Spaniards to his village. This middle-aged chief, who lived atop a mound where a dozen structures housed both him and his family, came out to welcome Hernando and his men once they had entered his town. The chief of the Casqui told the commander of the Spaniards that their arrival had been foretold and graciously offered food and lodging for their comfort. The bitter experiences of the past made de Soto wary of housing all his troops in one confined area. The army was therefore divided between those who were housed inside the town and those who were camped at a nearby orchard.

To show his appreciation for the hospitality of the Casquin people, and as part of a concerted effort to convert heathen souls to Christianity, Hernando had Maestro Francisco, a master carpenter, turn a huge pine tree felled by the Spaniards into a giant holy cross. Chief Casquin and his subjects expressed their thanks for this magnificent offering by permitting it to be planted on one of their sacred mounds. A lavish ceremony climaxed with the baptism of a great many natives. An odd coincidence helped to convince many more to accept the faith of the Christians. Chief Casquin had asked de Soto to pray to his god for much needed rain for their crops. These prayers were answered the following night when a steady rain began to fall and continued for several days. This apparent miracle convinced the natives that the Spaniards were blessed by a god of great power.

After more than a week at the village of Casquin, and with no signs of gold or silver to entice him to stay, Hernando decided the time had come to seek out more prosperous realms. To ensure their safety, Casquin asked if he might accompany them to the border of his province. The chief made the request even more attractive by offering to provide a host of porters who would shoulder the burden of the Spaniard's provisions. Hernando could not refuse such a generous offer.

Hernando de Soto would soon learn that Chief Casquin had an ulterior motive in mind. His tribe had a long-standing dispute with the rulers of Pacaha, a chiefdom that stood at their border, and Casquin saw the arrival of the conquistadors as an opportunity to forge an alliance that would strengthen his chances of winning a war against his enemy. The suspicions of the commander should have been aroused when the chief assembled five thousand armed warriors and three thousand porters to accompany the Spaniards on what was supposed to be a brief excursion through his province.

After a march of several days, the expedition arrived at a large swamp that served as a natural boundary for the provinces of Casqui and Pacaha. Three more days of trekking over difficult terrain brought the Spaniards and their numerous allies within sight of Pacaha, a fortified town consisting of five hundred large wooden houses that was further protected on three sides by a large moat. Hernando de Soto sent a message to the ruler of Pacaha to announce their arrival but the messenger soon returned to say that the chief and many of his subjects had fled in fear. Casquin told Hernando that he would go on ahead with his warriors to make sure the way was safe. De Soto ordered his men to march on the town of Pacaha shortly after the head start of his allies.

The chief of Pacaha, who is referred to as Capaha by Garcilaso de la Vega, had good reason to believe that the friends of his enemy were surely his enemy as well. Finding himself unprepared for such a large assault, Chief Capaha ordered his subjects to leave the town at once and seek shelter at a nearby islet. Unfortunately, the vengeful Casquin warriors stormed the village before all had a chance to escape. They slaughtered every Pacaha male they could catch and removed their scalps as trophies to take back home, trophies which were to serve as proof of their great valor in this victory. A great many women and children were taken prisoner, a haul that included two of Capaha's wives. The Casquins further vented their fury by desecrating the ancient burial grounds of their enemy. They emptied the temples and disturbed the bones of the ancestors of those who dwelled at Pacaha. The warriors were about to set fire to the temples but decided to forgo such an act, fearing that it might anger the Spaniards, who could now be seen approaching the town.

Realizing he had been unwittingly drawn into a tribal feud, Hernando ordered an immediate halt to the rampage perpetrated by his native allies. De Soto then sought to make amends by sending several captured natives to the nearby island fortress with an apology for the unseemly behavior of those who accompanied him and to assure Chief Capaha that no further harm would come to his people. When it was learned that the chief of Pacaha had sent urgent messages to other tribes requesting their help against those who had invaded his land, the Spanish commander decided he needed to quickly take the island fortress by force before the situation escalated into a major conflict. Chief Casquin advised him to wait for the arrival of the fleet of canoes he had already summoned before launching any attack.

A few days later, a total of two hundred conquistadors and three thousand Casquin warriors began boarding the sixty large canoes that were to transport them to the island fortress of Chief Capaha. To many Spaniards, the drowning death of Francisco Sebastián at the very moment they made landfall seemed to portend that a terrible tragedy was about to befall them all. The soldiers soon learned that their allies were not quite so brave when faced against an equally armed enemy. From the safety of their island stronghold, Pacaha warriors hurled a slew of verbal threats that caused the Casquin warriors to lose courage and entirely abandon the fight. The frightened allies of the Spaniards rushed back to the docked canoes and paddled as fast as they could back to the town they had recently sacked. They even tried to take the canoes that transported the Spaniards, and they would have succeeded if the soldiers left to guard the boat had not put up such a determined fight.

Finding themselves suddenly pitted against a foe far greater in number, the two hundred Spaniards feared their end was near and thus began an orderly retreat to the boats. Sensing that victory was well within their grasp, the Pacaha warriors prepared to finish off those who had been left behind. Fortunately for the fleeing soldiers, Chief Capaha ordered his warriors to stand down. Knowing that the will and strength of his tribe had already been proven, the chief believed that a show of mercy would not only save lives, but might also save his town from ruin. Capaha certainly made a wise choice: Hernando appreciated the fact that his men had been permitted to leave unharmed and therefore was receptive to opening up a dialogue that might lead to a peaceful resolution to their situation.

After an exchange of friendly messages, Capaha agreed to return to his village to meet with the Spaniards. The young chief, who the Spaniards estimated to be in his mid-twenties, made an inspection of the extensive damage that had been done to his beloved town, especially the desecration of the sacred burial grounds, before speaking with de Soto. After a cordial meeting that helped to settle many differences, Capaha turned to the chief who was responsible for inflicting so much death and destruction and said, "You must be exultant, Casquin, to have realized what you never dreamed or hoped to obtain with your own forces; that is revenge for your injuries and affronts. For this be thankful to the power of the Spaniards. They will go away and we shall remain in our lands as we were before. Pray to the Sun and the Moon, our gods, that they give us good seasons."[4]

Knowing that the deep-seeded hatred between the two tribes would make for an uneasy alliance, Hernando de Soto publicly ordered that no one was to cause any more harm to the town or the people who dwelled there. The governor also made sure that the two young and beautiful wives of Chief Capaha were released along with all the other captives. Capaha, Hernando, and Casquin continued to meet but, for the most part, the rival chiefs refused to talk to one another. A grand banquet was held to celebrate their newly forged friendship, but even this quickly turned into a squabble over which chief should be permitted to sit at the right hand of the governor. De Soto deftly handled this delicate matter by telling the quarrelsome chieftains that Christians believed that one side was just as good as the other.

Though disappointed to learn there was no gold to be found at Pacaha, the Spaniards were, however, extremely grateful to receive numerous animal skins and blankets that could be used to make clothes to replace what had been lost and moccasins to substitute for their badly worn shoes. The food and shelter was also much appreciated. Unfortunately, the explorers were now in dire need of a basic substance that is essential to the human body. Despite all the meticulous planning that took place at Spain and Cuba to make sure there were sufficient provisions for the conquest and settlement of this vast New World region, Hernando de Soto and his officers had failed to include salt in their list of necessary supplies. It wasn't long before many became ill and as many as sixty deaths during the first year of the expedition are believed to be attributable to a severe deficiency of salt. Many of these deaths could easily have been prevented if the soldiers had been willing to take an herbal remedy that the natives used for themselves. The ash of certain plants could serve as a suitable substitute for salt, but the proud Spaniards felt it was beneath their dignity to take medicinal advice from those whom they considered savages. Many paid a dear price for such arrogance.

Hernando learned from some tribesmen of Pacaha that at a region approximately forty leagues away there could be found salt, which he desperately needed, and gold, which he greatly desired. Hernando de Silvera and Pedro Moreno volunteered to travel with guides provided by Chief Capaha to see if this land possessed all that the natives claimed. At the same time, the

Spanish commander sent out another expedition, which traversed a different route, to learn if there were any promising leads worth investigating. After eleven days, Silvera and Morena returned with a large quantity of much needed rock salt crystals and a fair amount of copper, the metal that the natives thought was the same as gold. They also reported that there were few villages in this region and little in the way of food to be found along this route. The second expedition returned with more discouraging news. Early into their adventure, the scouts happened upon a wandering tribe of hunter-gatherers who told them that by following a northwesterly course they would find many large villages. The quest was abandoned when a march of eight days brought them to a vast uninhabited plain that was entirely devoid of trees.

Taking these disappointing reports as irrefutable evidence that there were no rich kingdoms to be found in this region, de Soto decided to return to Casquin, where he hoped to find a way to restore the waning confidence of his troops. After a stay of nearly a month in this province, Hernando and his troops bade farewell to Chief Capaha and departed in the company of Chief Casquin and his warriors. The return to the town of Casquin helped provide the much needed lift to the downtrodden spirit of the troops that Hernando had hoped for, which was especially important after coming off yet another failed adventure to discover the rich native kingdoms they had been promised would be found. After rewarding his soldiers with five days of rest, the governor led his men on yet another expedition, this time to explore the possibilities that awaited at a province called Quiguate.

A five day march through fertile and well-populated lands brought the expedition to Quiguate, a town that proved much larger than expected but not quite as rewarding as Hernando and his soldiers had hoped. Shortly after the Spaniards made their presence known, the natives of Quiguate suddenly abandoned their homes. Most, however, returned after just two days, begging de Soto's forgiveness for their rude behavior. Their return was most likely prompted by a fear that their unexplained absence would give these uninvited guests a reason to wreak havoc upon their precious homes and fields. Worried that the disappointment realized at this town might spark a mutinous scheme, Hernando decided not to linger any longer than necessary at Quiguate. A stay of roughly a week (some accounts state they stayed for three weeks) was long enough to obtain the interpreters, guides, and porters they needed for the next journey. The plan was to follow a course that would lead them across an immense plain that they were told would eventually bring them to the vast "Other Sea" that washes up against the shores of the New World.

The Quiguate guides led the weary Spaniards through yet another region laden with swamps, parts of which were home to a large number of alligators. What made this particular trek more bearable were the abundant amount of fish they were able to catch with little difficulty. Instead of leading them to the "Other Sea," this march across flatlands brought them to a range of hills that are part of the Ozark Mountains. Hernando de Soto once again saw this as a fortuitous sign. The Spanish commander still believed that a rich and powerful native kingdom would be found nestled within the mountains.

On or about the 4th of September, the Spaniards reached Coligua (Colima), a village situated along a river that cut through the mountains. Despite the friendly welcome extended by the tribe, de Soto resorted to his old methods and made the chief his prisoner. The soldiers followed his example and captured a number of natives, all of whom were pressed into service as porters or guides. Those who could, quickly fled to the safety of the forest, thus leaving the Spaniards to help themselves to the food and clothes that had been left behind. What started out as a dignified and hopeful Spanish expedition had now been reduced to simply a band of wandering marauders. While at Colima the Spaniards had a chance encounter with a herd of buffalo, which they enjoyed hunting for mere sport.

Once Coligua had been exploited for all it was worth, the conquistadors then marched southward into the thick forests of the Ozarks. They followed the course of the White River for a good way before veering west and then turning north. The army marched for several days through a sparsely populated mountain region. Once again, the expedition was in a desperate search for yet another rich native kingdom, this time it was located in a wealthy province called Cayas.

The Spaniards continued on to the Arkansas River where, just to the north of present day Little Rock, they found several small villages that were part of the Cayas province. Once again, de Soto decided to go on ahead with several soldiers to reconnoiter the region. His efforts were soon rewarded with the discovery of Tanico, a large town that the Spaniards were delighted to learn was the center of a fairly extensive native trade in salt. Even though he was again disappointed to find a village that lacked any items considered to be of material value, Hernando was at least glad to have found a town large enough to suit the basic needs of his troops. The conquistadors would call Tanico home for the next month.

While camped at Tanico, Hernando sent out several small expeditions for the sole purpose of enslaving Indians. One such raid led to the capture of the principal chief of the Cayas province who, while bound in chains, was personally interrogated by de Soto regarding the location of chiefdoms that might possess any precious metals or valuable stones. The tortured chief of the Cayas eventually told Hernando de Soto what he wanted to hear: to the southwest there was a rich province called Tula. The commander decided that the southern location of Tula would probably make for a better camp to sit out the winter that was fast approaching.

Just as he had done on so many occasions, Hernando decided he would lead the way with a small company of men while the rest of the army followed in his wake. As they made their approach to the town of Tula, de Soto and his soldiers attempted to capture some Indians they encountered but were surprised to suddenly find themselves coming under attack from those they intended to enslave. Several horses and soldiers were wounded during a fierce altercation that left between thirty and forty natives dead. Fearing that the strength of his soldiers was on the verge of faltering, the governor issued the order to retreat. Hernando planned to resume his advance on Tula once the entire army was at his side.

When Hernando returned to where his army was encamped, he learned, much to his dismay, that most of the recently captured natives had managed to escape. This left him without an interpreter to help smooth out any differences with the Tulans. Any thoughts by the soldiers that these Indians would freely submit following a show of Spanish strength were quickly shattered when the Tula warriors came out in full force to confront them. Even the women fought alongside the men, with each displaying a skill and strength of purpose equal to their male counterparts. According to Garcilaso de la Vega, a hapless soldier by the name of Francisco de Reynoso would learn firsthand just how tenacious an opponent the women of Tula truly were. Upon entering the upstairs room of a Tula home, Francisco was wrestled to the floor by five women, who pinned him down by grabbing hold of each limb while one female placed a vise-like grip on his genitals. While Reynoso desperately struggled to extricate himself from the women, who were biting and hitting him with all their might, his leg broke through the thin cane mat floor. Luckily for Francisco, a soldier saw his dangling leg and after hearing the commotion he rushed upstairs with several other soldiers and together they saved their comrade from further harm by killing all five women.

Meanwhile, the rest of the conquistadors had their hands full fighting an enemy determined not to yield any ground. The Tulans were experienced buffalo hunters who employed long pointed poles to bring down their prey. They used these same weapons against the Spanish horses with great success. Many Tulans chose not to flee their village and continued to carry the fight to the death, even after it was clear that all hope of victory was lost. In the end, it was the Spaniards who prevailed, which they did in such a convincing manner that the Tulan warriors bided their time before mounting another attack.

Once they had gained control of Tula, Hernando and his men were free to enjoy the spoils of their hard fought victory. They helped themselves to the generous stockpiles of buffalo meat and hides. On the fourth night after having lost their battle to the Spaniards, the Tulans attempted to retake their town by attacking in great numbers from three different directions. They were close to claiming victory, but luckily for de Soto and his troops the tide turned when the charge of the horses disrupted the ranks of the warriors and caused them to flee in all directions. A dialogue was opened with the arrival of several Tulan emissaries. Through the use of signs, Hernando made it clear that he wished to leave their land very soon but he was in dire need of guides and interpreters who could aid him. The only thing that the emissaries were willing to offer de Soto was the advice that he would have to lead his men to the distant east if he expected to find villages large enough to accommodate his army.

After twenty difficult days at Tula, Hernando de Soto and his forlorn troops resumed their search for those ever-elusive kingdoms of gold. The guides and interpreters that de Soto so desperately needed were once again obtained in the usual manner—they were seized. Scouts probed into present day Oklahoma only to return with the disappointing news that the land had become very flat and barren, a terrain they deemed unfavorable for supporting the rich native kingdoms they sought. They also failed to find any signs to indicate that the expedition was anywhere near the aforementioned "Other Ocean."

Unwilling to admit that his expedition had been a failure, Hernando led his soldiers up into the Ouachita Mountains, while clinging to the faint hope that this highland region would reveal evidence of gold that could be found either in the rocks or along the streams. The governor, however, was forced to abandon this quest when an exhaustive five day search failed to turn up any trace of gold. It was now late October and de Soto did not want to risk being stranded in the mountains when winter ushered in its bleak mixture of cold and snow.

15

NEARING THE END

A Renewed Effort

The sense of frustration that had long plagued many members of this expedition regarding the lack of wealth that this land and its people had to offer finally gained a hold over the thoughts of Hernando de Soto. What was equally annoying to the governor was the fact that, unlike Mexico or Peru, there was not one omnipotent tribe whose defeat would earn him control of an entire native empire. Instead, de Soto and his men were forced to fight a seemingly endless succession of skirmishes that earned them very little for their effort. Just as bothersome was the realization that their sense of direction was guided entirely by Indian stories of rich kingdoms, tales that were calculated to simply lead the conquistadors far from their town or to deliver them into the lands of their enemy, where they would either kill, or be killed, by their rival tribe.

Fearing that his expedition had now lost its sense of purpose, de Soto decided the time had come to return to the Mississippi River. Such a turnaround did not mean that he was ready to abandon his grand quest; with his hard earned reputation and fortune on the line, there was simply too much at stake for Hernando to quit. Despite the misgivings of his troops and the fact that his men, horses, and provisions were rapidly dwindling from the debilitating effects of war, fatigue, famine, and pestilence, the governor was still determined to proceed with his search for those ever elusive kingdoms of gold. His new plan was to establish a temporary settlement along the banks of the Mississippi River where his men would concentrate their efforts on building two ships. One boat was to sail back to Cuba while the other ship sailed to New Spain, with both departing for the purpose of obtaining new recruits and much needed provisions to continue the expedition. De Soto was also anxious to get a message back to his wife, whom he hadn't seen in nearly three years, to let her know that he was still alive and well.

The march back to the Mississippi River was not without incident. The Spaniards were periodically harassed by Indian attacks, most of which were of minor consequence but certainly served to demonstrate that the inhabitants of these regions were every bit as warlike as the natives of Tula. Hernando and his beleaguered troops eventually made their way to the town of Autiamque (Utiangue), which was believed to have been located near the present site of Redfield, Arkansas. Finding the town abandoned, the commander decided that Autiamque would make for an excellent winter camp. This certainly proved to be a wise decision on de Soto's part. The heavy snow fall, deep drifts, and bitter cold of the ensuing winter kept the Spaniards confined to the fortified town for several weeks, during which time they managed to survive off the abundant supply of food and firewood the natives had collected and stored for the inclement weather to come.

The displaced residents of Autiamque harassed the Spaniards on numerous occasions, but their best efforts never succeeded in dislodging the intruders. The most devastating blow to the expedition was the sudden death of Juan Ortiz, who became sick and passed away during that terrible winter of 1541–42. The loss of Ortiz was of great concern to all the Spaniards: besides being well liked by nearly everyone, he was the integral link in a long chain of interpreters needed to communicate their needs and wishes to those who inhabited these strange lands.

According to the account provided by Garcilaso de la Vega, once the snows had passed Hernando de Soto led a company of soldiers to find natives to serve them on their journey. This search brought them to the province of Naguatex, near the northern border of Louisiana. A surprise raid on a village led to the capture of a great number of Indians, who were returned to camp as slaves to the needs of the Spaniards.

Hernando led his entire army out of Autiamque during the spring thaw of 1542. They would once again pass through the province of Naguatex, where they hoped to find food that would sustain them during their quest to reach the banks of the Mississippi River. The Spaniards, however, were disappointed to discover that news of their previous raid in this province had preceded them and that the natives were quick to flee with all of their food once they learned of their approach. The expedition would suffer yet another loss during its march through this province. Diego de Guzmán, a soldier who had a penchant for gambling, went native after losing everything he owned, including his horse and weapons, in a game of cards. He did not wish, however, to give up his most prized possession — a young and beautiful Indian maiden who had recently come into his possession. This was made clear to his commander and creditors when it was discovered that both had slipped away to return to her Naguatex tribe. De Soto and his soldiers continued on after it was realized that there was nothing they could say or do to convince Guzmán to return.

A five day march brought the Spaniards to the province of Guancane, where they were surprised to find many natives wearing what seemed to bear a strong resemblance to Christian crosses. Even though they had never traveled through this region, these Indians had heard of the legendary miracles performed by Cabeza de Vaca and his comrades and decided to adopt the sign of the cross as their talisman. Unfortunately, this did not mean that they were willing to accept these trespassers who also revered the cross. This was made clear when the natives began massing in a very threatening manner.

Determined not to dally at any town or province, especially one that showed itself to be hostile, Hernando continued to lead his soldiers as quickly as possible toward the Mississippi River. After several days the Spaniards reached the province of Anilco (Nilco) and after continuing for another thirty leagues they caught sight of the banks of a river where the main town, also called Anilco, was situated. Their advance was stalled by the sudden appearance of the chief, who bore the same name as both the town and province, and fifteen hundred accompanying warriors who were prepared to oppose them. However, the chief and his warriors unexpectedly made a hasty retreat to their village, which de Soto and his soldiers attributed to the intimidating sight of their hurriedly arranged battle formations.

The Spaniards soon learned that this show of strength by the Anilco warriors was merely done to buy enough time for the women and children to safely get across the river by canoe. The warriors fled in the same direction once they believed enough time had passed for their families to escape harm. Once he realized what was really happening, Hernando feared that the natives might be taking all their possessions with them, including the food, and therefore ordered his men to attack. The Spaniards rushed in with enough speed and fury to overtake and capture a great many men, women, and children who had yet to reach the canoes.

Hernando de Soto dispatched messages to inform Chief Anilco that he had come to his land in peace and that his people were free to return to their homes without fear of any harm coming to them. The chief had good reason to doubt the sincerity of such flowery words and refused to even bother with a response. The Spaniards made Anilco their home for four days, during which time they built barges and assembled enough confiscated canoes to carry the entire expedition across the river. Once on the other side, de Soto and his men marched toward the province of Guachoya.

Near where the Arkansas River joins the Mississippi River, the fatigued Spaniards caught a glimpse of the principal town of the Guachoya realm. The chief, whose name was also Guachoya, had advance warning of these intruders and readied his warriors to defend their homeland. But the chief had a change of heart once he saw how many Spaniards were headed his way. He gave the command to evacuate and, just like the inhabitants of Anilco, they crossed to the other side of the river in a fleet of canoes.

When it was learned that the Anilco and Guachoya tribes were bitter enemies, Hernando sent word to Chief Guachoya that he would welcome the opportunity to become his ally in a campaign against the tribe that had been so unkind to both of them. After several friendly correspondences passed between them, the chief decided to trust the governor and agreed to meet with him. After de Soto and Guachoya greeted one another in person, a grand banquet was held at the town to celebrate their newly forged alliance and plan their strategy against the town of Anilco.

Captain Juan de Guzmán and a squad of soldiers were assigned to accompany four thousand armed Guachoya warriors who were to make their way to Anilco in an armada of canoes. At the same time, Hernando de Soto and the rest of the soldiers would join Chief Guachoya and two thousand warriors on an overland march. It was agreed that they would rendezvous near Anilco after three days. The residents of Anilco saw the approach of the fleet and desperately tried to halt its advance. With their chief away at the time of the attack, and realizing they were about to be overwhelmed, the decision was made to once again abandon the town. Many, unfortunately, were unable to outrun the Guachoya warriors who rushed in for the kill.

Guachoya's warriors committed a number of atrocities that shocked and horrified their Spanish allies. Their wrath was so great that they butchered any Anilco inhabitant they could lay their hands on. The elderly were struck down alongside the very young. Mothers were forced to watch as their infants were thrown into the air and mercilessly pierced with arrows before their tormentors turned on them. The Guachoya warriors further vented their long pent-up rage by desecrating the sacred Anilco graveyard, where they took delight in trampling over the bones that belonged to the ancestors of their enemy.

Disturbed by the extreme acts of violence committed by his new allies, Hernando had his troops intervene on behalf of the afflicted Anilco Indians. His soldiers managed to bring a halt to the carnage just as the Guachoya warriors were preparing to burn the town to the ground. By this time, however, more than a hundred helpless souls had already been slaughtered. The Spanish commander chastised Chief Guachoya for sanctioning such a barbarous raid and demanded that he command all his warriors to return at once to their homeland. Believing that a peaceful resolution had been achieved, the conquistadors joined the march back to Guachoya. The Spaniards hadn't traveled very far before they noticed billows of smoke emanating from the town of Anilco. Determined to finish what they had started, the vindictive warriors secretly placed live embers in several of the huts as they were preparing to leave with the Spaniards. De Soto and his men were relieved to see that the survivors at Anilco were busy putting out the fires.

Once back at Guachoya, the Spaniards immediately began collecting wood and other materials that could be used to build ships large and strong enough to sail to Cuba and New Spain. While this task was underway, the chief of Quigualtum (Quigualtanqui), a powerful native empire located on the other side of the Mississippi River, sent a message demanding to know exactly what the Spaniards intentions were in this land. Meanwhile, an armada of war canoes assembled on the river to impress upon the conquistadors that they were a mighty people determined to defend their homeland.

The Death of de Soto

Hernando de Soto had previously sent Juan de Añasco and several other cavaliers on a search downriver to learn just how close they were to the sea. The governor hoped to hear from his scouts before responding to the inquiries of the curious chief across the river who, just like the other rulers of these lands, bore the same name as his province. Añasco returned after a week to report that he was unable to discover where the river meets the sea. He told his disappointed commander that the dense woods and tangle of thickets limited their travels to a mere "fourteen or fifteen leagues," and added that there were no native settlements along the way.

After receiving this disconcerting news, Hernando contracted a fever that steadily sapped his strength and weakened his will to carry on. Realizing that he would have to remain in this region longer than he had anticipated, the sickly commander decided it would be best to make peace with the antagonistic chief across the river. The Gentleman of Elvas wrote: "Before he [Hernando de Soto] took to his bed, he sent an Indian to tell the cacique of Quigualtum that he was the son of the sun and that wherever he went all obeyed him and did him service. He requested him to choose his friendship and come there where he was, for he would be very glad to see him."[1]

Hernando knew that many of the tribes of the Mississippi region worshipped the sun, and on several occasions he tried to persuade a chief to submit peacefully by having his interpreters proclaim that he was a true "son of the sun," a lesson learned from his dealings with the Incas of Peru, who considered themselves the true "children of the sun." He decided to use this tactic on Quigualtum. (De Soto was also known to employ other cunning practices to try to get the natives to submit to his will before resorting to force. One such method was to claim that the reflection of a mirror captured not only a person's image but also their thoughts and even their soul.) When the message sent by the ailing commander was received, Chief Quigualtum replied that he would be inclined to believe such a divine claim if Hernando used his god-given powers to dry up the great river that separated them. He went on to say that where he lived all obeyed him and paid him tribute. The chief closed by stating that if the ruler of the Spaniards wished to see him then he must cross the river and present himself.

Such a response from Quigualtum surely must have made Hernando think that perhaps he was the one who had been naive in his dealings with the ruler of this land. The governor undoubtedly realized he was no longer in a position to enforce his demands and therefore would have to be more diplomatic in his relations. But by this time, Hernando was no longer strong enough to visit the chief — his fever had worsened and he was now confined to a bed. The frustrated and delirious commander was convinced that Chief Guachoya was now in league with Chief Quigualtum and decided his men needed to teach the natives that they must respect the might of the Spaniards.

A company of foot soldiers under the command of Juan de Guzmán and several horsemen led by Nuño de Tobar were sent across the river to launch a surprise raid. According to Garcilaso de la Vega, the soldiers returned to camp shortly after encountering several abandoned villages. The Gentleman of Elvas, however, claims that a terrible slaughter occurred. In his account, the Spaniards descended upon a town so swiftly that the warriors did not have time to arm themselves and the women and children had nowhere to hide. Elvas writes that "The cries of the women and little children were so loud that they deafened the ears of those who pursued them." A hundred or more natives died during the lightning raid that surprised them as they slept in their huts. Regardless of which account is correct, this was the last official directive of Hernando de Soto before he turned over command of the expedition to another officer.

Three days after contracting the fever, Hernando de Soto's condition deteriorated to a point where many, including the governor himself, believed that the end was very near. The famed conquistador who had been a witness to so much death, much of which had been delivered by his own hand, now had to face his own mortality. Upon dictating his last will and testament, in which he remembered his wife, his two illegitimate children, and Hernán Ponce de León, and after confessing his sins to a priest, the bedridden and febrile Hernando de Soto summoned his officers to inform them that he was turning over command of the expedition to Luís de Moscoso, a loyal and competent officer who had stood by his side ever since the conquest of Peru. After demanding that all of the officers pledge their fealty to Moscoso, Hernando spent his remaining waking hours saying his goodbyes to those who came to pay their respects. Weakened by fever and a growing sense of despair, de Soto soon lapsed into a coma from which their was no awakening. He exhaled his last breath on May 21, 1542, the seventh day of his lingering fever.

Even though most of the troops mourned the death of Hernando de Soto, there were many who welcomed his passing, hoping that this would finally bring closure to this disastrous expedition and that they would now be free to return to Cuba. There were, however, other concerns that needed to be addressed first. The natives had suspected for some time that Hernando was gravely ill. The Spaniards, who had good reason to believe that the warriors would attack once they knew their commander was dead, sent messages to inform the chiefs of Quigualtum and Guachoya that their leader was on the road to recovery. Realizing that spies would soon discover their claim was a lie, Luís de Moscoso attempted to conceal the death of his former commander by keeping the corpse hidden in a house while a secret grave was dug at the entrance to the town. The body was laid to rest under cover of night.

The Indians surmised that the Spaniards were trying to deceive them and several were soon spotted snooping around Hernando's unmarked grave. Moscoso feared that the warriors were about to disturb the burial site and commit terrible atrocities to the body of their fallen leader, something that the Spaniards had witnessed the natives of this region do to the buried bodies of their enemy on more than one occasion. To keep this cadaver from being desecrated, the new commander had the body of their recently interred commander dug up and taken to a site where he hopefully would never be found.

After being weighted down to ensure it would remain submerged in the deep water of the Mississippi River, the lifeless body of Hernando de Soto was stuffed inside a hollowed out tree trunk, the open end of which was boarded up. Taking care to make sure that the suspicious natives did not see what they were up to, several soldiers transported this improvised sepulcher to the middle of the river, where it was lowered until it sank to the very bottom. It is commonly believed that the watery grave of Hernando de Soto rests somewhere along the mighty river's path at Ferriday, Louisiana.

16

The Long Way Home

A Search by Land

Luís de Moscoso, the newly appointed commander, let it be known that he was just as eager as the rest of the survivors to return home. However, the most pressing matter for Moscoso and his troops at this moment was to find a safe means of escape from this region before Chief Quigualtum decided to launch a full scale attack. After consulting with the other officers, Luís determined that their best hope of finding a way out of their present predicament was to blaze a path that would lead them to one of the many Spanish settlements of New Spain, and from there they could sail back to Cuba. Once this new objective had been announced, the soldiers collected their few belongings and marched westward, a course that Moscoso believed would bring them closer to home.

The route followed by Moscoso and his troops soon crossed into east Texas, where the Spaniards saw evidence of bison that had recently passed that way, but they never actually saw any of these wandering herds. It was during this time that the expedition happened upon a native woman who had once been claimed as the property of Juan de Zaldívar, a captain in Francisco Coronado's army. The young woman told the soldiers who had found her that she had walked eastward after eluding her captors while they were camped at Palo Duro Canyon. She also "told them she had fled from the Spaniards nine days distant and she named the captains."[1] Moscoso, however, chose not to believe her story and therefore missed an opportunity to link up with the Coronado expedition and the chance to find a surer route to New Spain.

The Spaniards continued on to the province of Auche, which is believed to be the present location of San Augustine, Texas. Here they were warmly received by the chief of the region, who was gracious enough to house and feed all of them for two days. The chief told Moscoso that a two day march from his village would lead to a vast wilderness that could be crossed in just four days. He assured them that on the other side of this barren land they would find a fertile and well-populated region, a territory that the Spaniards hoped would prove to be a gateway to Mexico. The kindly chief of Auche provided the Spaniards with many porters, who carried enough corn to feed the entire army for their six day journey, and an elderly guide who would show them the way.

As expected, Moscoso and his soldiers reached the wilderness in just two days. However, after wandering for eight days in a barren region that the chief had said would take them no more than four days to cross, Moscoso summoned the guide for an explanation. When the elderly Indian offered up a multitude of excuses, none of which satisfied the concerns of the commander, Moscoso had him tied to a tree and then unleashed a snarling mastiff that savagely bit into the flesh of the guide. Terrified by the fierceness of this large dog, the wounded native cried out that he would tell the truth if they called off the beast. Once the animal was pulled away, the frightened guide said he was merely following his chief's instructions to lead the Spaniards to their death by taking them through lands that would deprive them of both food and water. He finished with a pledge to lead the soldiers to safety, a journey of perhaps three days. Moscoso and his fellow officers were so outraged by the deceitfulness of the chief they thought was their friend and the guide they had trusted that they momentarily let their anger get the better of their judgment. The hounds were released and allowed to freely feast upon the flesh of the guileful guide.

The Spaniards now found themselves stranded in the middle of nowhere without a guide. Previously, in an effort to conserve their rapidly dwindling supply of food, many of the native porters were permitted to return to their village. The famished soldiers were forced to eat grass and roots while continuing westward in the hope of stumbling upon an Indian settlement. Luckily for them, their former guide's claim of finding food and shelter in three days proved to be true. The weary and tattered Spaniards entered a village that the inhabitants abandoned once they saw their approach. Here they would regain their strength by feasting on buffalo meat and other available foods.

A peculiar incident occurred on the second day in this region that the Spaniards called the Province of the Herdsmen. An Indian decked in elegant plumage on his head stepped out of the woods as if he were an emissary sent by a local chief. He continued walking toward the soldiers who eagerly waited to receive him. The native suddenly affixed an arrow to his bow and immediately launched it in the direction of the conquistadors. The startled Spaniards scattered in all directions to get out of the path of this projectile. The arrow penetrated the body of one of the native women still in their company with such force that it pierced the breast of another woman standing directly behind her, thus killing both with one shot. The warrior then turned and ran back toward the forest, but he was unable to outrun the cavaliers who immediately gave chase. The Spaniards punished him with a quick but extremely brutal death.

Three days later a similar event took place as Moscoso and his men were continuing their trek across the Province of the Herdsmen, only this time it was two warriors who came out to confront them. The mounted Juan Páez accepted the challenge and swiftly raced toward the two armed Indians. One of the warriors excused himself from the encounter that was about to take place so that his partner could demonstrate his skill and valor in single combat. The stoic fighter patiently waited for the charging horse and rider to get as close as was safely possible before drawing back on his bow and unleashing an arrow that pierced Páez's left arm. After losing his grip on the reins, the wounded Spaniard suddenly found himself lying helpless on the ground. A group of soldiers who saw what happened rushed to the aid of their bested comrade and slew both of the warriors.

Guided by the faint hope that they might run across a Spanish outpost, Luís de Moscoso continued to lead his men westward. However, by the time they reached the Trinity River, where the city of Dallas now stands, Moscoso had found sufficient reason to pause and reconsider their approach. The lack of villages along this route that could provide sustenance and the uncertainty of which direction would led them to a Spanish settlement were now life-threatening concerns. Moscoso sent out three squads of cavaliers in different directions to reconnoiter the land. All had returned after fifteen days to report that they were unable to find any evidence of a settlement. The natives encountered by each group were nomadic tribes that moved from one place to another to find food, which was not that much different from what the Spaniards had been doing ever since they landed at Florida. The natives told the Spanish scouts that they would have to continue westward for quite a long way before finding permanent settlements large enough to house and feed them.

Moscoso did not relish the idea of continuing westward into unsettled lands with little food for an army that was already at the brink of starvation. The severe heat also played a factor in the commander's decision to return to the banks of the Mississippi River. There they would spend the winter season building boats that would carry them downriver to the sea and collecting corn and other food items to sustain them during this long voyage.

Fearing a confrontation with the tribes of those lands they had recently passed through, the Spaniards marched as quickly and quietly as possible, taking care not to commit any offense that might arouse the ire of the natives. Despite these efforts, the soldiers still found themselves having to fend off numerous attacks. Most of these conflicts were the result of ambushes by warriors who deftly concealed their whereabouts by hiding behind trees or tall grass. Once the soldiers had passed their way, the hidden warriors let loose a barrage of arrows and then retreated before the Spaniards had an opportunity to retaliate. A great many soldiers and horses were either killed or wounded in this manner.

The pace of the expedition was greatly slowed by the soldiers' constant need to forage for food. There were other hardships to endure besides the severe lack of food and incessant native attacks, a list that included finding adequate shelter for much needed rest and replacement articles for clothes that were tattered by wear and rot. The steady accumulation of adversities caused the Spaniards to perish at a rate of roughly three per day. The horses also expired at an alarming rate and nearly every native porter died during this arduous trek. Because of their rush to reach the river, there was simply no time for Moscoso and his men to give the dead a proper burial. While accounts may vary over the number that died on this brutal march back to the banks of the Mississippi, it is reasonable to speculate that anywhere between fifty and one hundred Spaniards and as many as eighty horses never made it to the end of this journey. The many perils of this leg of the expedition reduced the number of men to slightly more than three hundred, which was roughly half the size of the expeditionary force that first landed at Florida.

After having been steered away from several villages by well orchestrated Indian attacks, the fatigued and famished Spaniards were delighted to see they had stumbled upon a town whose inhabitants were not yet aware of their presence. Because of their urgent need for food, Moscoso ordered his men to rush the town in order to prevent the natives from taking advantage of any opportunity that might deprive them of what they so desperately required. The Indians fled at the sound of the charge, which left the Spaniards free to help themselves to the stores of food left behind. A second town was gained in the same manner. Unfortunately for several soldiers, the consumed food was not timely enough to stave off the harsh effects of malnutrition.

Escape Along the River

The Spaniards resumed their march to the Mississippi River once they felt a slight return of their former strength and health. They finally reached their destination in late 1542, arriving near the area where their previous commander had been laid to rest. It was the beginning of January before Moscoso and his men undertook the daunting task of building seven boats large and sturdy enough to transport the entire company downriver and back to civilization. Just like the soldiers of the Pánfilo de Narváez expedition who were stranded at the Bay of Horses, the survivors of the Hernando de Soto expedition had to improvise with what materials were readily accessible. The chains used to shackle the natives were melted and forged into tools for cutting down trees and building the boats. The melted chains were also fashioned into nails, as was the metal of the arquebuses, which had been rendered useless ever since the powder was destroyed by the fires at the battle of Mabila. Blankets and animal skins were used to make sails, and tree resin was made into a caulking compound. Plant fibers and horsehair were woven into rope.

When it was learned that the Spaniards had returned and were camped at the nearby province of Aminoya, the chief of the twice abandoned town of Anilco sought to avoid another Spanish incursion by sending emissaries who carried an offering of his tribe's friendship and assistance. Meanwhile, the chief of Guachoya came in person to greet Moscoso. These enemies of one another competed for the favor of the Spaniards by offering them all the food, provisions, and help they required. Both tribes were further inspired to render aid once it was known that these conquistadors planned to leave their lands for good.

Chief Quigualtum also learned of Moscoso's return to the banks of the Mississippi. Fearing that the boats they were building would one day be used to ferry the soldiers across the river to plunder his village, Quigualtum was not inclined to offer any help to the Spaniards. Instead, this chief formed an alliance with ten other tribes, all of whom feigned friendship with the Spaniards while secretly preparing an armada that would be used to drive off these intruders. A warrior captain of Anilco, who had befriended the Spaniards, informed Moscoso of this sinister plot.

Adding to Luís de Moscoso's list of worries was the growing dissension between the warrior captain, who the Spaniards called Anilco, and the chief of Guachoya, the latter being offended that the Spaniards showed so much attention to a lord of lesser rank than himself. Guided by the lesson learned from Hernando de Soto's savvy dealings with the bitter rivalry between Chief Capaha and Chief Casquin, Moscoso was able to mediate a temporary peace between the rival nobles. Chief Quigualtum, on the other hand, continued to plot against the Spaniards.

As the Spaniards continued to work at a feverish pace to build their boats, a new danger emerged that threatened to undo all they had done so far. At the beginning of March the Mississippi began to overflow and flooded the town where Moscoso and his men spent the winter. The Spaniards now understood that one of the purposes of the many manmade mounds of this region was to provide a higher ground to escape the periodic flooding of the river. The Spaniards had been warned that the Mississippi was expected to flood, but they chose to consider such advice as nothing more than a native superstition. Even though the river steadily rose for a period of forty days, Moscoso and his men were able to continue their work on the boats by simply moving to an elevated spot. An unforeseen advantage to the flood was that Quigultum and his allies had to postpone their plan to attack the Spaniards, as they were forced to tend to their own villages during this calamitous event.

Anilco warned Luís de Moscoso of the renewed plans of Chief Quigualtum and his allies to attack their camp. He said that the devious chief would first try to get the Spaniards to let their guard down by sending emissaries who would pay them many compliments while expressing Quigualtum's desire for forging a peaceful and prosperous accord. The warrior from Anilco offered protection by stating that the Spaniards were welcome to settle at his homeland. Moscoso told Anilco that he appreciated his generous offer but he did not want to place the kind people of Anilco, who had already suffered the enmity of these tribes, in any further harm. The commander closed by saying that the time had come for him and his men to return to their homeland.

Shortly thereafter, a great many emissaries representing the confederation of tribes allied to Quigualtum strode into the Spanish camp and acted in the very manner that the Anilco captain predicted they would. Thirty of these supposed ambassadors of goodwill were seized and each suffered the loss of one of their hands. The bloodied emissaries were then sent back to serve as a stern warning to the chiefs who were conspiring against them. The extreme nature of this message compelled the scheming chiefs to alter their plan of attack: instead of assailing the Spaniards by land they would concentrate their assault along the path of the river.

Knowing that it was just a matter of time before Chief Quigualtum responded with a show of force, Moscoso had his men finish with the construction of the boats as quickly as possible. The hogs and lame horses were butchered to provide food for the upcoming voyage. Specially rigged canoes were to transport the remaining horses, which now numbered barely thirty. Before setting sail, Luís de Moscoso bade a fond farewell to Chief Guachoya and the captain-general of Anilco after beseeching each to put aside their differences and try to live in peace and harmony.

It was already July of 1543 by the time three hundred twenty-two Spaniards and one hundred native slaves began to board the seven completed boats to begin the voyage down the Mississippi River. There were seven oars on each side of each brigantine, and every man was expected to take a turn at rowing. Each ship was commanded by one of the few surviving officers and the entire flotilla was guided by the astrolabe that had been saved from the fires at Mabila. Fortunately for the Spaniards, the flood made it easier to launch their boats.

The Spaniards were thankful that their first two days downriver passed without incident, which led many to believe that Chief Quigualtum no longer planned to make good on his threats now that they had departed his realm. Such wishful thinking was shattered when on the third day they found themselves under attack from a confederation of ten tribes who owed their fealty to Quigualtum. A fleet of canoes carrying hundreds of armed warriors with black and blue war paint on their faces gave chase while a concerted attack of similarly attired warriors occurred from along the banks of the great river. The Spaniards shielded themselves and their horses as best they could from the steady barrage of projectiles hurled at them, occasionally returning fire with shots from their few remaining crossbows. The frightened soldiers paddled as fast as they could, but there seemed to be no escaping the wrath of these warriors.

During their frantic flight down the Mississippi, the beleaguered Spaniards caught sight of a town that rested alongside the river that was abandoned the very moment the frightened inhabitants saw their approach. A number of soldiers went ashore to quickly gather additional food for the long voyage ahead. Because they had become too much of a burden to shield from the onslaught of arrows, the few surviving horses were brought ashore and set free. The sudden return of the natives forced the Spaniards to rush back to the ships in order to resume their escape from these persistent pursuers. All of the recently freed horses were slaughtered by a barrage of arrows.

When Moscoso saw that a foolhardy soldier and five equally foolish followers had decided on their own to slip away in one of the empty canoes that previously hauled the horses so as to execute an ill-conceived scheme to scare off the natives with a show of bravado, he immediately dispatched four canoes carrying a squadron of soldiers to bring them back. Seeing the confusion ahead, the confederation of warriors quickened their pace. The armada of native canoes soon caught up with the five Spanish canoes and rammed them with full force. Several soldiers drowned when their vessels capsized and many more were killed by arrows or blows to the head when they came up for air. Only four of the fifty-two soldiers managed to survive this brutal assault.

Shortly after this confrontation, Quigualtum's warriors declared victory and returned to their homes. They all took delight in knowing that their efforts had forced Moscoso and his men from their lands and in the process they had the satisfaction of killing many Spaniards and all of their horses. Another brief encounter downriver with a different tribe resulted in the death of yet another soldier, but after this it was relatively smooth sailing for the remainder of the voyage down the Mississippi.

It took the crew of the seven Spanish ships three painfully long weeks to complete the roughly six hundred mile voyage down the Mississippi River. Once they were safely deposited onto the waters of the Gulf of Mexico, Luís de Moscoso steered the flotilla westward in the general direction of New Spain. A lack of navigational instruments and a fear that they would run out of freshwater and food if they attempted to sail to Cuba were just a few of the reasons why the commander felt compelled to follow a course that stayed well within sight of the coast. Despite all these precautions, ten more men would fail to survive this leg of the voyage to New Spain.

Fifty-three days after having left the mouth of the Mississippi — twenty-three of which were spent anchored along the Texas coast in order to make necessary repairs to their badly leaking vessels — a terrible storm suddenly swept in and threatened to carry the entire flotilla far out to sea. The Spaniards waged a desperate battle against the elements to reach an estuary that would offer some protection. Many soldiers had to swim ashore when their boats began to sink.

Once all were safely ashore and the tempest had passed, Moscoso sent out several small expeditions to try to get a bearing on their present whereabouts. One of the scouting parties soon returned with good news that had been learned from some local natives. All were delighted to hear they had landed at Tampico, a harbor where the Panuco River meets the Gulf of Mexico, and that just fifteen miles inland rested the Spanish settlement of Panuco.

On September 10, 1543, Luís de Moscoso and the rest of the survivors of the tragic Hernando de Soto expedition straggled into the town of Panuco. Having received advance notice of their approach from the natives, the excited residents of this Spanish outpost made numerous preparations while they eagerly awaited the arrival of the soldiers who had long been given up for dead. The citizens of Panuco, however, were shocked by the pitiful sight of the haggard Spaniards who paraded before them. News of the survivors' arrival and their frail condition was immediately sent to Viceroy Antonio de Mendoza at Mexico City. The concerned viceroy quickly dispatched provisions and medicine to aid in their care as well as instructions that these poor souls were to be shown every possible courtesy.

Once they had sufficiently recovered, Luís de Moscoso and his troops were escorted to Mexico City, where they were greeted with a grand reception and a warm welcome from Antonio de Mendoza. New clothes, shoes, and any other accessories required were freely provided for the returning Spaniards. Food and bedding were also made available to all, the latter being a comfort they had not experienced since leaving Cuba. Moscoso and his men returned with only tales to tell of their long ordeal, none of which were encouraging to those who still believed there were rich native kingdoms to the north of New Spain. For many survivors, their arrival at Mexico City marked the end of their days of adventure in the New World. Many soldiers, however, clung to their dreams of finding fame and fortune by venturing to Peru to enlist in the upcoming expedition led by Gonzalo Pizarro and his trusty lieutenant, Francisco de Orellana, that would set out to find El Dorado, the legendary golden city rumored to be rich beyond their wildest dreams.

CHAPTER NOTES

Chapter 1

1. John Mandeville, *The Travels of Sir John Mandeville*, trans. C.W.R.D. Moseley (London: Penguin, 1983), 123.
2. Ibid., 189.
3. Samuel Morison, *The European Discovery of America: The Southern Voyages, A.D. 1492-1616* (New York: Oxford University Press, 1974), 504.

Chapter 2

1. Paul Schneider, *Brutal Journey: The Epic Story of the First Crossing of North America* (New York: Henry Holt, 2006), 21.
2. Alvar Nunez Cabeza de Vaca, *The Narrative of Cabeza de Vaca*, trans. Rolena Adorno and Patrick Charles Pautz (Lincoln: University of Nebraska Press, 1999), 59.
3. Ibid.
4. Ibid., 82.
5. David Ewing Duncan, *Hernando de Soto: A Savage Quest in the Americas* (New York: Crown, 1995), 260, cites The Gentleman of Elvas.

Chapter 3

1. *The Narrative of Cabeza de Vaca*, 87.
2. *The European Discovery of America: The Southern Voyages*, 523-524.
3. Ibid., 522.
4. *The Narrative of Cabeza de Vaca*, 134.
5. Ibid., 140.

Chapter 4

1. *The Narrative of Cabeza de Vaca*, 159.
2. Irvin Block, *The Real Book about Explorers* (Garden City, NY: Garden City Books, 1952), 87.

3. Herbert Eugene Bolton, *Coronado: Knight of Pueblos and Plains* (Albuquerque: University of New Mexico, 1949), 12.
4. Donald E. Chipman, *Spanish Texas, 1519-1821* (Austin: University of Texas Press, 1992), 34.

Chapter 5

1. *Hernando de Soto: A Savage Quest in the Americas*, 6.

Chapter 6

1. *Coronado: Knight of Pueblos and Plains*, 18.
2. *Brutal Journey*, 316.
3. *Coronado: Knight of Pueblos and Plains*, 27.
4. Ibid., 36.
5. *Hernando de Soto: A Savage Quest in the Americas*, 239.

Chapter 7

1. *Coronado: Knight of Pueblos and Plains*, 100.
2. Ibid., 100-101.
3. Ibid., 107.

Chapter 8

1. *Coronado: Knight of Pueblos and Plains*, 117.
2. Ibid., 118.
3. Richard Flint, *Great Cruelties Have Been Reported: The 1544 Investigation of the Coronado Expedition* (Dallas, TX: Southern Methodist University Press, 2002), 281.
4. Editors of Reader's Digest, *America's Fascinating Indian Heritage* (Pleasantville,

NY: Reader's Digest Association, 1991), 211 (no source cited).

5. *Coronado: Knight of Pueblos and Plains*, 143.

6. Albert Marrin, *Empires Lost and Won: The Spanish Heritage in the Southwest* (New York: Atheneum, 1997), 39.

7. Stewart L. Udall, *Majestic Journey: Coronado's Inland Empire* (Santa Fe: Museum of New Mexico Press, 1987), 90.

8. *Coronado: Knight of Pueblos and Plains*, 183.

9. Ibid., 186.

10. *Majestic Journey*, 98.

Chapter 9

1. *Majestic Journey*, 103.

2. *Empires Lost and Won*, 45-46.

Chapter 10

1. *Coronado: Knight of Pueblos and Plains*, 245.

2. Ibid., 262 (Castenada quote).

3. *Majestic Journey*, 108.

4. *Coronado: Knight of Pueblos and Plains*, 258.

5. Ibid., 300.

6. Ibid., 302.

Chapter 11

1. *Empires Lost and Won*, 54.

Chapter 12

1. *Hernando de Soto: A Savage Quest in the Americas*, 259.

2. Garcilaso de la Vega, *The Florida of the Inca*, trans. John Varner and Jeannette Varner (Austin: University of Texas Press, 1951), 118-119.

3. *The Florida of the Inca*, 120.

4. *Hernando de Soto: A Savage Quest in the Americas*, 260 (cites the Gentleman of Elvas, chapter XVII).

Chapter 13

1. *The Florida of the Inca*, 245.

2. *A Savage Quest in the Americas*, 325.

3. Ibid., 328.

4. George E. Stuart and Gene S. Stuart, *Discovering Man's Past in the Americas* (Washington, D.C.: National Geographic Society, 1969), 140 (cites Vega).

5. *The Florida of the Inca*, 311-312.

Chapter 14

1. *The Florida of the Inca*, 348.

2. *A Savage Quest in the Americas*, 370.

3. Editors of Reader's Digest, *Mysteries of the Ancient Americas: The New World before Columbus* (Pleasantville, NY: Reader's Digest Association, 1986), 180, cites Garcilaso de la Vega.

4. *The Florida of the Inca*, 445.

Chapter 15

1. *A Savage Quest in the Americas*, 420.

Chapter 16

1. *Coronado: Knight of Pueblos and Plains*, 356.

BIBLIOGRAPHY

Acosta, Jose de. *Natural and Moral History of the Indies*. Durham: Duke University Press, 2002.

Bakewell, Peter. "The Hispanic World in the United States." In *The Spanish World: Civilization and Empire, Europe and the Americas, Past and Present*, edited by J.H. Elliott. New York: Harry N. Abrams, 1991.

Block, Irvin. *The Real Book about Explorers*. Garden City, NY: Garden City Books, 1952.

Bolton, Herbert Eugene. *Coronado: Knight of Pueblos and Plains*. Albuquerque: University of New Mexico, 1949.

Burland, Cottie. *North American Indian Mythology*. Middlesex: Hamlyn House, 1965.

_____. *The People of the Ancient Americas*. Middlesex: Hamlyn House, 1970.

Casas, Bartolome de las. *The Devastation of the Indies: A Brief Account*. Baltimore: Johns Hopkins University Press, 1992.

Chipman, Donald E. *Spanish Texas, 1519–1821*. Austin: University of Texas Press, 1992.

Descola, Jean. *The Conquistadors*. New York: Viking, 1957.

Duncan, David Ewing. *Hernando de Soto: A Savage Quest in the Americas*. New York: Crown, 1995.

Editors of Reader's Digest. *America's Fascinating Indian Heritage*. Pleasantville, NY: Reader's Digest Association, 1991.

_____. *Mysteries of the Ancient Americas: The New World before Columbus*. Pleasantville, NY: The Reader's Digest Association, 1986.

Fagen, Brian M. *Kingdoms of Gold, Kingdoms of Jade: The Americas before Columbus*. New York: Thames and Hudson, 1991.

_____. "Who Were the Mound Builders?" In *Mysteries of the Past*, edited by Joseph J. Thorndike, Jr. New York: American Heritage, 1977.

Feest, Christian F., ed. *The Cultures of Native North Americans*. Cologne: Konemann Verlagsgesellschaft mbH, 2000.

Flint, Richard. *Great Cruelties Have Been Reported: The 1544 Investigation of the Coronado Expedition*. Dallas, TX: Southern Methodist University Press, 2002.

Galloway, Patricia, ed. *The Hernando de Soto Expedition: History, Historiography, and "Discovery" in the Southeast*. Lincoln: University of Nebraska Press, 1997.

Irwin, R. Stephen. *The Indian Hunters*. Blaine, WA: Hancock House Publishers, 1984.

Kamen, Henry. *Empire: How Spain Became a World Power, 1492–1763*. New York: Harper Collins, 2003.

Mandeville, John. *The Travels of Sir John Mandeville*. Translated by C.W.R.D. Moseley. London: Penguin, 1983.

Marrin, Albert. *Empires Lost and Won: The Spanish Heritage in the Southwest*. New York: Atheneum, 1997.

Morison, Samuel. *The European Discovery of America: The Southern Voyages, A.D. 1492–1616*. New York: Oxford University Press, 1974.

The New Encyclopaedia Britannica. 23 vols. Chicago: Encyclopaedia Britannica, 1972.

Nunez Cabeza de Vaca, Alvar. *The Narrative of Cabeza de Vaca*. Translated by Rolena Adorno and Patrick Charles Pautz. Lincoln: University of Nebraska Press, 1999.

Restall, Matthew. *Seven Myths of the Spanish Quest*. New York: Oxford University Press, 2003.

Schneider, Paul. *Brutal Journey: The Epic Story of the First Crossing of North America.* New York: Henry Holt, 2006.

Snell, Tee Loftin. *The Wild Shores: America's Beginnings.* Washington, D.C.: National Geographic Society, 1974.

Stirling, Stuart. *The Last Conquistador.* Gloucestershire: Sutton, 1999.

_____. *Pizarro: Conqueror of the Inca.* Gloucestershire: Sutton, 2005.

Stuart, George E., and Gene S. Stuart. *Discovering Man's Past in the Americas.* Washington, D.C.: National Geographic Society, 1969.

Thomas, David Hurst, Jay Miller, Richard White, Peter Nabokov, and Philip J. Deloria. *The Native Americans: An Illustrated History.* Atlanta: Turner, 1993.

Thomas, Hugh. *Rivers of Gold: The Rise of the Spanish Empire from Columbus to Magellan.* New York: Random House 2003.

Udall, Stewart L. *Majestic Journey: Coronado's Inland Empire.* Santa Fe: Museum of New Mexico Press, 1987.

Underhill, Ruth. *Life in the Pueblos.* Santa Fe: Ancient Press, 1991.

Vega, Garcilaso de la. *The Florida of the Inca.* Translated by John Varner and Jeannette Varner. Austin: University of Texas Press 1951.

Wood, Michael. *Conquistadors.* Los Angeles: University of California Press, Berkeley, 2000

INDEX